COLUMBUS AND LAS CASAS

The Conquest and Christianization of America, 1492–1566

David M. Traboulay
College of Staten Island
City University of New York

UNIVERSITY
PRESS OF
AMERICA

Lanham • New York • London

Copyright © 1994 by
University Press of America,® Inc.
4720 Boston Way
Lanham, Maryland 20706

3 Henrietta Street
London WC2E 8LU England

Library of Congress Cataloging-in-Publication Data
Traboulay, David M.
Columbus and Las Casas : the conquest and Christianization of
America, 1492–1566 / David M. Traboulay.
p.   cm.
Includes bibliographical references and index.
1. America—Discovery and exploration—Spanish.   2. Indians—
Missions—History—16th century.   3. Conquerors—America—
History—16th century.   4. Columbus, Christopher.   5. Casas,
Bartolomé de las, 1474–1566.   I. Title.
E123.T73   1994   970.01'6—dc20   94–21742 CIP

ISBN 0–8191–9641–X (cloth : alk. paper)
ISBN 0–8191–9642–8 (pbk. : alk. paper)

The paper used in this publication meets the minimum requirements of
American National Standard for Information Sciences—Permanence
of Paper for Printed Library Materials, ANSI Z39.48–1984.

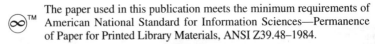

DEDICATION

This book is dedicated to Mom, Dad, my sister Joyce and my brother Mickey. The memory of their passing still brings a tear; the memory of their love, compassion and humor continues to inspire us and enables us all to go on.

TABLE OF CONTENTS

PREFACE

Columbus's accidental landing in the Caribbean marked the dawn of modern history that would be characterized by the development of modern capitalism, its gradual expansion into a global market, and the domination of non-Western peoples and societies by the West. On the other hand, the Americas felt the heavy hand of Western colonialism with greater cruelty than in Africa, Asia, and the Near East. Here the population was almost totally destroyed by brutality and disease; here the resources and wealth were extracted to enrich Europeans, not the native peoples. On the other hand, economic development, political democracy, and the prestige of capitalism in Western Europe and North America serve as justification for celebration of the discovery by Columbus in 1492. Although a large percentage of the population of the Americas is of mixed racial ancestry, and peoples have come in large numbers from Europe, Africa, Asia, and the Near East to the Americas, the dominance of European cultures, languages, and varieties of Christianity in the nations of the Americas attests ironically to the pervasiveness and strength of European colonial systems. Should Columbus be considered the representative of the European Renaissance spirit of adventure and curiosity? Should he be glorified as the precursor of capitalism's rise to dominance and the colonial mission to Christianize the other?[1]

The study of Columbus and his times allows us once again to undertake the journey to discover the truth about that encounter between Europeans and Americans. The awareness of this truth may move our minds and wills in a more useful and human direction. Bartolome de Las Casas found this remark in a memorandum Columbus had written as he lay sick in 1505: "The Indians of Hispaniola were and are its wealth, because they are the ones who till the land, provide the bread and other victuals for the Christians, dig the mines for gold, and do all the work which men and beasts usually do."[2] Columbus said that he was aware that six out of every seven Indians had been "butchered, beaten, starved and ill-treated to death but that he was out of the island when it happened." He argued that he brought Indian slaves back to Spain to be sold but "it had been for the purpose of instructing them in our Faith, our customs, crafts and trades, after which he intended to reclaim them and return them to their lands so that they could instruct others." The reaction of Las Casas was: "His was a crafty ignorance, if it was ignorance and not greed." Las Casas, an admirer of Columbus, saw the ambiguity in the man. As the age of exploration was followed by conquest, Spanish and Portuguese imperialism and Christianity were imposed on the peoples of America. What followed was a long period of native suffering and death and the replacement of native cultures by Christianity. Although many voices cried out and protested against this inhumanity, like those of Las Casas and Montesinos, the close relationship between Church and State implicated the Church in the cruelties visited on the native peoples by European imperialism.[3]

Should Columbus be held accountable for the horrors that befell native American society? Was the "discovery" also a conquest? What are we to make of his declared religious motives juxtaposed so frequently to the materialistic objectives of his voyages? Is there a single explanation that can provide the key to understand the mind of Columbus? An examination of the text of Columbus's journal and letters, the texts of contemporaries who wrote about the event, and the context of historical movements that were reshaping the history of Europe around 1500 provide clues to the answers to these questions.[4]

How seriously must we accept Columbus's frequent assertions that the purpose of the discovery was religious?[5] His first impressions of the natives were that "they have no religion, and I believe that they would very readily become Christians." "I have no doubt that were proper devout and religious persons to come among them and learn their language, it would be an easy matter to convert them all to Christianity." "Your Highnesses ought not to suffer any trade to be carried on, nor a foreign foot to be set upon these shores except by Catholic Christians, as the object and sum of the present undertakings has been the increase and glory of the Christian religion." In his log on Wednesday December 12 he said that he placed a large cross at the entrance of the harbor "as an indication that your highnesses possess the country and principally for a token of Jesus Christ Our Lord, and the honor of Christianity." "The admiral ordered every civility to be shown them because these are the best and most gentle people in the world, and especially, as I hope strongly in our Lord, that your Highnesses will undertake to convert them to Christianity." Columbus had this to say about the natives of Española: "There is not upon earth a better or gentler people, at which you may rejoice, for they will easily become Christians and earn our customs."[6] As Columbus sailed back to Spain, he "felt the most anxious desire to have his great discovery known, so that the world might be convinced that the assertions made by him had been correct, and that he had accomplished what he professed himself able to do: the thought of this not being done gave him the greatest inquietude, and he was perpetually in apprehensions as the smallest trifle might defeat his whole undertaking. He ascribes this to his want of faith and confidence in the Divine Providence...And as he had made the service of God the aim and business of his undertaking...he indulges a hope that he will continue the favor and secure him a safe arrival."

But if the spread of Christianity was a constant preoccupation with Columbus, what are we to make of his obsession with the search for gold?[7] The desire for gold looms large from the beginning: "And considering the indications of it among the natives who wear it upon their arms and legs...I cannot fail, with the help of Our Lord, to find the place which produces it." "This day I launched the ship...for the South East in quest of gold and spices." They directed their course "in search of an island where...the inhabitants collected gold at night by torchlight upon the shore, and afterwards hammered it into bars." On every island he plied the natives with questions about the location of gold. Columbus saw this as redounding to the glory of Christianity and the greatness of Spain: "A very short space of time would suffice to gain to our holy faith multitudes of people, and to Spain great riches and immense dominions, with all their inhabitants; there being without doubt in these countries vast quantities of gold; for the Indians would not without cause give us such descriptions of places where the inhabitants dug it from the earth, and wore it in massy bracelets at their necks, ears, legs, and arms. Here are also pearls and precious stones and an infinite amount of spices." With her new found wealth, Spain could then undertake a crusade to recover the holy land from the Muslims: "For I have before protested to your Highnesses...that the profits of this enterprise shall be employed in the conquest of Jerusalem." In Columbus's mind, the contradiction between the spread of Christianity and the desire for gold was reconciled by the ultimate project of financing a crusade to liberate Jerusalem from the infidels.

Nor did these preoccupations prevent him from describing the places and peoples of this new world in a favorable manner.[8] The trees are the "most beautiful I have seen": He delights in the aromas of the flowers and leaves: "Everything looked as green as in April in Andalucia." "All the night they were entertained with the melody of the birds and crickets; the air was mild and soft throughout the night, neither hot nor cold." "Those who went for water informed me that they had entered their houses and found them very clean and neat with beds and coverings of cotton nets." "They are an inoffensive, unwarlike people." "For I have observed that these people...are a very gentle race, without the knowledge of any iniquity; they neither kill nor steal nor carry weapons." Of their generosity, he remarked: "They are ready to barter anything they possess for whatever we choose to give them, without objecting to the small value of it." Whatever thing they were in possession of and knew the Spaniards wanted, they offered with great pleasure and the utmost liberality. Columbus offered in return glass beads, hawks bells, and brass rings and charged his men not to inflict any wrong on the Indians. Above all, nothing should be taken from them without paying for it. Even if it is possible that the narrative of the encounter in Española was embellished to win the support of the Crown for further voyages, the description of the encounter is moving especially in light of the narratives of later voyages where the description changes from gentle to savage. Natives came to greet them in one hundred and twenty canoes, "all filled with people and everyone bringing something, in particular bread, fish, and water in earthen pitchers." This kindness allowed him another opportunity to stress the gentleness of the peoples. King Guacanagari came in for special praise. When the Santa Maria was wrecked, he sent his people to assist the Spaniards carry their supplies safely to his town. So charmed was Columbus by their hospitality that he declared that the native peoples were "a very loving race, and without covetousness." There was one exception to this happy description. Columbus wrote that he was told by his hosts that there were warlike Indians who inhabited neighboring islands who were accustomed to attack the natives of Española. They were called Caribs. Columbus admitted that he had not encountered any Caribs whom he called cannibals because, as he was told, they ate human flesh.[9]

Notwithstanding this brief mention of the Caribs, the picture of America and the native Americans that emerges is an idyllic one. The narrative of the first encounter does little to prepare us for the cruelties of what came after. The nature of the first voyage was, of course, exploration, to determine whether it was possible to reach Asia by sailing westwards; the later voyages were motivated not only by exploration but also by the desire to conquer and colonize. Yet, in his journal of the first voyage, there were references that contained the seeds of later exploitation. Columbus informed the king that he was determined to pass none of those lands without taking possession. The native peoples were "such cowards that ten men might put ten thousand of them to flight."[10]   Before leaving Española for Spain, he ordered the construction of a fort with a tower and a ditch, not as a defense but "that the natives may understand the genius of the peoples of your highnesses...so that they may be held in obedience by fear as well as love." Columbus demonstrated to the Indians the power of his firearms and got his crew to stage a mock battle to strike terror into their hearts. With seven Indians as slaves, Columbus returned to Spain in 1493.

The controversy over Columbus and his voyages is essentially about the European legacy in America and the world.   There are scholars who point to capitalist development, constitutional democracy, and individual rights as some of the central achievements of the European dominated modern world.   Other scholars have raised criticism of European hegemony, not so much against democracy, development, and individual rights as their treatment of native Americans and Africans who were brought as slaves.   These scholars emphasize the mixing of cultures in America and the tragedy of the colonial encounter.   Some have responded to this perspective by arguing that this criticism was not historical and that it was unfair to apply twentieth century moral values to Columbus and his times.   Yet, the contemporary criticism of the conquest in Spain and in America was strong and coherent.

The work of Bartolome de Las Casas and others in the movement for justice for the indigenous peoples of America is eloquent testimony that some of Columbus's contemporaries saw the injustice of Spanish conquest and imperialism, cried out passionately at the destruction, and struggled to defend the human rights of native Americans to liberty and property. Las Casas argued that native people were certainly not slaves by nature, as his critics had contended. He pointed to the high quality of their minds as demonstrated by their political and social order, the beauty of their art and artifacts, and their personal achievements. Colonists charged Las Casas with embellishing native society. But his narrative was no more glowing than that of Columbus after his first encounter. Columbus remained preoccupied with the ideas of wealth, glory, and crusades; Las Casas developed from being a colonist to a social reformer. Influenced and assisted by the liberal intellectual climate at the university at Salamanca and the courage of friars like Anton de Montesinos, Las Casas could not turn a blind eye to the genocide that was taking place before his eyes. His sense of urgency over the decline of the indigenous population proved prophetic. Surely that was the greatest and swiftest demographic catastrophe in history. Critics through the centuries have condemned the "vehemence" of his rhetoric and raised questions about his view of what had taken place. Perhaps he was quick to become angry, but the death and destruction that took place made the matter of human destruction more important than the manner of telling the story. The works of scholars like Woodrow Borah and Sherwood Cook, among others, have tended to confirm the truth of Las Casas's narrative.

The struggle on behalf of the native Americans occurred within the larger purpose of converting them to Christianity. Even where one isolates and highlights the struggle for Indian rights, one should not forget that Christianization was part and parcel of imperial conquest. New Christian and European institutions, buildings, and ideas were constructed; but at almost the same time, conquistadors and religious destroyed native American institutions, temples and books. The current dualism between western and non-western civilizations has caused us to overlook the fact that for several centuries the polarity in European intellectual life was between Christian and non-Christian which was linked to the earlier distinction of antiquity between civilized and barbarian. The desire for domination and wealth was justified by claims of civilization and Christianity. How Bartolome de Las Casas, Francisco de Vitoria, Alonso de la Vera Cruz, and Alonso de Zorita, among others, answered those weighty arguments in order to remove the obstacles to their defense of native American rights is an exemplary narrative.

The significance of Las Casas and his friends has been a matter of controversy since the sixteenth century. Each age revises its picture of Las Casas in accordance with its prevailing intellectual climate. In the European conflict between Catholic Christians and Protestants, Las Casas's works were used as propaganda by Protestant nations against Catholic Spain. The defenders of Spain and its colonial empire have blamed Las Casas for creating the Black Legend of Spain. Later, the Enlightenment doctrine of progress and civilization made some question

Las Casas's glowing narrative of native peoples and their society. Cornelius de Pauw, an admirer of Voltaire, saw the people and world of America as inferior to Europe and condemned the works of Las Casas as being nothing but lies and exaggerations. In his *Wealth of Nations*, Adam Smith shared DePauw's dismal view of American civilizations and maintained that European arts, tools and livestock have improved American societies.

In the nineteenth century social Darwinism and the notion of the civilizing mission of the white race created a white legend of Spanish colonialism. William H. Prescott, Lewis Morgan, and Adolph Bandelier wrote as if the "savage" American Indians were fated to be destroyed on contact with the superior European civilization. Prescott admired Las Casas as saintly, but blamed him for his obsession with the idea of Spanish persecution of the Indian. E.G. Bourne's *Spain in America* (1904) and Lesley B. Simpson's *Encomienda in New Spain* (1929) continued the tendency towards a more favorable view of Spanish colonialism. Benjamin Keen noted the coincidence of the rise of this school of historians with the rise of an American empire in the Caribbean and the Pacific.[11] Simpson attacked Las Casas for his "violent partisanship."

However, when anti-imperialism, anti-racism, indigenism, and human rights make an impact on the climate of opinion, interest in the figure of Las Casas and his movement become significant. The Cuban poet and revolutionary, Jose Marti, lauded Las Casas for "half a century of lonely struggle against Indian slavery." In *Canto General*, the Chilean poet, Pablo Neruda, gave what Raymond Marcus called a moral tribute to Las Casas as a defender of native peoples.[12]

> Father (Las Casas), enter today this house with me.
> I will show you the letters, the torment of my people, of oppressed humanity.
> That I would not fall but hold my head over the Earth and continue the struggle, Leave in my heart the wandering wine
> And the implacable bread of your sweetness.

I am indebted to many friends for their encouragement and advice. I thank Dr Astrik L. Gabriel, Terry Julien, Fr Thomas Harricharan, Jyoti Sharma, Suresh Sharma, Kyu Kim, and Sarah Rachel Walters for their suggestions and kind words. I also thank Harold Sirsena and his daughter, Surani, and Ramu for their help in preparing this manuscript.

NOTES

1. For an excellent review of the current literature on the topic, see "New Worlds for Old: Columbus and His Consequences," in *History Today*, May 1992, 58-59.

2. Bartolomé de Las Casas, *Historia de Las Indias,* 3 vols. ed. by Augustin Millares Carlo and Lewis Kanke (Mexico City, 1951), English trans. New York, 1971 [cited as *History*], p. 141, 147.

3. Pedro de Leturia, "Origen Histórico del Patronato de Indias," in *Relaciones entre la Santa Sede e HispanoAmérica.* Analecta Gregoriana, CI. (Rome, 1959), 3-31.

4. Cristobal Colon, *Raccolta Colombiana*, I, vol. I and II (Rome, 1892-94); trans: *Journals and Other Documents*, (New York, 1963), [cited as *Journal*].

5. *Journal*, pp. 36, 65, 91, 117

6. Ibid., p.90.

7. *Ibid.*, pp. 33, 66.

8. *Ibid.*, pp. 58, 65, 67, 89, 133, 140, 145.

9. See Peter Hulme, *Colonial Encounters* (London, 1986), pp. 13-43.

10. *Journal*, p. 149

11. Benjamin Keen, "Introduction: Approaches to Las Casas, 1535-1970," in *Bartolome de Las Casas in History*, ed. by Juan Friede and Benjamin Keen (De Kalb, I11., 1971) 3-61.

12. Raymond Marcus, "Las Casas in Literature," *Ibid.*, 581-597.

Chapter 1

COLUMBUS: THE LEGEND

The Image of Columbus:

It is difficult to pin down the figure of Columbus. Buried in controversy almost from the time of the voyages, a sharp and consistent image of Columbus has eluded even the most disinterested scholars. The claim of the Pinzon family that some of the credit for the discovery should redound to them, the story of an anonymous pilot as source for Columbus's voyages, and the litigation between Columbus and the Spanish Crown which sought to trim the sails of his political power in the Indies have colored sixteenth century narratives about Columbus and the significance of his role in the European voyages to America from 1492.[1] In agreements of 1492 and 1493, the Spanish Crown had promised generous property and political rights to Columbus. They soon became jealous of a possible independent political power in the Indies and used the rebellion against the rule of the Columbus family in Española to replace Christopher Columbus as governor with their appointee Francisco de Bobadilla. Although some of his property rights were restored, his political rights were not. After his death in 1506, his sons, Diego and Fernando, continued the litigation against the Crown. Agents of the Crown sought to diminish Columbus's achievements, stating that he got the idea from someone else and that Columbus's role in the enterprise was minor. The Council of the Indies finally ruled in 1536 that his heirs could not hold the title of viceroy but would receive a perpetual income of 10,000 ducats and the duchy of Panama.

To reclaim credit for the discovery was an important issue for the supporters of Columbus. The enthusiastic days of the jubilation and the celebration in Spain after the first voyage soon came to an end. Another issue that his heirs had to deal with was the question of what Columbus had set out to discover by sailing westward. Was it Asia or an unknown continent? Writing at a time when the earlier confusion about the relation between America and Asia had been resolved, Gonzalo Fernandez de Oviedo, perhaps favoring the Crown's side of the lawsuit, stated that the discovery of the Indies was really a rediscovery.[2] The recently discovered lands were, in his mind, the Hesperides, the subject of numerous treatises by ancient writers. Lopez de Gomara, whose *General History of the Indies* was published in 1552 or 1553, followed Oviedo in arguing that Columbus's discovery was a rediscovery in that it was the anonymous pilot who led Columbus to the Indies.[3] This was the political climate that led his son, Ferdinand, to write a biography of his father in order to answer his detractors.[4] Unfinished at the time of his death in 1539, the manuscript was translated into Italian and published in 1571. Ferdinand argued that no one knew of the existence of the lands called the Indies until his father discovered them in 1492. He denied that the purpose of the voyages was to reach Asia. The name "Indies" was given because those lands had to be near Asiatic India and to obtain the support of the Crown. The figure of Christopher Columbus described by Ferdinand shows us a calculating and rational man prompted by "natural reason, the authority of writers and the testimony of sailors." Ferdinand claimed that his father attended the university of Pavia and had developed his hypothesis from the serious study of the following sources: Aristotle, *De Coelis*; Seneca, *Questiones naturales*; Strabo, *Geography*; Pliny, *Natural History*; Solinus, *Collectanea*; the *Travels* of Marco Polo; the *Books of Travels* of John Mandeville; Pierre D'Ailly, *Imago Mundi*; Capitolinus, *Geography*; and the correspondence of Paolo Toscanelli.

This scientific approach which, according to Ferdinand, lay behind Columbus's purpose would endear Ferdinand's account to late eighteenth and nineteenth century European historians who interpreted the significance of the discovery according to the ideas of their own time. Bartolome de Las Casas supported the view of Ferdinand that it was his father who discovered the Indies and that he arrived at the knowledge of the existence of the Indies by scientific reasoning. Where Las Casas differed, however, was his recognition that Columbus was attempting to reach Asia by sailing westward from Europe. While the works of historians were linked by an interest in certain political questions, the study by las Casas raised at least two issues that went beyond the question of the rehabilitation of Columbus. First, Las Casas focused on the consequences of the European discovery and conquest of the Indians. The other writers included little comment on the native peoples. For Oviedo, the Indians were "lazy, vicious, idolatrous, cowardly and without responsibility."[5] This did not mean that he was blind to the cruelties of the colonists. He was forced to admit that "some Spaniards overburdened the Indians with work." Ferdinand Colon, too, did not have a high regard for Indians and said little about the treatment if the Indians. He supported Gines de Sepulveda's position that the natives should submit to the colonists for their own good and offered as an explanation of the destruction of the native peoples the justice of God's avenging hand. For Las Casas, however, it was their encounter with peoples they had not known previously that made the voyages of Columbus important. In his eyes it was God who furnished the ultimate significance: "God gave this man the keys to the awesome seas, he and no other unlocked the darkness...He showed the way to the discovery of immense territories...whose inhabitants form wealthy and illustrious nations of diverse peoples and languages...the boundaries of Christ's empire could be vastly extended."[6] Belief in providence made Las Casas see the achievement of Columbus as essentially the work of God's plan to propagate his teaching to all peoples. But how could Las Casas reconcile his belief in providence with the suffering and destruction of the native peoples that he described so powerfully? His response was paradoxical. In the face of injustice, human beings, individually and collectively, had to work creatively to mitigate and end injustice.

Washington Irving's *Life and Voyages of Columbus* (1828) and Alexander von Humboldt's *Cosmos* (1866-1867) set the lines of interpretation that would continue until the first half of the twentieth century.[7] There were some one hundred editions of Irving's biography of Columbus. The heroic image of Columbus in the United States of America was in large part due to the popularity of Irving's biography. The depiction of Columbus by Randolph Rogers who was commissioned to do the Columbus doors in the Capitol building in Washington, D.C. between 1855 and 1858 drew heavily from that work. Rogers did not care that Columbus never landed in territory that would become the United States of America. The expansion of the United States of America and Europe was the frame of his perspective. For Rogers, Columbus came to symbolize their success story.[8] Significance was achieved by combining history and legend. In one of the panels depicting scenes from the life of Columbus, the meeting of the council of Salamanca to discuss the merit of Columbus's proposal, Rogers distorted history altogether by presenting Columbus as a modern, scientific man harassed by superstitious, ignorant, Catholic priests.

Relying on documents published by the Spanish scholar, Martin Fernandez de Navarrete, Irving's biography depicted Columbus as an exemplary hero, bold and courageous in the face of adversity, skillfully using European history to shape the view of U.S. history. For Irving, it was not particularly significant that Columbus was the first European to reach America. Irving like Humboldt admitted the possibility that Norse seamen had reached America in the late tenth century.[9] But, in their lights, these expeditions were casual and soon forgotten. What mattered for both was the purpose behind Columbus's voyages. It was for them a scientific project carried out by intellectual activity, one that held out great opportunities to humanity for progress. Alexander von Humboldt articulated his doctrine of progress very well. He argued that the discovery of America represented one of those advances in scientific knowledge which speeded up man's progress towards fulfilling his historical destiny. Columbus was therefore the instrument of history, opening up a new field of observation for Europe, the seat of history. Samuel Elliot Morrison's *Admiral of the Ocean Sea* (1942) and *The European Discovery of America* (1971;1974) continued this line of interpretation. Ostensibly written with the objective of studying Columbus as a navigator and to leave his psychology, his "motivation", and all that to others, this study nevertheless presented a favorable image of Columbus as a scientific navigator, familiar with the technical developments in navigation and courageous in undertaking the voyages. Morrison acknowledged that Columbus's intention was to reach Asia and he died believing that he had indeed reached Asia. Morrison insisted, nevertheless, that Columbus discovered America. His celebration of what he saw as the modern, western, scientific and courageous spirit of Columbus echoed still the view of nineteenth century historians. It was a view that had a certain resonance among the peoples of Europe and the United States of America and was linked to western imperialism and nationalism.

The Decadas (1530) and *Letters* of the Italian humanist, Peter Martyr, who had come to Spain in 1487 and held important governmental positions, including membership in the council of the Indies, revealed the first European response to the discovery.[10] Peter Martyr never traveled to the Americas, but drew his impressions from conversations with those who had made the voyages to the Indies. He was skeptical over Columbus's story that he had reached Asia but did not reject it altogether. Martyr felt that the major significance of the discovery was the possibility of increasing knowledge about an unknown part of the world. It was Martyr who used the term "New World" to describe the recently conquered lands. This was a term that was rich in possibilities. While Martyr may have meant the term to be ambiguous in so far as Columbus's assertions were concerned, his choice of "New World" was entirely appropriate because "the notion of world...refers to a moral or spiritual order." This encounter with different peoples could have become the significant consequence of the voyages. It was left to Bartolome de Las Casas to develop this theme.

The Mexican historian, Edmundo O'Gorman, in his thoughtful study, the *Invention of America* (1961), analyzed carefully the history of the classical interpretation of Columbus and his enterprise. But his own thesis did not fundamentally depart from it. For him, the invention of America was the idea of "the liberation of man...from an archaic way of understanding himself."[11] The American was the "new Adam of western culture." Developing this European perspective, he stated that even in antiquity the Greeks considered Europe "the place of origin and development of the forms of human life that embody human values with the greatest purity." He continued: "Europe, therefore, the seat of culture and of Christendom, represented the only true interests of mankind...European history, therefore, was not conceived as that of one particular civilization among others, but was lived and felt as the history of the only truly significant culture; European history was universal history. Europe became history's paradigm, and the European way of life came to be regarded as the supreme criterion by which to judge the value and meaning of all other forms of civilization." Given such a view, the significance of America lay in how successfully it received and fulfilled the values and ideals of European culture.

In his review of the historical interpretations of the voyages, Alfred W. Crosby, Jr. made the distinction between the dominant or bardic interpretive tradition and the more recent analytical schools.[12] Skilled in their craft, bardic historians were found to focus on "great white men". Their presentation emphasized Columbus's voyages, the exploration and colonization, but treated scantily Amerindians and African-Americans. Shaped during the nineteenth century, these works came out of a social context of rampant individualism, nationalism, and racism. This version of history, Crosby cautioned, was "deceptive as it is popular" because it was a selective view of history; it was "dangerous as it is deceptive" because its Euro-centered premises were now obsolete." The analytical historians found favor with Crosby because they focused on new ways of looking at the world. Rather than celebrants of white heroes, they emphasized "paradox" and sought to illuminate the "power of the humble, even the invisible." Some historians traced the roots of European imperialism and evangelization back to the age of the crusades and saw the Spanish treatment of the Guanches in the Canary Islands as the precedent for the New World encounter. The Annales school in France and the so-called Berkeley school adopted a more global thrust in their inquiries. A feature of their methodology was openness to other disciplines like archeology, geology, geography, and epidemiology. The works of Fernand Braudel, Eric Wolf, Carl Sauer, Sherburne F. Cook, Woodrow Borah, and Lesley Byrd Simpson have done much to reassess the Amerindian and Columbian past. They have placed alongside the older and still influential heroic tradition another which sees the conquest and its significance operating within a global context and, very importantly, records and analyzes the responses of the vanquished.

Not surprisingly, this revisionism has been subjected to considerable criticism. In his review of Kirkpatrick Sale's The *Conquest of Paradise* (1990), the historian William H. McNeill called this study of the Columbian legacy of environmental destructiveness "lopsided."[13] He found the image of Columbus as "cruel, greedy, and incompetent" simply a caricature that distorted "the complexity of human reality." "Ridiculous" was his response to Sale's contention that "American Indian society, technology, religion, and ethics were all superior to their European counterparts." What Sale had set out to do was to look at the European conquest of America from an ecological point of view, a vital global issue. He obviously had an important ideological axe to grind. But, in establishing the centrality of the dualism between good Indian and bad European, he tended to simplify the encounter. The dualities he created disabled his legitimate inquiry about the ecological consequences of the encounter. It is nevertheless ironic that an older tradition of civilized European and savage Indian was accepted as true, but a version which reversed the descriptions would cause such anger. How different was the review of the English translation of the Cuban novelist Alejo Carpenter's novel, *The Harp and the Shadow* (1979), by the Mexican writer, Ilan Stavans.[14] For Stavans, the novel "dares to awaken Columbus from his glorious eternal rest to denounce his foolishness, his mendacity, his insatiable greed for gold." To the question whether Columbus truly discovered the New World, Stavans answered: "Only from a European point of view."

Columbus's Spirituality

In the early 1980's, some scholars focused on religious sources of influence on Columbus.[15] Tzvetan Todorov (1982), whose interpretation of the figure of Columbus is hardly laudatory, insisted that greed was not Columbus's true motive, but the spread of Christianity.[16] Wealth for Columbus signified his achievement as discoverer and was to be used to advance the cause of the universal victory of Christianity. In locating his religious sensibility within an inflexible medieval Christian system and vision, Todorov argued that this was one of the causes of Columbus's inhumanity to the Indians. Columbus "discovered America but not the Americans." Todorov contrasts the stubborn, obsessive medieval mentality of Columbus with that of Hernan Cortes, "the first to have a political and even a historical consciousness of his actions." Possessing a modern mentality, Cortes was first interested in comprehending the situation in Mexico and acquiring information. But Cortes destroyed the Indians and their world no less effectively than Columbus because he used information to manipulate, exploit, and colonize. For Todorov, archaic ideology and liberal individualism were causes of human destructiveness. While it is useful to attempt to distinguish Columbus from Cortes, it must be stressed that religious feelings were important to Cortes as well. During and after the conquest of Mexico, it was Cortes who was most zealous in uprooting Aztec religious practices and converting the native peoples to Christianity.[17] The missionary, Fray Bartolome de Olmedo, had to urge Cortes to be more prudent. The break between the medieval and modern worlds in Western Europe was not sudden. The transition to modernity would take a long time.

Pauline Moffitt Watts (1985) and Alain Milhou (1983) made a more sustained inquiry into the "spiritual dimension" of Columbus's personality and the religious environment in which he was nurtured. Rooting their line of argument in the millennial movements of the late fifteenth and early sixteenth centuries, they concluded that Columbus's apocalyptic vision was a major motive for the voyages. They were both indebted to John Leddy Phelan (1956) who, in his pioneering study of the influence of Joachim of Fiore on the Franciscans in the New World and Columbus, had stressed the significance of Columbus as a religious visionary influenced by a centuries-old apocalyptic tradition.

Pauline Moffitt Watts built her argument on Columbus's use of the works of Pierre D'Ailly and the *Book of Prophecies* (1501-1502), a collection of materials drawn from the Bible and well-known ancient and medieval authors assembled by Columbus at the time of the later voyages with the assistance of a Carthusian monk, Gaspar Gorricio.[18] Columbus's use of D'Ailly's *Imago Mundi* (1410), a compendium of medieval cosmology and geography, was well-known. D'Ailly had borrowed much from Roger Bacon's *Opus maius*. Other works by D'Ailly came into the hands of Columbus, among which were the *Tractatus de legibus et sectis* and other prophetic treatises. One of the major purposes of these works by Bacon and D'Ailly which combined the study of history, astronomy, and mathematics was to predict the end of the world, the rise and fall of religions, and the coming of antichrist. From the *De legibus et sectis*, Columbus lifted the statement that the law of Islam would last 693 years; he noted the passage that said that Moslems would be defeated by the Tartars or Christians. Among the main themes in the *Book of Prophecies* were the preoccupation with recovering Palestine and the conversion of non-Christians. Columbus also described his role in this apocalyptic drama. His discovery of the islands near the alleged archipelago of Asia and the conversion of the peoples to Christianity were part of God's plan to convert all the peoples of the world before the world came to an end. Columbus came to see himself as the Christ-bearer, the one who would inaugurate the age of one flock and one shepherd. For Pauline Moffitt Watts, the liberation of the holy land was Columbus's "ultimate goal, the purpose of all his travels and discoveries." Columbus found the inspiration for this vision in the works of Pierre D'Ailly, not in Joachimism.[19]

In his wide-ranging study of the apocalyptic tradition of Europe and its influence on Columbus, Alain Milhou made a strong case for the powerful and enduring force of millenialism.[20] For Milhou, however, the major influence came from the mendicant orders, particularly the Franciscans. He argued that the voyages of Columbus were not simply to reach and tap the riches of Asia by sailing west. Their purpose responded to a global vision which "combined the tradition of Atlantic discoveries, the commercial and missionary undertakings to Asia, medieval legends about unknown lands and the messianic and eschatological universalism of the medieval crusade." The enterprise embraced the expansion of Christianity to the limits of the world, to establish an alliance with the Grand Khan of Cathay and "roll back" the influence of Islam on peoples who did not have an organized religion, to defeat the Muslims and recover Jerusalem.

For his narrative of the intellectual currents of late fifteenth century Spain, Milhou used the life and works of a contemporary of Columbus, Martin Martinez de Ampiez. A Spanish aristocrat who was both soldier and humanist, Ampiez published in 1496 his version of the *Book of the Antichrist*, followed by several other treatises. What his works demonstrated clearly was the heightened anxiety of Europe around 1500, caused principally by the obsessive fear of the Turks. In the *Book of the Antichrist*, Ampiez dramatized a global struggle between Christianity and the Antichrist assisted by Judaism and Islam, the two "sects of perdition." Anxiety at the prospect of the end of the world, interest in Jerusalem and unknown peoples and lands, the global struggle against Islam, curiosity about the part played by Jews in the history of civilization, respect for Rome and the pope, and an affinity for the Franciscan tradition and a deep-seated devotion to Mary, were the dominant themes of the works of Ampiez and formed the spiritual climate of the Spain that Columbus knew. Franciscan influence helped shape Columbus's religious vision. They were in the vanguard of missionary activity in the Canary Islands and Portuguese West Africa in the late fifteenth century. The Franciscan convent of La Rabida where Columbus stayed in 1485 was especially active in this work and was highly regarded at the Spanish court. At La Rabida Columbus found support for his project both from scientific and politico-religious points of view.

The portrait of Columbus described by Las Casas revealed a deeply religious person. He was accustomed to recite prayers at the canonical hours regularly. Las Casas noted an incident in 1494 when he made the cacique Ornofay wait until he had completed his prayers. In his administration of Espanñola, he wanted to impose the regulation that colonists had first to go to confession and receive the eucharist before obtaining the required license to go to the gold mines. Such scrupulous religiosity was hardly likely to make him popular among the colonists. As early as 1493 Columbus signed a memorandum to Ferdinand and Isabella, *Christoferens*. From 1493 until his death in 1506 he signed every letter with the following cryptic sigil:

.S.
.S. A .S.

X   M   Y

Milhou offered this interpretation of the symbols. The letters of the bottom line stood for: Christophorus - Maria - Johannes (Baptista); The middle line: Sanctus - Ave - Sanctus; The symbol S at the top, again Sanctus. The triple repetition of Sanctus represented the Trinity, a popular devotion around 1500. There developed at that time, too, an interesting iconography - the Virgin Mary crowned by the Trinity, an image that reflected the popular devotion to the Trinity and Mary. What all this meant was that Columbus saw himself as another John the Baptist, preparing the way for bringing Christianity to the peoples of the Americas.

In his seminal study, *The Millennial Kingdom of the Franciscans: The Apocalypse in the Age of Discovery*, John Leddy Phelan considered Christopher Columbus to be the first to see "the possibility of converting all the races of the world as an apocalyptical and messianic vision."[21] For Phelan, this tendency could be seen more clearly during the third voyage and afterwards. The identification of the Orinoco river as one of the four rivers of the garden of Eden and the inclusion in his will of Feb. 1498 of a clause setting aside a portion of his estate to finance a crusade to liberate Jerusalem could be attributed to this frame of mind. The letter to Ferdinand and Isabella which was to serve as an introduction to the *Book of Prophecies* illuminated Columbus's apocalyptic vision. In it Columbus seemed certain that the world was rapidly coming to an end. The gospel had therefore to be preached to all the peoples of the world. He said that the Holy Spirit had inspired him in his enterprise of the Indies. He insisted in this letter that the Holy Spirit would help in the project to liberate Jerusalem. According to Phelan, Columbus's mindset belonged to a Franciscan spiritual tradition of the thirteenth and fourteenth centuries, particularly the tradition influenced by Joachim of Fiore. For Columbus, "the discovery of the Indies, the conversion of all the gentiles, and the deliverance of the holy sepulcher were considered to be the three climactic events which foreshadow the end of the world."

But how does one square all this evidence of Columbus's spirituality with his insensitivity to the suffering of the American Indians, his obsession with finding gold, and the vanity with which he pursued and demanded recognition? It was Columbus who sent back to Spain in 1494 some five hundred Indian slaves with the expectation that trade in Indian slaves would compensate for not finding a large quantity of gold;

from the first voyage to the last Columbus seemed overcome by a
hunger for gold; he demanded and received the 10,000 maravedis that
the Crown had promised to the person who first sighted land when the
reward should have been given to Rodrigo de Triana; after he fell from
grace in 1500, he made countless petitions to have his privileges
restored. The answer to this predicament may be that there is no
necessary connection between spirituality and ethics. The history of that
time showed the coexistence of religion and slavery as well as the desire
for God and gold. Christian Genoa did not have too many qualms
about selling Christian slaves to Muslim Turks despite their fear of the
Turks; Portuguese merchants were not disturbed unduly about selling
African slaves in Lisbon; and Spanish merchants were engaged in the
slave trade of the Guanches of the Canary Islands.

The search for gold reflected the revival of commerce in Europe
since the middle of the thirteenth century. As the monetary instrument
of long-distance trade, the Italian cities of Genoa, Venice, and Florence
engaged in several projects to obtain gold from Asia and Africa.[22] This
desire, less urgent during the plague-ridden fourteenth century, revived
again in the early fifteenth century, especially after the Portuguese
seizure of Ceuta in 1414. In many ways, Portuguese activity in Africa
was a mixture of religious crusade and the search for gold and slaves.
With the revival of economic expansion in the fifteenth century, there
arose a considerable interest in finding new sources of precious metals.
The search for gold in the Americas by Columbus and the conquistadors
was part of a general European thirst and was a powerful illustration of
the dynamic spirit of nascent European commercial capitalism. In the
great mercantile cities of the western mediterranean-Genoa, Florence,
Montpellier, Perpignan, Barcelona, Valencia- there existed an excessive
commercial spirit alongside a radical calling to a life of poverty.[23] It
was in these cities that radical Franciscan sects like the Spirituals,
Fraticelli, and the Beguinage developed. Guardians of the holy places
in Palestine, the Franciscans were behind the last two great calls for a
crusade by pope Calixtus III in 1455 and Pius II in 1463. Although
unsuccessful in rallying the people of Europe, they nevertheless
stimulated a resurgence of interest in the pilgrimage to the holy land at
the end of the fifteenth century. Moreover, Columbus knew about the
tradition that held that a Spanish monarch would recover Jerusalem
from the Muslims. When he arrived in Spain in 1485, the tide in the
war in Granada had begun to turn in favor of the Christians. History
seemed to be supporting myth. The defeat of the Muslims of Spain, the

reconquest of Granada, and the expulsion of the Jews in 1492 had united Christian Spain and seemed to point the way to the reconquest of the holy land.

Columbus continued to cling stubbornly to his apocalyptic ideology. The narratives of the third and fourth voyages indicated that Columbus comprehended more than ever his experiences in prophetic terms. Sailing along the coasts of Trinidad and curious about the fresh water of the gulf of Paria in 1498, he concluded that it came from a very long river and imagined that he was close to the earthly paradise.[24] He saw himself now as the herald of the enterprise of the Indies, sent by the Trinity. In a letter of 1500, the earthly paradise became the "new heaven and earth." As his personal disappointment became more bitter, his prophetic language was more marked. He still had not reached Asia; he did not find gold in large quantity; he was not liked by both colonists and Indians; and, in 1500, he was arrested and put in chains by Bobadilla who replaced him as governor of Española. His response to the bitter pill of the loss of power and prestige was to see himself as another Job, persecuted unjustly. Writing from Jamaica in 1503, he lamented: "I am ruined, as I have said. Hitherto I have wept for others; now, Heaven have pity on me, and earth, weep for me! Of things material I have not a single *blanca* to offer; of things spiritual, I have even ceased observing the forms, here in the Indies. Alone, desolate, infirm, daily expecting death, surrounded by a million savages full of cruelty...weep for me, whoever has charity, truth, and justice."

Columbus's religious and millennial mentality was shaped by the prevailing spiritual climate of Europe and Spain. The main lines of this ideology developed in large part out of the European attempt to understand and resolve the experience of their long encounter with Islam and Judaism. Anxiety about the Muslim threat loomed large again at the Turkish conquest of Constantinople in 1453. The Spanish victory in Granada, the expulsion of the Jews in 1492, and the Portuguese successes in Africa offered hope for a successful outcome of a global struggle with Islam. The fears that this crisis produced led to the resurgence of the prophetic tradition. It obviously influenced Columbus. The Turkish seizure of Belgrade (1521), Rhodes (1522), and Hungary (1526) meant that this anxiety would remain until the victory at Lepanto in 1571. Even then the fear of Islam persisted. In 1609 the Moriscos, Muslims converted to Christianity, were expelled from Spain. How ironical it was that Spain, where Christians, Muslims, and Jews had lived for centuries with relative tolerance and which could have been a model for a pluralistic empire had become with the expulsion of Jews and Muslims a model of purity and homogeneity, a reversion to an archaic, Visigothic past.

NOTES

Chapter 1

1. See Fernandez Duro (ed.), *De Los Pleitos de Colon,* 2 vols. (Madrid, 1892-94); see also F. Morales Padron "las Relaciones entre Colon y Martin Alonso Pinzon,"*Revista de Indias,* 21(1961), 95-105..

2. Born in Madrid in 1478, Oviedo distinguished himself in both arms and letters. He was introduced to the royal family at the age of 13, and remained loyal and devoted to the Crown throughout his life. He knew Columbus, his sons, the Pinzon family, and Ovando, later to be governor of Española in 1502. Oviedo spent two years in Italy studying painting and served in the army in 1503 and fought against the French. In 1513 he was sent to the Indies in the expedition of Pedrarias Dávila. He died in 1557. His works exercised enormous influence, especially the *Historia General y Natural de Las Indias* (Paraguay, 1959).

3. See López de Gómara, *Historia de Las Indias,* (Madrid, 1852).

4. Ferdinand was born in Cordoba where his father was awaiting word from the commission established to discuss his project. He spent his early years with his mother and, on the triumphant return of his father from his first voyage, went to the royal court where he was page to prince Don Juan and queen Isabella. There he developed his taste for books and scholarship. He accompanied his father on his fourth voyage in 1502. In 1509 he again went to Española to supervise the erection of churches and monasteries but returned to Spain after a few months. He was considered an expert on colonial affairs. His library was considered one of the finest private collections in Europe. He died in Seville on July 12, 1539. See Fernando Colon, *The Life of the Admiral Christopher Columbus by His Son Ferdinand,* trans. by Benjamin Keen (Rutgers, 1959) [cited as Ferdinand]

5. Oviedo, 16.

6. Las Casas, *History,* 35, 36.

7. Edmundo O'Gorman, *The Invention of America*, (Bloomington, Ind., 1961).

8. Carla Rahn Phillips, "The Blurred Image: Christopher Columbus in the United States Historiography," in *Humanities News*, Jan. 1992.

9. See Gwyne Jones, *The Norse Atlantic Saga*, (Oxford, 1964).

10. Peter Martyr was a secular priest and humanist. Born in Italy in 1447, he lived in Spain from 1487. See *De Orbe Novo. The Eight Decades of Peter Martyre Anghera*, 2 vols., edited by F.A. Macnutt, (New York, 1912).

11. O'Gorman, *op.cit.*, 87-137.

12. Alfred W. Crosby made a distinction between bardic and analytic historians of Columbus. See *The Columbian Voyages, the Columbian Exchange, and their Historians*, (Washington, D.C., 1987).

13. For recent works that are critical of Columbus, see Kirkpatrick Sale, *The Conquest of Paradise*, (New York, 1990); Ronald Wright, *Stolen Continents*, (New York, 1992).

14. Alejo Carpentier, *The Harp and the Shadow*, English trans. (San Francisco, 1979).

15. This was not a new observation. Even Humboldt had detected a certain mystical disposition on the part of Columbus. But he did not think it was central. It might be useful to balance this inquiry by recalling the judgement of the Spanish historian Ramon Iglesia on this issue: "I believe that Columbus was not at all a religious man. The piety that is claimed for him was fabricated, conscious, extroverted, ritualistic...the religiosity of Columbus is as secondary in his spirit, is as self-interested and dependent upon practical results, as his supposed feeling for nature." See Ramon Iglesia, *Columbus, Cortes, and other Essays*, trans. and edited by L.B. Simpson, (Berkeley, Cal., 1969) 8-33.

16. R. Todorov, *The Conquest of America*, English Trans. (New York, 1984).

17. R. Ricard, *The Spiritual Conquest of Mexico*, (Berkeley, Cal., 1966) 16. It was originally published in Paris, 1933, as *Conquête Spirituelle de Mexique*.

18. P. Moffitt Watts, "Prophecy and Discovery: On The Origin of Christopher Columbus's Enterprise of the Indies," *American Historical Review*, 90(1985) 73-102.

19. Joachim of Fiore (d. 1202 A.D.) divided history into three epochs: the age of God the Father from Adam to Christ, corresponding to the layman's church; the age of God the Son from Christ to 1260, the church of priests; and the age of the Holy Spirit to begin in 1260 and known as the friars' church. The third age was to be the millennial kingdom of the Apocalypse. The transition from the second to the third would be characterized by the contemplative life of apostolic poverty and angelic nature. See John Leddy Phelan, *The Millennial Kingdom of the Franciscans*, 2nd ed., (Berkeley, Cal., 1970), 14-15.

20. Alain Milhou, *Colon y su Mentalidad Mesiánica*, (Valladolid, 1983).

21. Phelan, *op. cit.,* pp. 2, 19; see also Delno West, "Medieval Ideas of Apocalyptic Mission and the Early Franciscans in Mexico," *The Americas* XLV(1989) 293-313.

22. See Ruth Pike, *Enterprise and Adventure. The Genoese in Seville and the Opening of the New World*, (New York, 1966).

23. Milhou, *op. cit.*, p. 48.

24. *Ibid.* p. 254.

Chapter 2

COLUMBUS: THE ENTERPRISE OF THE INDIES

Life and Context

Born in the great commercial and shipping city of Genoa in 1451, Christopher Columbus was the son of Domenico Columbus, a weaver, and Susanna Fontanarossa.[1] Apprenticed as a wool-carder, he eventually joined a shipping firm linked to the Genoese banking firms of Spinola and Di Negri which had interests in both the eastern and western mediterranean. In 1474 he sailed to the Greek island of Chios either for business reasons or with a group of weavers from Savona, a neighboring town to which his father had moved his family. The fleet returned home, refitted, and set out for the west. Off the coast of Cape St. Vincent, Portugal, the fleet was attacked by French pirates and several ships sank, including that of Columbus who swam to shore. Columbus settled in Lisbon.[2] Ferdinand's biography of his father insisted that Columbus's achievements were the product of his training at the university of Padua where he studied navigation and the sciences.[3] But no evidence had been found to support this. It is more likely that Columbus's knowledge of navigation was derived from his experience.

Columbus was fortunate to have settled in Portugal which was the center of navigational science in the fifteenth century and was actively engaged in the project of finding a route to Asia around Southern Africa.[4] Having expelled the Muslims from their last stronghold in 1249, Portugal was among the earliest European nations to establish a cohesive state. The encouragement of maritime exploration had a long history in Portugal. Beginning with king Dom Diniz's invitation to the Genoese Admiral Pessanha to enter Portugal's naval service in 1317 and culminating in Dom Henrique's (1394-1460) famed nautical school, Portugal encouraged exploration and recorded in the fifteenth century some impressive achievements. At the ports of Faro and Lagos, no less than Sagres, many of the best pilots and navigators were trained. The capture of Ceuta in Morocco in 1415 signalled the beginning of projects of exploration and conquest. It was, however, king Dom João II (1481-

1495) who should receive major credit for Portugal's voyages of discovery. Benefitting from the Treaty of Alcaçovas in 1479 which ended the bitter rivalry between Spain and Portugal, Dom João sent Diogo Cão on voyages down the coast of West Africa in 1482 and 1485. He commissioned Bartholomew Diaz in 1486 to continue the project of discovering the sea-route to India. The hope of breaking the Venetian-Near Eastern monopoly of the Levant trade in spices and oriental luxury products was a spur to this project. In 1488 Diaz rounded the Cape of Good Hope, but a tired, mutinous crew forced him to return to Portugal. It was left to Vasco da Gama to complete the celebrated voyage in 1497-1498.

Columbus married Felipa Perestrello e Moniz whose father was first captain-general of Porto Santo, the island neighboring Madeira, and a former squire to Dom Henrique. In 1480 a son, Diego, was born. Columbus gained first-hand knowledge of the Portuguese voyages from contact with Portuguese seamen. He said that he made at least two voyages to West Africa and had visited A Mina, the trading post and castle constructed on the Gold Coast of lower Guinea; he intimated that on one occasion he sailed with the astronomer, Jose Visinho, and that he observed closely the pilots at work. He must have reflected on, too, the general Portuguese greed for gold, slaves, and spices. It was likely that his own proposal for reaching Asia was shaped by the impact the Portuguese exploration had on him. His son Ferdinand stated that Felipa's mother gave his father access to her late husband's library, allowing Columbus to develop his idea of reaching Asia by sailing west. The key to his conclusion was that the sea-voyage was much shorter than that calculated by astronomers and navigators. This was not an original idea. In 1459 a Florentine physician, Paolo Toscanelli, and some of his colleagues had presented this notion to King Alfonso V, repeating this thesis in 1474 in a letter to Fernão Martins, the king's representative. Ferdinand asserted that his father corresponded with Toscanelli and received a reply from him. But Columbus's correspondence with Toscanelli has been disputed. It is likely that he had seen the letters of Toscanelli and that they served to confirm his own conclusion.[5]

Columbus presented his proposal to the king of Portugal in 1488, requesting, if accepted, the fitting of a fleet, rights over all discoveries, the titles of viceroy and admiral, to be passed to his descendants, and a share in all the wealth obtained. The proposal was rejected because the Portuguese had already committed themselves to the project of sailing to Asia by sailing around southern Africa. To add to his disappointment, his wife Felipa died that year. With his son Diego, he journeyed to Spain to try his luck with the Spanish Crown. Portuguese successes and wealth from their explorations were already well-known. The prospect of an alternative route to the riches of Asia might well be attractive to the Spanish monarchs. In addition, he must have expected at least financial support from the large Genoese merchant community in Seville.

The Spanish monarchy was, however, too engaged in the final stages of the conquest of Muslim Granada to consider seriously the proposal and rejected the first presentation. The political history of Spain was different from Portugal. By the middle of the thirteenth century, Christians had reconquered most of Spain as in Portugal. But long, bitter civil and dynastic wars in Spain prevented them from launching a concerted attack against the remaining Spanish Muslim province of Granada. The marriage of Ferdinand of Aragon and Isabella of Castile in 1469, the authorization of the Spanish Inquisition in 1478, and their decision to launch a crusade against Granada in 1482 provided the political and ideological means for the unification of Spain. A second presentation was made in late 1491 with the help of Juan Perez, a priest at the Franciscan convent of La Rábida who was confessor to queen Isabella. In January, 1492, the Spanish Muslims were defeated and Granada taken. After initially rejecting it, the monarchs reconsidered and accepted the proposal. Of course, they were brimming with confidence after the victory against the Muslims and, in the changed political climate in Spain, were more disposed to consider carefully the opportunities that Columbus's project offered. The Portuguese success in rounding the Cape of Good Hope and the prospect that the wealth of Asia would be controlled by Portugal compelled the Spanish Crown to take a second look at Columbus's proposal of reaching Asia by sailing west. A significant financial obstacle was removed when friends and supporters of Columbus were able to obtain the funds necessary to equip the expedition. The support of the Duke of Medina Sidonia, a wealthy landowner with extensive shipping interests, Luis de Santangel, a converted Jew and royal treasurer, and Francesco Pinelli, an influential financier among the Genoese community in Seville, created the instruments to finance the expedition. Through the persuasive request of Santangel and Pinelli, a loan was raised from the *Santa Hermandad*, a corporation established in 1476 to protect the rural population from bandits. This loan was guaranteed by Pinelli.[6]

What scientific merit did Columbus's project have? Ever since the ancient Greeks discovered that the earth was spherical, there had been dispute as to its size. The *Orbis Terrarum* or Island of the Earth was located in the northern hemisphere and divided into three parts - Europe, Asia, and Africa.[7] The 7th century Spanish scholar, Isidore of Seville, held out the possibility of a fourth part in the southern hemisphere but contended that it was inaccessible. The medieval view that the Island of the Earth was a large island was held by Roger Bacon (1214-1294) and transmitted to Columbus through the works of Pierre D'Ailly (1350-1420). This view was replaced by one that held that it was relatively small, and therefore, the only practical sea-route to Asia was to sail east because the distance westward was too great. Columbus's proposal ran counter to the established view of the expert opinion. It is nevertheless possible that his Italian friends in Spain had consulted the Toscanelli papers before giving their financial support. The Colombian historian, Roberto M. Tisnes, has argued that Antonio Geraldini, papal nuncio to the Spanish monarchs, and his brother Alejandro Geraldini, preceptor to the monarchs' children, had done much to convince the king and queen about the merit of Columbus's project.[8] Both were well known Italian humanists who were at the court of Spain at this historic moment. Antonio died in 1489 and Alejandro would eventually become the first bishop of Santo Domingo.

Apart from the commercial possibilities of trade with Asia, one cannot ignore the weight of the religious argument. Defeat of the Spanish Muslims in January 1492 was followed in March by another decree expelling Spanish Jews from Spain. In recommending Columbus's project to queen Isabella, Fray Juan Perez must have persuaded her that the expedition would bring many Asian converts to Christianity. The ideas of commerce and crusade were certainly linked in European culture of that time.

In April 1492, the capitulations were drawn up and agreed upon. Columbus was to be made admiral and viceroy in "all the islands and mainlands" discovered; he was to receive a tenth of all profits of the venture after expenses and to be given the right to contribute an eight of the expenses of equipping any ship engaged in future trade in return for a similar proportion of the profits; the administration of the new lands would be shared by both the Crown and Columbus. These concessions seem generous, but the work of exploration, conquest, and colonization had to be left largely to private enterprise in light of the difficult financial situation after the war against Granada. It was also the legal means by which all lands to be discovered would be possessed by the Crown, not by feudal lords; it was also the instrument whereby the Crown could direct the purposes and institutions of colonization. They guarded jealously their responsibility for conversion to Christianity and the allocation of land.

There is no denying the influence of the rich commercial history and talents of his native Genoa nor that of the remarkable Genoese communities in the western Atlantic. But there was also a well-developed urban and commercial civilization in Spain.[9] Medieval Catalonia and Aragon (united in 1137) had a long and respectable history of trade with the Levant and North Africa. The *Llibre del Consolat*, one of the most famous maritime codes to regulate trade in the mediterranean, was a product of the city of Barcelona. Castile was also developed commercially. The sheep and wool industries brought Castile in contact with the outside world and made its northern towns important commercial centers. The reconquest of Seville by Fernando III in 1248 gave Castile an atlantic city which bustled with commerce.

Columbus was undoubtedly influenced by the spirit of this dynamic, mediterranean, commercial civilization. But his stay in Portugal and Spain coincided with another historical force- the resurgence of a crusading mentality, whose dominant interests were reconquest, conquest, and conversion. This was in large part due to the rise of Castile economically and politically and the decline of the commercially oriented and relatively tolerant, pluralistic civilization in the federation of Catalonia, Aragon, and Valencia. The strength of the reconquest movement against Islam in Castile meant that the church occupied a privileged position there and gave a militantly religious character to its culture. The capture of Constantinople by the Turks in 1453 and the papal appeal for a crusade in 1455 added fuel to the crusading fires. Through the marriage of Ferdinand and Isabella and the later union of the two Crowns, the interests of Castile came to be dominant.

Columbus observed at first hand this crusading spirit in the battle of Granada against an old enemy of Christian Europe, Islam;[10] in the journal of his first voyage, he mentioned but did not comment upon the expulsion of Jews from Spain. But he must have witnessed also the conquest and colonization of a people who were neither Muslims nor Jews. In 1478 Ferdinand and Isabella sent an expedition to occupy the

Grand Canary and subjugate its people, the Guanches.[11] The Guanches resisted and it was not until 1483 that the Grand Canary was taken; Palma was captured in 1492 and Tenerife in 1493. Columbus set out from the Canaries on all four of his voyages. Indeed, many of the strategies of Spanish colonization were first attempted in the Canaries. During the first period of Spanish conquest between 1350 and 1450, the Crown pursued a policy of a military conquest of the northern islands and religious conversion by missionaries in the south. Civil and dynastic wars did not allow the Crown to continue its colonization. Still, the result of its policy in the northern islands was the enslavement of the natives; in the south there were few conversions. Ferdinand and Isabella renewed the policy for the Canaries. Within a generation, two-thirds of Canarians had died. Native Canarian culture was effectively destroyed.

On Aug. 3rd. Columbus set sail with three ships, the flagship Santa Maria, and two caravels, the Pinta and Niña, from Palos for the Canary Islands. The Santa Maria was chartered from Juan de la Cosa, a vizcayan pilot who had become wealthy through trade with the islands off the coast of West Africa. The Pinzon and Niño families were a significant presence in the first voyage. Experienced seamen and respected members of the communities of Palos and Moguer, Martin Alonso Pinzon was captain of the Pinta; His younger brother Vicente Yañez was captain of the Niña. Three members of the Niño family accompanied Columbus; Juan was master of the Niña and Peralonso, the pilot of the Santa Maria. With a crew of ninety men, Columbus set sail on Sept. 6. Two hours after midnight on Oct. 12, he sighted land. Later that day, he went ashore the island its people called Guanahani.

The Encounter

As he sailed by the Bahamas islands to Cuba and Española, he encountered the native peoples, describing them as attractive and kind, and their villages as clean and well-ordered. He recorded that he was told that there were some who were fierce and ate human flesh.[12] Asia was the main reference to comprehend what he was encountering. On arriving at Cuba, he at first felt that it was Cipangu but rejected this for the belief that made Cuba part of Cathay. On Dec. 5 a favorable wind took him to the island of Española where he found some quantities of gold, thereby giving him and his crew encouragement. Friendly relations were established between Europeans and American Indians, exemplified by the warm friendship between Columbus and cacique Guacanagari. Columbus was certain that they would be ripe for conversion to Christianity. But conquest was on his mind, too. He insisted that the native people were cowardly and could be easily defeated. It was clear that he had a second voyage in mind, one with a different purpose, when he built a garrison at Puerto Navidad on the north coast. He left thirty nine men to await his return and embarked on the Niña on Jan. 16, 1493 with six Indian captives and a cargo of parrots, plants and gold.

Caught in a storm, he was anxious and fearful that his glory and credit for the success of the enterprise of the Indies would be lost. He described his experience on a piece of parchment, wrapped it in waxed cloth, sealed it in a wooden barrel, and threw it out to sea with the expectation that those who found it would take it to the Spanish monarchs. He was concerned for the safe return of his crew and for his two sons at school in Cordoba if he met misfortune. He was afraid that Martin Alonso Pinzon who had set sail on the Pinta might reach Spain earlier than he and claim credit for the discovery. Antagonism had broken out between both men in Española. Columbus did not like Pinzon's independent spirit as he left the main party to search for gold on his own. The Niña weathered the storm, however, and Columbus disembarked in the Azores and Portugal before proceeding to Spain on Aug. 3rd., three hours before Martin Alonso Pinzon did. In 1511 the Pinzon family brought a lawsuit against the Columbus family, challenging their claims and titles, asserting that it was Martin Alonso Pinzon, who died less than a month after he returned to Spain, who should be given credit for the enterprise.

After receiving Columbus's letter that he wrote from Portugal announcing the wonders of his voyage, Ferdinand and Isabella at once invited "Don Cristobal Colon, their admiral of the Ocean Sea, Viceroy, and Governor of the islands that he had discovered in the Indies" to thank him for having "rendered an immense service." The impact of Columbus's letter must have been significant.[13] There were several editions printed in Spain and Italy and versions soon appeared in Spanish, Italian, Latin and German. The narrative of his letter differed little from his journal. The letter captured the arrogance of Columbus: "I found very many islands filled with people without number, and of them all I have taken possession for their Highnesses by proclamation and with the royal standard displayed, and nobody objected." Statements like this make his description of the people and places he met bitterly ironic: "Of anything they have, if you ask them for it, they never say no; rather, they invite the person to share it, and show as much love as if they were giving their hearts." The islands are "most beautiful, of a thousand shapes..."

Although Columbus insisted that he was in Asia, others remained skeptical while still acclaiming his achievement. The Italian humanist, Peter Martyr, who lauded Columbus as one of the great heroes, had enough doubts to call the lands Columbus came upon "antipodes" or "New World."[14] Still, what must have convinced the monarchs to support a second voyage was the impressive display of samples of gold, spices, plants as well as the native Americans. The recommendations of the Duke of Medinacelli and Italian financiers created a favorable atmosphere at the Spanish court. In their minds, Columbus's enterprise matched the Portuguese maritime successes. After the papal confirmation of Spanish rights over their discovery, Spain and Portugal negotiated an agreement in 1494, the Treaty of Tordesillas, defining each other's sphere of influence. The Portuguese agreed to limit their western influence to 370 leagues beyond the Cape Verde islands. This was fortunate for them because they could legally claim Brazil after Cabral landed there in 1500.[15]

The preparations for Columbus's second voyage were more elaborate than the first and its purpose clearer. Columbus intended to colonize some of the islands in order to control and exploit the production of gold and cotton, and to use these islands as bases for continued exploration west and south. He hoped to settle in Española and build three or four towns for two thousand Spanish colonists. Mindful of their religious obligations, the monarchs sent Fr. Buil and a Franciscan to christianize the native people. The fleet numbered seventeen ships and the total number of personnel was about 1300 men.[16] Included among the military contingent were twenty horsemen whose animals were to terrorize the native warriors. Among those accompanying Columbus were: his younger brother Diego Colon; Pedro de Las Casas, father of Bartolome de Las Casas; Michele de Cuneo, a Genoese, Dr. Diego Chanca, the medical officer, and Guillermo Coma, all three of whom wrote accounts of the second voyage and their stay in the Caribbean; Juan Ponce de Leon, Alonso de Hojeda, and Juan de La Cosa. Armed with legal authorization from pope and monarchs and driven by ambitious plans to exploit the resources of the Indies, Columbus and his fleet set sail on May 29, 1493.

The Conquest of the Caribbean

The conquest and colonization of America began as early as the second voyage in 1493.[17] It explained in large measure the deterioration of relations between Europeans and native Americans. Events in Española were already headed in that direction. After landing on other islands from Dominica to Puerto Rico, Columbus reached the port-town of Navidad on the northern coast of Española where he had left thirty nine of his crew on his first voyage to search for gold and guard the garrison. He was shocked to learn that they were all killed. This was how Guillermo Coma explained what had happened: "Bad feeling had arisen and had broken out into warfare because of the licentious conduct of our men towards the Indian women, for each Spaniard had five women to minister to his pleasure...although they had resisted strongly to the last, our men were unable to withstand the close-order attacks of the enemy very long, and they were at length ruthlessly cut down."[18] There was no stopping Columbus from embarking on his project of colonization. Under his rigorous supervision, a new town, Isabella, was constructed, situated forty leagues east of Navidad and near the river where Pinzon had found samples of gold. But the experience was no bed of roses for the colonists and Columbus. The unaccustomed diet led to sickness and many died. Columbus's insistence that everyone take part in everyday work did not sit well with the men and led to bickering against Columbus. After the town of Isabella was built, Columbus set out for the gold mines of Cibao with a column of horsemen and infantry. Several forts were built on the way, especially in the plains of the Yaque river which he named Vega Real. But the quantity of gold was disappointing. To make matters worse, clashes arose between Indians and Spaniards in which several Indians were killed.

Despite his difficulties, Columbus set out west hoping to find Cathay. He sailed to the southern coast of Cuba, then Jamaica, and again for Cuba with the intention of determining whether it was an island or the mainland. But sailing conditions were bad. In the face of shallow waters, declining food and water supplies, storms, and discontent among the crew, he decided not to continue westward and ordered his crew to sign a declaration that Cuba was a peninsula, not an island. Explanation of this action remains baffling. Is this proof that Columbus lied about the enterprise of the Indies? Was he so obsessed by faith in his project of reaching Asia that he would brook no doubts?

He returned to Española where another brother, Bartholomew, had joined Diego in administering the colony. Criticism of the administration of the Columbus family had become serious. Father Buil who was jointly in charge of the settlement returned to Spain with a list of bitter complaints. By the end of 1494 the native Indians were in open revolt. Columbus had hoped to put down the resistance by kidnapping Caonabo, the chief of the Cibao region, and making an exemplary spectacle of him. To put a stop to the unravelling of the political order of the colony, to give it a firmer economic base, and, by no means least, to silence his critics, Columbus introduced a series of practices and institutions that, while they pacified the colony, had a crushing effect on the native people and environment. He sent troops to occupy the north east of the island and had more forts built in the Cibao region. A given tribute in gold was demanded quarterly, calculated according to the number of people over the age of fourteen. He introduced Indian slavery, suggesting that Indian slavery would be lucrative enough to compensate for the meager supply of gold found. He sent back 500 Indian slaves to Spain. His brother Bartholomew, Alonso de Hojeda, and he undertook a series of military expeditions all over the island. Villages that could not pay the tribute were brutally repressed. Las Casas charged that two thirds of the population were wiped out; Oviedo who was sympathetic to the interests of the colonists simply said that there were victims without number. In October 1495 Ferdinand and Isabella sent Juan Aguado to investigate the complaints of the colonists, not those of the native people. Stung by their criticisms, Columbus returned to Spain in March 1496 to plead his case before the royal court, leaving his brother Bartholomew in charge as adelantado.

His reception was favorable but questions were raised about the expected gold and spices of Asia. Columbus spent a year engaged in discussions and plans with the Crown for his next voyage. He was reminded that the Indians should be approached by peaceful means to serve the Crown and be converted to Christianity. On July 22, 1497 the monarchs authorized the distribution of lands (*Repartimiento*) to individual Spanish colonists to sow wheat, plant gardens, and to cultivate cotton and sugar cane. This land policy was designed to encourage permanent Spanish settlers in Española who were expected to establish small farms with Spanish labor. The *Repartimiento* that Columbus actually instituted was the allocation of native communities to Spaniards.[19]

At the end of May 1498, Columbus set sail with a fleet of six ships, three for exploration and three with supplies for Española.[20] On reaching the Canary Islands, he sent the supply ships to Española. His own point of departure was the Cape Verde Islands, arriving at the island of Trinidad on July 31. Sailing along the Gulf of Paria, he came upon the southern continent. His crew went ashore and were entertained by the native people. Mixing his scientific and religious perspectives, Columbus concluded that he had found another world and that this was the earthly paradise. The furious currents of fresh water he encountered in the Gulf of Paria suggested to him that such a large river could only flow through a continent, but this was not the continent of Asia. His fleet then turned north to Española.

During the two years he was in Spain, political order had collapsed in Española. Francisco Roldan, chief administrator of Isabella, resented that the administration of Española should be in the hands of Bartholomew Columbus and revolted and occupied the western parts of Española. Native Indians suffered at the hands of all the Spanish antagonists. To heal the division among the colonists and to put down Roldan's rebellion, Columbus curried favor with Roldan by introducing the institution called *Encomienda*. This fateful institution was destined to produce catastrophic consequences for the native peoples of the Americas. Native communities identified by their chiefs were allocated to individual Spaniards to do whatever labor the colonists demanded. To counter the decline in the economy because of the diminishing supplies of gold, Columbus sought to bolster the colony's revenue by encouraging trade in Brazilwood and Indian slaves. He felt that enormous profits could be made from Indian slavery. Admitting that the first Indian slaves soon died, he responded that that was also what happened to African and native Canarian slaves but deaths were not likely to continue as they grew accustomed to the work they had to do. This resoluteness on the part of Columbus did not halt the sense of drift, the disappointment, and criticism of the administration of Columbus and his brothers. The Crown sent Francisco de Bobadilla to conduct an inquiry into the state of affairs in Española. When he arrived in Santo Domingo in 1500, he witnessed two Spaniards hanging from two gallows and learned that five others were to follow. The three Columbus brothers were reportedly then hunting down Spanish rebels in different parts of the island. Acting decisively, Bobadilla sent all three back to Spain in chains.

Queen Isabella ordered Columbus's immediate release and received him well at court, promising to return most of what was taken from him. To return as viceroy, however, was out of the question. The monarchs were persuaded by the colonists that Columbus was too arbitrary an administrator. He nevertheless began to nudge the monarchs to give their approval for one more voyage to reach Asia. The millennial character of his spirituality expressed itself more clearly now than previously as he tried to link a new voyage to Asia with a crusade to liberate Jerusalem from Islamic control. He claimed that a Spanish victory was certain and that king Ferdinand would sit in Jerusalem as the last world emperor. In the end, it was a more mundane argument that won the day for Columbus. The Portuguese under Vasco da Gama had already reached South India and returned to Lisbon with accounts of great cities, spices, and gems. In July 1499, Dom Manuel of Portugal wrote to Ferdinand and Isabella announcing that their explorers had reached India and had found great quantities of cloves, cinnamon, pepper and other spices, in addition to precious gems. Dom Manuel intimated his intention of seizing control of the Indian ocean spice trade from the Muslims. In the race to find a route to Asia, it seemed that the Portuguese had triumphed. It is possible that the monarchs decided to allow Columbus one more opportunity to achieve his goal and to match the Portuguese success.

It was not simply blind faith that motivated support for Columbus. The discoveries of Columbus on his previous voyages were beginning to be economically productive. The reorganization of the economy under Bobadilla and later by governor Nicholas Ovando led to a mining boom. A substantial amount of gold was sent to the Crown in 1501. The discovery and conquest of these new lands were beginning to pay dividends. In addition, the crew who went ashore the mainland of South America during Columbus's third voyage had reported that the Indians were rich with pearls. The Gulf of Paria was conceived as a potentially new area for trade and exploration. It was bishop Juan Rodriguez de Fonseca who sought to impose his own colonial vision in America now that Columbus's star was on the decline. Empowered to look after the affairs of the Indies since Columbus's second voyage, Fonseca set up an organization to exploit the fruit of the discoveries of Columbus and to control the administration of the Indies. With Columbus relieved of his position as viceroy and Bobadilla now titular governor, he encouraged and granted contracts in 1499 to mariners like

Juan de la Cosa, Alonso de Hojeda, and the Pinzon and Niño family, to go on enterprises of trade and exploration. All of these voyages focused on the Gulf of Paria. Before his fall from grace, Columbus had tried to block others from access to the Indies. The rebellion in Española had prevented him from establishing an outpost on the mainland. Voyages by Alonso de Hojeda, Peralonso Niño, Vicente Yañez Pinzon, and Diego Lepe were undertaken in 1499. Pinzon and Lepe landed in Guyana and Brazil but did not sail to the Caribbean. The expedition by Niño and Cristobal Guerra discovered the Pearl Coast and Venezuela. For six months they sailed westwards and engaged in trade in pearls with the native people. Hojeda's expedition included Juan de la Cosa as chief pilot and Amerigo Vespucci who, representing the interests of the Medici family in Seville, had at his disposal two ships. They reconnoitred almost 1,000 miles of the mainland westward from the Gulf of Paria and the islands of Margarita, Curacão, and Aruba. Landing on the Guyana coast, Hojeda and his main party headed towards the Gulf of Paria while Vespucci sailed towards Brazil before rejoining the fleet. Peter Martyr, who had interviewed Niño for his account of this voyage, described the American Indians as hospitable. He also said that they had markets where the products of each region were traded. The discoveries achieved by these expeditions gave new interest in the western voyages.

There was a rush for licenses. Cristobal Guerra returned to Venezuela where he loaded brazilwood and slaves. He continued his slave hunting along the coast as far as Cartagena in present-day Colombia and the island of Bonaire. Juan de la Cosa joined forces with Rodrigo de Bastidas and explored as far as the Gulf of Uraba where they found the natives in possession of abundant gold pieces. Relations between the Indians of Colombia and the Spaniards were friendly, so different from later expeditions. Vespucci meanwhile was in the service of the king of Portugal and had as his project the exploration of Brazil. In giving Hojeda the contract for his second expedition, Fonseca urged him to establish a government at Goajira and to forestall English interests. This was futile as Hojeda as well as Guerra preferred raiding the shores of the mainland. Fonseca's plan for the mainland was clear. East of the Gulf of Paria up to Portuguese territory was to be controlled by Vicente Yañez Pinzon; the middle by the Guerras; and the west by Hojeda.

As Columbus was beginning to set sail on his final voyage, the enterprise of the Indies was already receding from his control.

Accompanied by his brother Bartholomew and his son Ferdinand, Columbus left Cadiz with a fleet of four ships on May 11, 1502. Intending to make Jamaica his base for the exploration of the mainland, he tried to dock at Santo Domingo, but was denied entry by the governor. His pilots were able to exchange charts, however, with members of the Bastidas expedition which was about to sail for Spain. A hurricane caused the shipwreck of most of the outgoing fleet. Columbus, who had in vain warned governor Ovando of the approaching storm, sheltered his fleet in an adjoining bay and then set out for Jamaica. The inhospitable seas took him to Cape Honduras. He then turned east, exploring Central America. At times he said that he was looking for a strait to the Indian ocean; at other times he thought he was near his original objective - the Chinese province of Mangi. An incident occurred which would point the way to future Spanish colonization, the significance of which escaped Columbus.   They encountered an unusually long, canopied, canoe with a party of some thirty Indians.   In the canoe they found attractive colored clothes, wooden swords and tools, grain, and wine. They obviously were on a trading expedition of greater sophistication than Columbus had observed previously. He did not consider trying to find out the source of the trading mission and its links to the Maya and Aztec regions. He spent nine months sailing up and down the coast just short of the Gulf of Darien. As expected, they were intoxicated by greed for gold and, making the same mistakes as in Española in seizing the chief and several Indians as captives and setting fire to their village, Indian hospitality turned to resistance. The Spaniards were forced to flee to Jamaica where they were marooned for almost a year. Ill and overcome by a profound self-pity, Columbus coped with the failure of this expedition by reminding the monarchs in a letter he sent to them that he "was arrested and cast into a ship with my two brothers, shackled with chains and naked in body...I came to serve you at the age of 28 [sic] and now I have not a hair on me that is not white, and my body is infirm and exhausted." His depression overwhelmed him. Gone was the confidence that nourished his stubbornness and obsession with the enterprise of the Indies: "Alone, desolate, infirm, daily expecting death, surrounded by a million savages full of cruelty and our enemies...weep for me, whoever has charity, truth, and justice." On his return to Spain, his gloom deepened when he learned that queen Isabella was dying. He was still able at times to bounce back, confident that he would return to Española as viceroy. Yet, he was so obsessed with regaining his entitlement that one would conclude that he had lost everything. But the remittances from the revived economy in Española made him a wealthy man. King Ferdinand was friendly to his interests, giving Columbus's son Diego an excellent pension. He even made a match for him with the duke of Alba's niece, Doña Maria de Toledo. Columbus, however, could not be satisfied. As he lay dying, he kept insisting to the new rulers of Castile, Juana and Felipe: "The untoward circumstances into which I have been plunged, contrary to all rational expectation, and other adversities, have left me in dire extremity...I very humbly beseech you to accept my purpose and intent...as one who hopes to be restored to his honor and estate." Columbus died on May 20, 1506.

The Colonization of the Caribbean

The arrival of Ovando in 1502 with some 2500 Spaniards infused a new dynamism in Española. No sooner had they arrived than they rushed to the gold mines where, crowded in camps with gangs of native workers, they came down with tropical diseases and, like the native people, died in large numbers. Ovando set out to pacify the island more completely than Columbus and Bobadilla had done. Spanish control of the island became dominant and the production of gold increased with a more efficient, coercive system. The royal share was reduced from one half to one fifth; Indians were allocated to individual settlers first for six months, then eight months, and then for an unlimited time. The cost of the pacification and efficiency was Indian suffering and death. The southeast island of Saona was totally ravaged; in the province of Higuey numerous captives were taken and the queen of Higuey slain. In 1503 Ovando marched into the western part of Xaragua where they were met and entertained by queen Anacaona and chieftains of the province. She and her brother Behecchio had earlier offered to Bartholomew Columbus and Roldan friendship and tribute. In the midst of festivities in the royal house, Ovando gave the signal to massacre the Indians. The higher Indian nobility, including queen Anacaona, were burned to death; those of less rank were cut to pieces. In 1504 Juan de Esquivel and Ponce de Leon utterly destroyed the province of Higuey.

More towns were established. By 1508 there were fifteen. Ovando organized a system whereby each Spanish town was governed by a council (Cabildo) consisting of those who held *encomiendas and repartimientos.* Many of the towns were constructed near pacified Indian villages whose inhabitants were allocated to encomenderos in the nearby Spanish town. There was no shortage of food. European livestock, cattle, horses, and pigs increased bountifully, and cassava bread was plentiful. The rub was that the native people were dying alarmingly.

In 1503 members of the Board of Trade (*Casa de Contratacion*) drew up elaborate plans for the exploitation of the mainland. They had persuaded queen Isabella to issue an order permitting the capture and enslavement of "cannibals" who refused to receive the Catholic faith, a policy that was to have unfortunate consequences for the Indians. This would serve as the rationalization for slave-raiding to meet the shortage of labor in the islands that were colonized. The colonists now had the legal means to twist her condemnation of Indian slavery in 1500 to serve their ends. The mainland was now fair game for slaves. Native Indians who resisted were lumped into the same category as Caribs and cannibals.[21] This duality in the European consciousness of the "guileless and ferocious" Indian began with Columbus's first voyage. In his Journal, he wrote that he "found no monsters, nor had a report of any, except in an island "Carib",...which is inhabited by a people who are regarded in all the islands as very fierce and who eat human flesh."[22] Columbus provided no evidence to support his statement. The myth of the native cannibal would grow into an obsession among Spaniards. In his letter to the Cabildo of Seville describing his experience of the second voyage with Columbus, the physician Diego Chanca wrote of "finding countless human bones and hollowed heads hanging from houses." Peter Martyr's letter to Pomponius Letto in 1494 described the Caribs in a manner that would stick to them forever: "They attack villages and eat raw the men they capture; they castrate boys as we, chickens; and when they have grown and fattened, they cut off their heads and eat them."[23] Perhaps, the most sensational treatment of this theme was undoubtedly the first woodcut portraying native Americans, inspired by Vespucci's *Mundus Novus* letter about his experience among the Brazilian Indians.[24] The commentary to the pictures was: "...the men take for wife those that please them, be it their mothers, sisters, or friends, for they make no distinction. They fight among themselves and eat each other, even those they massacre, and hang their flesh over smoke." European explorers like Vespucci had not yet mastered Indian languages and hence their knowledge of native customs had to be at best sketchy. Yet, this portrayal of cannibal Indians would persist until the eighteenth century. Few Europeans attempted to verify whether this description was accurate. One of the few contemporary narratives which tried to analyze the reports of cannibalism was provided by Cuneo who accompanied Columbus on his second voyage: "We heard it said that when the father of someone is ill, the son goes to the temple, tells the idol that his father is ill and asks whether his father will be cured or not and waits for a reply. If the answer is no, the son returns to his home, cuts his father's head and cooks it: I do not believe that they eat it, but when it is white they place it in the temple. They do this only for lords of high rank."[25] Cuneo then was trying to place what they or others had seen within a religious context. At any rate, the lurid descriptions of allegedly cannibal Indians influenced queen Isabella to issue the order permitting the enslavement of Carib Indians.

Between 1504 and 1506 Juan de la Cosa and Alonso de Hojeda were licensed to make another expedition to the mainland with the hope of establishing settlements.[26] But the urge for gold and slaves again overcame any thought of settlement. Cartagena was attacked by practically every Spanish expedition and its people resisted fiercely. Their hostility earned them the category of Caribs and cannibals and left them prey to slave raiders. In the meantime, Ferdinand called a meeting at Toro in 1505 to discuss the affairs of the Indies. He invited Amerigo Vespucci, who had now become a Spanish citizen, and Vicente Yañez Pinzon to attend. The uncertain political climate in Castile following queen Isabella's death forced Ferdinand to abort the conference. The conference resumed in 1508 in Burgos. Vespucci was made chief pilot, an office that supervised the training and licensing of navigators. Juan de la Cosa and Juan Diaz de Solis, who had been sailing in Asian waters under Portuguese patronage, also attended the meeting. The conference reached agreement on several projects. Yañez Pinzon and Solis were urged to sail north and west from the Gulf of Honduras with the hope of finding a strait that would take them to Asia. They sailed up the coast of Mexico to the north of Tampico, but found no strait. Diego de Nicuesa was given rights to mainland South America west of the Gulf of Uraba; Alonso de Hojeda, east to Codera. Both parties sailed in Dec. 1509 from Española to Cartagena where they encountered stiff resistance. Juan de la Cosa was killed in 1510; Nicuesa embarked on a mission of killing and looting; Hojeda and his group built a fort in Uraba but had to retreat due to Indian attacks and a shortage of provisions. Wounded by a poisoned arrow, Hojeda sailed to Española. The command of the fort at Uraba was given to Francisco de Pizarro, who twenty years later would be involved in the conquest of Peru. It was Vasco Nuñez de Balboa who persuaded the Spaniards to seize the town of Darien, west of Uraba. This was a stroke of luck. Food was plentiful as were native houses. It seemed that the native people in this town wished to live in peace with the Spanish strangers. There were indications, too, that prospects of finding gold were good. So, the Spaniards established a town here, Santa Maria La Antigua de Darien, which became the base for explorations into the interior of the continent.

The boom in the mining of gold in Española was short-lived. The decline in the supply of gold paralleled the decline in population. It was therefore decided to colonize Puerto Rico, Jamaica, and Cuba. Governor Ovando had sent Juan Ponce de Leon in 1508 to pacify and colonize Puerto Rico. That island was initially classified as Carib but rumors that it possessed great mineral wealth persuaded that authorities to remove it from that category, thereby saving it from the ravages of the slave traders. Ponce de Leon had become wealthy from this enterprise. Upon Ovando's retirement in 1509, Columbus's son Diego became governor of Española. Diego ordered Juan de Esquivel and Panfilo de Narvaez to occupy and colonize Jamaica. Columbus had visited Jamaica on his second and fourth voyages, spending almost a year in that island.[27] Contemporary accounts indicated that Puerto Rico and Jamaica were densely populated islands.[28] There was no gold in Jamaica but all commentators had marveled at its food supplies and the peaceful nature of its inhabitants. The Spanish colonists introduced the repartimiento in both Jamaica and Puerto Rico.[29]

In Jamaica, Indians grew cassava, maize , and cotton for export to the settlers on the mainland in Panama and also for those in Cuba. They also had to build roads with the hope that new Spanish migrants might settle. Indian women made cloth and hammocks from Jamaican cotton. The colonization of Jamaica was no different than in Española. The native population declined catastrophically. Esquivel stayed as governor until 1515 when he was replaced by Francisco de Garay. Horses, pigs and cattle had replaced human beings as the inhabitants of Jamaica.

Diego Colon authorized in 1511 Diego Velasquez to occupy Cuba, the same Velasquez who had earlier massacred the assembled chiefs in the western part of Española. Velasquez was joined by Narvaez from Jamaica. Their soldiers then proceeded to pacify the island. After the unprovoked massacre at Caonao by Narvaez, the native people and their chiefs fled from wherever the Spaniards approached. Gold was discovered near the Bay of Xagua and precipitated a rush there from Española and the mainland. The repartimiento was predictably introduced. By 1514 six Spanish towns were founded and Velasquez established his capital at Santiago de Cuba. In less than ten years the population of Cuba had also dramatically declined.

In the face of a declining native population and the consequent shortage of labor, Spanish colonial administration pushed at full steam the policy of designating certain islands as Carib, thereby permitting slave raiding there. The Lucayan Indians of the Bahamas, portrayed by Columbus on his first voyage as gentle and kind, were lured to Española by Spaniards who promised that they would meet their departed loved ones in that island. On Española they found "neither father, mother nor loved ones but iron tools and instruments and gold mines instead, where they perished in no time." When pearls were discovered around Cubagua island near Venezuela, the Lucayans were dragged there to swim and dive for pearls. To find "a single Lucayo alive was almost a miracle." Pedro de Isla, hoping to bring the remaining Lucayans to Española to teach them Christianity, journeyed to the Bahamas in search of the native peoples. After three years, he found only eleven people.

The islands of the Bahamas, Trinidad, Barbados, Curaçao, Aruba, Bonaire, and Margarita were classified as Carib.[30] But knowledge about the inhabitants of these islands was arbitrary. Trinidad, for example, was initially designated as Carib in 1511 but was taken off the list after Las Casas challenged this in 1518. It was reclassified as Carib in 1533 along with Guadeloupe, Dominica, and Tobago. The lifting of Carib designation in 1520 was motivated in part by prospects for the mining of gold in Trinidad. When this proved futile, its importance lay in providing Indian slaves to Española and Puerto Rico and, above all, in its strategic location to the new centers of Spanish colonization in South America and the pearl fisheries. Antonio de Sedeno was sent from Puerto Rico in 1530 to colonize the island. Native resistance was fierce. As late as 1569 armadas of slave raiders would pounce on the island, depopulating the island in the process. As for Curacão, Bonaire, and Aruba, when these islands were reclassified as not being Carib in 1520, there were few natives left.

It was becoming clear by the second decade of the sixteenth century that a colonial system was coming into place. The organization established by Christopher Columbus was arbitrary and haphazard. It seemed that he had in mind initially establishing trading posts which he had observed the Portuguese create in West Africa. The settlement, pacification, and the introduction of the encomienda after his second voyage to the Indies, leave little doubt that Columbus conceived of Española and the Indies more like the Canary Islands than Portuguese trading-posts. The island peoples and economies were conquered and organized to enrich himself and other Europeans. But the project of reaching Asia by sailing west consumed him. It was left to bishop Fonseca and the royal treasurer, Miguel de Pasamonte, to organize the discoveries into a colonial system. Built around the exploitation of gold, the production of sugar, the provisioning of food, and the export of European livestock, Fonseca and Pasamonte, while not abandoning the dream of a western route to Asia, were already creating the structure of their vision of the new found world with the hope of bringing a bonanza for Spain. The shortage of labor caused by the decline in the native population threatened the system with collapse, but they tried cleverly to solve this problem with native American and African slave labor. It was Hernan Cortes who understood the political and economic significance of this new world of America after his conquest of Mexico in 1521, and organized Mexico into an imperial system. But the outlines of this system were already beginning to take shape in the Caribbean. As the first act of the European conquest of America was coming to an end in the Caribbean, the most significant consequence of the encounter between Europeans and native Americans was not the wealth that was discovered nor the colonial system that was established, but the destruction of the native peoples.[31]

NOTES

Chapter 2

1. For the Genoese origin of Christopher Columbus and his family, see *Journals and other Documents on the Life and Voyages of Christopher Columbus*, trans. and ed. by Samuel Eliot Morison, (New York, 1963), 7-10.

2. There are several histories of Columbus and his voyages. Among the more recent in English are: Felipe Fernandez-Armesto, *Columbus*, (Oxford, 1991); John Noble Wilford, *The Mysterious History of Columbus: An Exploration of the Man, the Myth, the Legacy.* (New York, 1991); Carla Rahn Phillips, *The Worlds of Christopher Columbus*, (Cambridge, 1992). In addition to the works

by Kirkpatrick Sale and Ronald Wright that criticize Columbus, see D.J.R. Walker, *Columbus and the Golden World of the Island Arawaks,* (London, 1991); Ian Wilson, *The Columbus Myth,* (New York, 1991); for works that deal with the encounter, see B. Litvinoff, *1492. The Year and the Era,* (London, 1991): Carlos Fuentes, *The Burried Mirror: Reflections on Spain and the New World,* (New York, 1992); Sardar, Z.,et Al., *The Blinded Eye,* Goa, India, 1993.

3. Fernando Colon, V-XVII.

4. C. R. Boxer, "The Politics of the Discoveries," in *Portugal and Brazil. The Age of Atlantic Discoveries,* eds. M. J. Guedes and G. Lombardi, (New York, 1990) 264-267, see also J. Martins da Silva Marques, *Descobrimentos Portugueses,* 3 vols. (Coimbra, 1940-71).

5. Paolo Toscanelli, a Florentine physician , met Canon Martins, a delegate from Portugal, at the church council of Florence in 1438-1445. They were interested in resuming contact with China after its disruption in the early 14th century. Toscanelli held that the land mass of China was extensive, as was held by Marco Polo, and consequently he calculated that the distance from the Canary Islands to China was about 3,000 miles. When Columbus came across Toscanelli's correspondence with Martins, he was of course excited by its confirmation of his own thesis and wrote to Toscanelli. The authenticity of some of Columbus's correspondence with Toscanelli is still disputed. For the Toscanelli letters, see *Journals and other Documents,* 11-17. For a discussion of the dispute, see H. Vignaud, *Toscanelli and Columbus,* (London, 1902).

6. See J. Manzano y Manzano, *Cristóbal Colón: Siete Años Decisivos de su Vida,* (Madrid, 1964) 321-328; Felipe Fernandez-Armesto, *op. cit., 45-65.*

7. O'Gorman, *op. cit.,* 54-69.

8. Robert M. Tisnes, *Alejandro Geraldini,* (Santo Domingo, 1987) 19-59.

9. J. H. Elliott, *Imperial Spain, 1469-1716,* (New York, 1966).

10. *Ibid.,* 44-55. See also the fascinating work by the Lebanese writer Amin Maalouf, *Leo Africanus,* paperback ed. (New York, 1992).

11. See Antonio Rumeu de Armas, *La Política Indigenista de Isabella,* (Valladolid, 1969); F. Fernandes-Armesto, *The Canary Islands After the Conquest,* (Oxford, 1989); E. Aznar Vallejo, *La Integración de las Islas*

Canarias en la Corona de Castilla, (Seville, 1984) 23-87.

12. *Journal,* 147-148. See also E. Jos, "El Libro del Primer Viaje. Algunas Ediciones Recientes," *Revista de Indias,* X(1950) 719-751. For a discussion of the significance of cannibals for Columbus in his journal, see P. Hulme, *op.cit.,* 13-87. The journal derived from the version of Las Casas who partly summarized the journal entries, partly quoted them directly from the original manuscript which was lost.

13. See Cristobal Colon, *The Letter of Columbus on the Discovery of the New World,* trans. by S.E. Morison, (Los Angeles, 1989) 31-38, 41-48; Las Casas, *History,* 38-39.

14. Pedro Martir, *Epistolario,* ed. by J. Lopez de Toro, (Madrid, 1953) p. 138.

15. The Treaty of Tordesillas of June 7, 1494 was ratified by the pope in 1506. O'Gorman, *op. cit.* p.156 n.16.

16. For Columbus's memorial to the sovereigns on colonial policy of April 1493, and the instructions of the sovereigns to Columbus for his second voyage, on May 29, 1493, see *Journal and Other Documents,* 199-208. In these documents it appeared that initially Columbus wanted to establish trading factories as the Portuguese did in West Africa. He changed his mind shortly after. For the second voyage, see also Michele de Cuneo's letter of October 28, 1495 in *Journal and Other Documents,* 209-228; also, the letter of Guillermo Coma translated into Latin by Syllacio in 1494, in *Journal and Other Documents,* 229-245. See also the letter of Dr. Alvaro Chanca in *Select Documents Illustrating the Four Voyages of Columbus,* ed. and trans. by Cecil Jane, 2 vols. (London, 1930-32) 18-103; also, the report of Andres Bernaldez in *Colección de los Viages y Descubrimientos,* ed. by Martin Navarrete, 3 vols, (Madrid, 1825) I, 308-310.

17. See S.E. Morison, "The Earliest Colonial Policy toward America: that of Columbus," *Bulletin of the Pan American Union,* LXXVI(1942) 543-555; Carl Ortwin Sauer, *The Early Spanish Main,* (Berkeley, Cal., 1965) 71-97; G.R. Crone, *The Discovery of America,* (New York, 1969 111-117.

18. *Journal and Other Documents,* 239-240.

19. Las Casas, *History,* bk. 1, 59-60.

20. See Columbus's letter on the third voyage, Oct. 18, 1498 and to Doña Juana de Torres in *Journal and Other Documents*, 284-298; Sauer, *op. cit.*, 97-103.

21. *Portugal and Brazil. The Age of Atlantic Discoveries*, p.267.

22. See the letter of Dr. Chanca of 1493 in *Select Documents*, 18-103; see also Jalil Sued Badillo, *Los Caribes: Realidad o Fábula*, (Rio Piedras, P.R., 1978) p. 42.

23. Pedro Mártir, *Epistolario*, letter 146; Badillo, p. 47.

24. *Portugal/Brazil*, pp. 93, 113. See Amerigo Vespucci, *The Mundus Novus Letter to Lorenzo Medici*, trans. with intro. by George Tyler Northup, (Princeton, 1916) p.6.

25. Michele de Cuneo in *Journal and Other Documents*, 209-228.

26. Las Casas, *History*, bk.2, 161-178; Sauer, 108-119.

27. Las Casas, *History*, 129-145; *The Lettera Rarissima* of July 1503 gave the first news of the fourth voyage. See *Journal and Other Documents*, 371-398.

28. *Journal and Other Documents*, p. 385.

29. Francisco Morales Padrón, *Jamaica Española*, (Seville, 1952) 260-261.

30. Badillo, 75-80.

31. Las Casas, *History*, bk.2, 154-161.

RESISTANCE: DEATH: SLAVERY

Resistance:Caonabo

In leaving some of his men to protect the fortress at La Navidad as he set out for Spain after his successful first voyage, Columbus felt certain that no harm would befall them because "these people are a friendly and amiable race." If the native inhabitants became hostile, however, he was in no doubt that his men would be victorious because the native people were "destitute of weapons, go naked, and are very cowardly." On his return to La Navidad, he learned that the entire party he had left had been killed. Theft of their property and women and an awareness that these powerful strangers intended to stay were the reasons that converted American Indians to hostility. The construction of a new capital town at Isabella and a string of forts along the way to the gold fields in the Vega Real left little doubt in the minds of native leaders that the foreigners intended to stay. The incident at the Yaque river in April 1494 in which Alonso de Hojeda humiliated Indian caciques by cutting off the ears of a chief was a grim portent of future relations. Fears over a possible Indian uprising were present in the minds of Columbus and the Spaniards. He had not forgotten the deaths of his men at La Navidad and blamed Caonabo, the cacique of the province of Maguana, for the disaster. Miguel de Cuneo heard stories that Caonabo's headquarters was near Fort St. Thomas and the gold fields.[1] It was felt that an attack by Caonabo was imminent. To be fair to Columbus, the condition of the Spaniards in Española in 1494 was miserable. The deaths of large numbers from disease and starvation added to his anxiety. He sent a plan to Pedro Margarite, commander of Fort St. Thomas, to capture Caonabo by deception: "Treat him with words until you have his friendship, in order the better to seize him."[2] Margarite, who had the reputation of rejecting the policy of violence to the Indian, did not carry out Columbus's plan, but Hojeda did. Marching with nine men across the central range to Caonabo's capital, Hojeda lavished gifts and words of friendship to Caonabo and then seized him.

Caonabo's imprisonment at Isabella led to the first native American uprising in late 1494. His brother rallied a force of some seven thousand Tainos with the intention of attacking the Spaniards and rescuing Caonabo. The support of a contingent of cavalry and a reserve sent by Bartholomew Colon enabled Hojeda to rout the Taino army. Caonabo's brother and other native leaders were imprisoned. Oviedo attributed the Taino defeat to the novelty of fighting against cavalry and the fact that "God wished to favor our men and gave them victory."[3] Fearing that the presence of Caonabo and his brother would encourage another insurrection, it was decided to send them to Spain. When they learned their fate, Caonabo and his brother died shortly after, according to Oviedo. Caonabo's wife, Anacaona, left Maguana to settle in the western region of Xaragua where her brother Behecchio was cacique. In this way Caonabo's territory was "pacified by the Christians." Las Casas interpreted this event differently. He blamed Columbus ultimately for what happened: "He inspired fear and displayed power, declared war and violated a jurisdiction that was not his but the Indian; and it seems to me this is not using the door but a window to enter a house." In the view of Las Casas, Columbus's guiding principle of relations with the native people was "first and foremost to instill fear in these people, to the extent of making the name Christian synonymous with terror."[4]

Guarionex

The crushing defeat of Caonabo and his brother forced the remaining Taino chiefs to adopt a realistic attitude towards Spanish aggression and their demand for tribute in gold. In the western region of Xaragua, cacique Behecchio and his sister Anacaona proposed to Bartholomew Colon that they would provide cotton and cassava bread because there was no gold in their region. The remaining native leaders hoped to preserve their authority and autonomy by making concessions on the issue of tribute. This was the policy, too, of Guarionex, the most important chieftain of the Vega Real, the area that witnessed the most extensive mining activity. He agreed to pay the tribute of gold, food and cotton. Guarionex had experienced the terror inspired by the Spanish use of cavalry and dogs in the first rebellion. By 1497, however, there was widespread grumbling among the Tainos. In the context of famine and sickness, the tribute seemed burdensome and harsh. Some Taino chiefs urged another rebellion; they saw Guarionex's accommodation as appeasement and cowardice.[5]

The division within the Spanish camp between the rival supporters of Francisco Roldan and Columbus made the current situation different from 1494 and gave hope to those who argued for insurrection. Roldan nudged Guarionex to attack the fort at Concepcion Real and promised assistance from his troops. Guarionex promptly massed his army near Vega Real. But Columbus's brother Bartholomew was more than a match for him. With some four hundred men, he marched to meet Guarionex. An attack at night on the surrounding villages caught the Tainos off their guard. Taino culture prohibited battles being fought at night. Fourteen of their leaders, including Guarionex, were captured. Bereft of their leaders and panic-stricken, the Tainos went in tears to Bartholomew's headquarters to ask that their leaders be released. Realizing that this rebellion was effectively crushed and wishing to preserve the existing tribute system, Bartholomew released Guarionex and other leaders. What Guarionex learned from this experience was that he had to steer his policies between the increasing demands of his people to do something to alleviate the burdens of the Spanish tribute system on the one hand, and to appease Bartholomew Colon on the other lest he come down on his people with a heavier hand. After a year this delicate political situation proved too difficult to manage. Guarionex fled with his family first to Vega Real and then to the north where he was hidden by Mayobanex, chief of the northern mountain region. Bartholomew Colon, fearing that the natives might rally around him in another insurrection, pursued and captured him. Chained, he was sent to Spain in 1502, but his ship sank in a storm.

Enriquillo

The defeat of Guarionex did not mean the end of native resistance in Española. The struggle of Cotubanama to preserve the autonomy of the eastern province of Higuey against the brutality of Juan Esquivel, and that of Hatuey against Diego Velasquez on the west coast were memorable. Both Cotubanama and Hatuey met their deaths by hanging. Spaniards encountered organized resistance in Puerto Rico as well as in Cartagena on the mainland of South America. The resistance of Enriquillo, however, was unique in that he harried the Spaniards for eighteen years and won an agreement that was sanctioned by the emperor Charles V.[6] This was the first agreement in the Americas between Europeans and native Americans as equals.

Guarocuya or Enriquillo, as he was known, was raised and educated in a Franciscan monastery. He returned as chief to his ancestral village in the province of Baoruco, near the southern coast. He and his wife Lucia were married as Christians. Repeatedly humiliated by a Spanish encomendero, Valenzuela, he restrained his anger until it was unbearable. Valenzuela seized his horse and later raped his wife. Enriquillo complained to the governor, Pedro de Vadillo, but was threatened with imprisonment. Determined to obtain justice, he took his case to the Audiencia in Santo Domingo, the supreme legal council, but was given the run around and told to take up the matter with the governor. As Las Casas put it: "They returned the plaintiff to his own enemies, the offenders." Enriquillo then led a full-scale native rebellion in 1519 which lasted until 1538.

One reason for the support that Enriquillo received was the recently introduced policy of the Jeronymite friars in 1517 to resettle the native people in artificially segregated villages of about 500 people. This policy had as its objective the conversion of the Tainos to Christianity. The toll from the small-pox epidemic of 1518-1519 convinced Tainos that this policy would expose them to disease and death.

Enriquillo and his followers returned to Taino ways of life. For more than a dozen years, he held his own against several Spanish contingents. With each victory, more native people joined him. He raised an efficient army by stealing Spanish weapons. He protected the old and women who had joined his movement: "For greater safety, he ordered various areas of land to be cultivated, and straw huts built in patches ten or twelve leagues apart over a surface of approximately 40 leagues; and in these huts he sheltered women, children and old people, sometimes here and sometimes there, according to his better judgement...The fame of Enrique's victories, diligence, courage, and war tactics spread more and more."[7] Native leaders from other parts of Española hastened to join Enriquillo. The rebellion had turned into a general insurrection.

News of this reached Charles V who was aware of the seriousness of this revolt. He saw the prospect of losing all of Española. He sent captain Francisco Barrionuevo with instructions for the Audiencia of Santo Domingo to negotiate a peace treaty with Enriquillo. After consulting with the Audiencia, Barrionuevo set out to find Enriquillo. Two months later, he presented him with letters from the king and the Audiencia, confirming the terms of peace: "He and his people would be allowed to live as free men on that part of the island Enrique would choose, and the Spaniards would not disturb them in any way." Enriquillo accepted. He died a year after the peace agreement. Las Casas said that the peace agreement lasted for four or five years.

Anton de Montesinos

On Sunday, Nov. 30, 1511, the Dominican friar, Anton de Montesinos gave the first sermon on the treatment of the native peoples of the new-found world in the presence of the admiral, Diego Colon, royal officials, and jurists of Santo Domingo: "I have come here in order to declare it unto you, I the voice of Christ in the desert of this island. Open your hearts and your senses, all of you, for this voice will speak new things harshly, and will be frightening...This voice says that you are living in deadly sin for the atrocities you tyrannically impose on these innocent people. Tell me, what right have you to enslave them? What authority did you use to make war against them who lived at peace on their territories, killing them cruelly with methods never before heard of? How can you oppress them and not care to feed or cure them, and work them to death to satisfy your greed?...Aren't they human beings? Have they no rational soul? Aren't you obliged to love them as you love yourselves?"[8]

Stunned by these sentiments, Spanish officials immediately went to see Montesinos and demanded a retraction. They threatened to take their complaints to the Crown and have the Dominicans sent back to Spain. What the colonists did not know was that the sermon was the product of a collective effort on the part of the Dominicans who, arriving in 1510, had reflected seriously on the treatment of the native people at the hands of Spanish colonists. They had found, for example, the account of the colonist, Juan Garces, persuasive. Garces had confessed to the "loathsome atrocities which he and others had committed in war and peace"[9] Officials and encomenderos crowded the cathedral in Santo Domingo the following Sunday, expecting a recantation. Montesinos surprised them once more by reiterating firmly that the words he uttered previously were true and insisted that Spanish rule was oppressive and illegal. The friars of his order, he said, would refuse to confess colonists who did not change their ways. He assured them that their threats did not bother him. They could take their complaints to anyone they pleased.

Anton de Montesinos had come to Española in 1510 with Fray Pedro de Cordoba, Fray Bernardo de Santo Domingo, and a lay member of the

Dominican order. Their number had grown to twelve, but they were in hot water with the colonists after the sermons of Fray Montesinos. The colonists sent a delegation under the Franciscan Alonso de Espinal to Spain to present their complaints against he Dominicans. That Espinal was persuaded to support the position of the colonists showed that the church was divided on this issue, much to the satisfaction of the colonists. Espinal had led some Franciscan monks to Española in 1502. They established convents in several towns and the process of conversion seemed promising. Some 3,000 Tainos were baptized in a short space of time. Espinal himself wanted to establish a Franciscan province in Española, but the colonists were not keen to assist the Franciscans establish a presence in the villages of Española. The number of conversions declined. Franciscans then shifted their interest to educating the sons of the native nobility in their monasteries.

Las Casas did not deny the virtue, religious zeal, and knowledge of Espinal, but charged that, in his ignorance, Espinal's support for the colonists would "further the cause of servitude and captivity." King Ferdinand favored the position taken by Espinal who had received support from the royal secretary, Lope de Conchillos. Montesinos found it necessary to go to Spain to present his point of view and to try to convince the king of the urgency of a solution to the issue of the cruel treatment of the native people. The king assembled a committee of jurists at Burgos in 1512 to discuss this question. Among the distinguished jurists were Lopez de Palacios Rubios and Matias de Paz. Montesinos presented his position before the committee in a treatise entitled *Juridicial Information on the Defense of the Indians*. Out of the presentations and deliberations of this committee came the Laws of Burgos of Sept. 27, 1512. This document insisted that Indians were free men and urged that the labor they provided be not oppressive. Yet, most of the propositions assumed that the native people would be allotted to the colonists. Pedro de Cardoba hurried to Spain to join Montesinos. They were both disappointed with the provisions of the laws and pleaded with the Crown to change some of them. Through their instrumentality, four propositions were added to the laws on July 28, 1513, declaring that Indian women and children were to be exempt from excessive labor.

Cordoba obtained permission to undertake a mission to Cumana in Venezuela and had hoped that Montesinos would lead it, but illness prevented him from doing so. His illness proved to be fortunate because Indians attacked the Dominican mission in Cumana in retaliation for the treachery of Spaniards who seized their chief. Pedro de Cordoba returned to Española where he completed his *Doctrina Christiana*, a handbook of Christian teaching which was to have enormous influence in the future evangelization of Spanish America. In 1514 the Dominicans in Española were joined by Bartolome de Las Casas, a man they had inspired and who would later be the center of the struggle for justice for the native people of America for over fifty years. As Pedro de Cordoba was anxious to keep the Indian question before the Crown, he sent Montesinos and Las Casas to Spain in 1515. Montesinos stayed for two years while Las Casas did not return to Española until the end of 1520. They held interviews with important officials like Cardinal Cisneros, Bishop Fonseca, and the jurist Palacios Rubios and built up a network of sympathizers which Las Casas would use effectively in the course of the struggle for the native American. Made regent upon Ferdinand's death in 1516, Cardinal Cisneros put into effect his plan of the Indies, sending Jeronymite friars to settle the differences between Franciscans and Dominicans and introduce his plan for conversion of the Indians. In essence, the plan involved resettling native Americans in segregated villages under their own chiefs. The amount of work was regulated, divided between tilling their own fields and producing food for the colonists. They were to follow the routine of Christian prayers and rituals. It was hoped that by this method they would be assimilated to Christianity. The experiment proved disastrous as the decline in the native population reached catastrophic proportions. In 1521 Pedro de Cordoba died. Montesinos and Fray Tomas de Berlanga, vice-provincial of the Dominicans, set out for Spain in 1528 to recruit more missionaries for work in the Indies and to keep the issue of Indian rights at the center of the enterprise of the Indies. Around 1536, he set out for Venezuela to evangelize and defend its native peoples. He died in Venezuela on June 27, 1540. Cesar Sepulveda, professor of law at the university of Mexico, summed up the significance of Montesinos in this way: "The original idea of the dignity of the human person, independent of his race or origin, of the natural equality among all human beings, and the liberty flowing from this equality has its first and indelible manifestations in America with the sermons of the celebrated Anton de Montesinos."[10]

Bartolome de Las Casas: His Struggle in the Caribbean

In 1514 Bartolome de Las Casas, who had a prosperous encomienda in Cuba, decided to join Anton de Montesinos and Pedro de Cordoba in the struggle to defend the rights of native American people. He came to Española in 1502 in the fleet that brought Nicholas de Ovando. His father Pedro had sailed with Columbus on his second voyage and had acquired property in Española. What awakened the conscience of Las Casas to the cruelties of the conquest? He was given an encomienda in Española and had participated in expeditions to eastern Española to seize Indians.[11] In 1510 he was ordained a priest. He spoke little about why he chose to do this. The Dominican friars had arrived that very year and it was possible that Pedro de Cordoba had ordained him. He came under their influence and was acquainted with the crisis that ensued after Anton de Montesinos denounced the colonists. At any rate, he was not yet persuaded to change his ways. The weight of property was heavier than principle. Writing later about this dilemma, he recalled his feelings: "He remembered how one day on Española, where he had owned Indians with the same carelessness and blindness as in Cuba, a Dominican friar had refused him confession. He asked why, was given the reason, and proceeded to refute the friar, giving frivolous arguments and vain solutions that had a semblance of truth, but the friar interrupted him with, "Enough, Father, truth has many disguises but so do lies."...as far as giving up his Indians, he paid no attention."[12]

In 1512 Las Casas accompanied Diego Velasquez in the pacification and colonization of Cuba. He and his friend, Pedro de la Renteria, were given a large encomienda near the Ariamo river, a major gold site. His interests were no different from other colonists: "He went about his concerns like the others, sending his share of the Indians to work fields and gold mines, taking advantage of them as much as he could." As he traveled across Cuba, however, the experience of witnessing the suffering of the native peoples persuaded him that he could no longer deny the cruelty of the Spanish colonization: "Death made speedier ravages among Indians here than in other places, starvation and hard labor helping. Since all able-bodied men and women were away at the mines, only the old and sick stayed in town with no one to look after them. So they died of illness, anguish, and starvation. I was traveling the Cuban roads then and it happened that entering a town I sometimes heard crying in the houses.   I would inquire and was greeted with the words "'hungry, hungry'." In 1514 he became convinced of the injustice of the system of colonization. He gave up his encomienda and, in a sermon on Aug. 15th, denounced the encomienda, demanding restitution to the Indians. Las Casas noted that the colonists were shocked: "Everyone was surprised, even astonished, to hear this and some walked away remorseful, while others thought they had been dreaming - the idea of sinning because one used Indians was as incredible as saying man could not use domestic animals." His efforts made little impact on the colonists. Early in his life as an activist, therefore, criticism of systems of forced labor and the recommendation of restitution became core political principles for him. As happened in Española, the attack on encomiendas created tensions in Cuba. Las Casas decided to argue his case before the royal officials in Spain. He journeyed to Española to consult with Pedro de Cordoba and the Dominicans on the issue before leaving with Anton de Montesinos for Spain. In the meantime, the Cuban colonists had sent Panfilo de Narvaez and Antonio Velasquez to Spain to present their side of the story. Las Casas and Montesinos were not unaware of the difficulty of their struggle. The economy in Spain was becoming increasingly dependent on gold from the New World. Although the gold boom in Española had declined by 1515, promising finds were located in Cuba and the Darien region. In addition, royal officials and men of power in Spain had a stake in the encomienda. The royal secretary, Lope de Conchillos, and the chief administrator of the Indies, Bishop Fonseca, were awarded large encomiendas in 1514. The promise of wealth for many in America and Europe depended upon the continuation of the encomienda.

Las Casas met the ailing king Ferdinand on Christmas eve, 1515, in Plasencia and discussed the affairs of the Indies with him. While waiting for a second meeting in Seville, he visited Conchillos and Fonseca, only confirming his opinion of them as opportunists. King Ferdinand died on Jan. 25, 1516 and the government of Spain was temporarily in the hands of Cardinal Ximinez de Cisneros. Las Casas presented proposals for a different kind of encounter between Europeans and native Americans. Cisneros was interested and formed a small committee to discuss the project, comprising Las Casas, Montesinos, and Palacios Rubios.

The committee came up with a detailed plan for a community project in Cuba. The allocation of native Americans to individual Spaniards was to cease. Instead, new native villages would be constructed near Spanish towns. Colonists would be allocated a number of Indians to work the mines and fields. However, Indian villages were to receive adequate farming and grazing land, cows, pigs, sheep, and horses and have access to a hospital. They were to be taught reading, writing, and Spanish. Working hours would be limited and they were to receive vacations. Indians were not to be forced to work far from their homes. Las Casas felt that this system of colonization was more humane.[13] As a concession to reality, he suggested that this approach would be profitable as well. It must be remembered, however, that the most important consideration for Las Casas was to put a stop to the deaths of native Americans. It was the urgency of this issue that caused him to recommend that "if necessary, white and black slaves can be brought from Castile, to keep herds and build sugar mills, and wash gold." Las Casas would later confess that African slavery was as cruel as Indian slavery.[14] Cardinal Cisneros liked these proposals and decided to send a team of Jeronymite friars to reform the government of the Indies and the condition of the Indians.[15]

Both the plan drawn up by the committee and the instructions given to the Jeronymite friars bore the unmistakable marks of Las Casas's influence.[16] They were to take a census of the Indian populations of Española, Jamaica, Puerto Rico, and Cuba, require a written account of the treatment of Indians by settlers, encomenderos, governors, judges, and other officials. The central idea was to congregate the Indians in towns of 300 families each. Indian towns were to be established on fertile land, "near rivers and on good soil so that the Indians may live near their places of work and may engage in their own occupations such as fishing and tilling their land." A church, a hospital, plazas, and streets would adorn each town. The government of these towns would be in the hands of native rulers. Las Casas described every part of his plan in minute detail. Men between the ages of 20 and 50 were to work in the mines in three shifts, rotating every two months. As for the dispossessed Spanish settlers, Las Casas suggested that they could earn their livelihood as administrators or salaried gold prospectors. Las Casas later objected that the initiative to remove Indians from encomiendas was not made compulsory. Cardinal Cisneros appointed him "Protector of the Indians" at a salary of 100 gold pesos a year. Judge Alonso de Zuazo, who would also have a distinguished career in the Indies as an advocate for the Indians, was placed in charge of investigations.

Las Casas was beginning to have doubts about the mission even before the fleet carrying the friars left Spain on Nov. 11, 1516. He indicated to Cardinal Cisneros that lobbyists for the colonists were badgering the friars with their arguments and appeared to be finding favor with them. Las Casas's ship stopped first in Puerto Rico where he learned of a massacre of Indians on the island of Trinidad by Juan Bono and some Spanish colonists. He complained about this to the friars who had arrived in Santo Domingo before him but they showed little interest in this or other protests of Spanish cruelty. In fairness to the Jeronymite friars, one could hardly envy their responsibility. On the one hand, the colonists were united in their opposition to any plan that undermined the encomienda; on the other hand, Las Casas had the support of the Dominicans and fourteen French Franciscans in denouncing the allotment of Indians. Speaking on behalf of the Dominicans, Fray Bernardo de Santo Domingo insisted that not only the holders of encomiendas were in sin but also priests who absolved them, and even the Jeronymite friars. If the uncompromising attitude of the Dominicans was not likely to endear them to the Jeronymites, it did not help to persuade them to initiate a policy that was certain to invite considerable resentment from the colonists. Las Casas was convinced that nothing would be done and returned to Spain in 1517 to complain to Cardinal Cisneros. Yet, to say that the Jeronymite mission had failed was not completely true. Although the encomienda remained intact, the encomiendas of absentee royal officials were expropriated. Their properties were sold and the former owners compensated. The friars did conduct an inquiry among officials and settlers in Española about the treatment of native Americans. For the most part, the consensus was that native Americans were not civilized enough to be capable of using liberty. The project of establishing Indian towns was not carried out because of a devastating small-pox epidemic. The Jeronymites returned to Spain in 1520.

Cardinal Cisneros died on Nov. 8, 1517, a week before young king Charles arrived in Valladolid from Flanders. Las Casas who had come to Spain earlier that year wasted no time in currying favor with Charles's most influential advisers-Chancellor Jean le Sauvage, Monsieur de Chievres, and Monsieur de la Chaux, chamberlains. After he had wormed his way into their confidence, he lashed out at the policies of Bishop Fonseca and secretary Conchillos who dominated the affairs of the Indies. The consequence was that Las Casas became the trusted adviser of the king and chancellor on Indian affairs. He again proposed congregating Indians in towns and releasing them from encomiendas as the way to put a halt to the decimation of the population of Española. This new project was different. Spanish farmers would be encouraged to settle in America; free passage, a year's wages, tools, animals, and land were offered as incentives to migrate; awards were promised for cultivating silk, cinnamon, pepper, and cloves; sugar mills were to be established. Those who signed up for this colonization project would receive licenses to take twenty Black slaves. On Sept. 10, 1518, the Crown authorized Las Casas's proposal. The matter of providing Black slaves took a different turn than Las Casas had intended. The contract to provide 4,000 slaves was given to one of king Charles's friends, Governor Bresa, who then sold the license to Genoese merchants. The fate of African slaves was linked to the importance of sugar as a profitable industry and the establishment of sugar mills.

The initial recruitment drives were successful. Many farmers signed up to go to America. But enthusiasm was short-lived. Spanish landlords complained of losing their peasants; another small-pox epidemic hit Española. To top it all, the confiscated lands of the encomiendas of absentee royal officials, which were to finance the project, were sold. When the king refused to guarantee more financial support, Las Casas saw no alternative but to abandon his project. An aide, captain Berrio, persisted and with 200 peasants sailed for Española in 1520. Many became ill, destitute, or died, and the project never really got started.

Between 1519 and 1522 Las Casas was occupied in winning support for a proposal to establish a mission colony in the north of Venezuela. The Dominicans already had a mission on the mainland, as well as the Franciscans. But these missions were near the pearl island of Cubagua. Pedro de Cordoba had written to Las Casas complaining of atrocities and slave-raiding by Spaniards and urged him to ask the council to grant him 100 leagues of territory so that they could carry out better their mission to convert the Indians. Las Casas presented his petition to the king in 1519 but asked for a grant of 1000 leagues. He offered to finance the project with the aid of fifty shareholders and held out the promise to the king of huge profits from trade and gold in the proposed mission colony. Francisco Hernandez de Cordoba had already informed Las Casas of his encounter in 1517 with a more sophisticated and richer Indian society in Central America. Juan de Grijalva had followed up the voyage of Hernandez de Cordoba and had brought back gold and other objects, thereby raising the hopes once more of a major source of wealth. The news of this discovery was to spur Diego Velasquez to raise a fleet to explore that region, naming Hernan Cortes as captain. This expedition would ultimately lead to the conquest of Mexico in

1521. Las Casas used the excitement over the news about Central America to whip up support for his own venture by suggesting that the north coast of South America was also rich. What he was proposing was that a system of trade between a free native population and Spaniards was a more effective way to produce wealth than forced labor systems.

Before he gained approval for his proposal, he had to answer criticism from opponents like Bishop Fonseca and the royal historian, Gonzalo Fernandez de Oviedo y Valdes. In his *History of the Indies*, Las Casas engaged in a bitter polemic against Oviedo.[17] The two major historians of the Spanish conquest of the Caribbean presented different views of the encounter. Oviedo had come to the New World in 1513 in the expedition of Pedrarias Dávila to Darien and was appointed supervisor of the smelting of gold on the mainland, a post he held until 1532. A friend of king Ferdinand and Charles V, he was commissioned by the Crown to write the history of the Indies. While his *Natural History of the West Indies* (1526) and the larger *General and Natural History of the Indies* (vol.1 1535; vol.2 1557) illustrated his curiosity and love for the Caribbean, his view of native Americans was derogatory. For Oviedo, they were irredeemable savages: "Indians are born lazy, idle, melancholy, cowardly, vile, and ill-natured, liars...They are an incorrigible people; no amount of punishment, reward, or admonition produces results...They are so thick-skulled that Christians hold as a basic principle never to hit them on the head in battle to avoid breaking their swords."[18] Oviedo was in Spain in 1519 to register his complaints about Pedrarias Dávila's cruelties and ineffectiveness in Darien and to get him removed from office. Oviedo proposed that the removal of Pedrarias Dávila would do the trick; Las Casas was adamant that the cause was the encomienda and the conquistador-dominated system of colonization. The support of the king's Flemish advisers, La Chaux and Chievres, the new chancellor Gattinara, and Diego Colon was enough to sway the court to favor Las Casas.

It was agreed that the size of the proposed colony would be two hundred and sixty leagues along the coast. The king agreed not to grant encomiendas in that territory and issued orders that no trader should mistreat the Indians, coerce them in any way, nor trade arms. Native Americans were free human beings and should be converted to Christianity only by peaceful means. Las Casas and his group of peasant farmers sailed from Spain on Nov. 11, 1520. On his arrival in

Puerto Rico, he learned that Indians had destroyed the Dominican mission in Venezuela and killed two Dominicans. The official report of the incident concluded that the Indian attack was without provocation. Whereupon, Spanish officials in Española gave their approval to a punitive attack against the offending Indians. Las Casas met the commander of the fleet, captain Ocampo, as he docked in Puerto Rico on his way to the mainland. Unable to persuade him to desist from the intended attack, Las Casas hurried to Española to argue against the attack, leaving his companions among the residents of San Juan. It was later learned that the Indian attack was indeed provoked. In one of their frequent slave-raids, Alonso de Hojeda and other colonists had visited the mission and then proceeded to Maracapana where they kidnapped thirty five Indians. The mission was therefore implicated in the slave-raids in the minds of the Indians.

Desperate to get his project on track, he worked out a deal with some officials in Española whereby he would be provided with ships and supplies and assistance from captain Ocampo in return for one half of the profits. When he landed on Puerto Rico to pick up his companions, he learned that they had all gone off on Indian raids. Shocked beyond belief, he nevertheless continued on and established his colony in Aug. 1521 with a few Franciscan friars, and salaried officials. Ocampo and his men helped him build a settlement which was called Toledo. With the assistance of an Indian interpreter, Maria, he did make contact with the Indians of Cumana. The tiny settlement was continually harassed by colonists in Cabagua and there were persistent rumors of an imminent Indian attack. Deeply disappointed, he left Cumana in 1522. Two weeks later, Indians attacked and destroyed the settlement.

Disheartened by a string of failures, Las Casas decided to become a Dominican friar in 1523. From then until 1531, he withdrew from the life of an activist. Appointed an official of the Dominican convent at Puerto de Plata on the north coast of Española, he began writing his great work, *The History of the Indies*. But the contemplative life was only a temporary stage, a kind of moratorium, to refresh his mind and will. In a letter from Puerto de Plata to the council of the Indies in 1531, Las Casas urged the councilors to stop the genocide of the native peoples of America. This was a sign that he had resumed his struggle on behalf of the Indians. This cause would take him to Central America and then Mexico. Before leaving the Caribbean, he was a participant in the peace treaty between Enriquillo and the Spanish authorities. Crediting Enriquillo and Barrionuevo for the magnificent achievement of the peace treaty, he felt nevertheless that the treaty was precarious because Enriquillo had returned to his retreat in the mountain. Without consulting the Audiencia but receiving permission from his Dominican superior, Las Casas visited Enriquillo, spent a month with him, and relieved them of their fears. He took Enriquillo to the town of Azua where the citizens honored and celebrated him.

In 1534 Las Casas left the Caribbean for Peru. The frontier of Spanish colonization had advanced to Central America, Mexico, and, more recently, Peru. In 1528 the conqueror of Peru, Francisco de Pizarro, had returned to Spain to validate his privileges. On his return to Peru in 1530 he took six Dominican friars. It was in response to a request to set up more Dominican convents that Las Casas set out for Peru. A storm dashed his hopes and he was forced to go instead to Central America.

Population Decline

The most devastating consequence of the conquest was without doubt the dramatic decline in the population of the native people. Other issues such as evangelization and exploitation pale into insignificance by the horror of this fact. Sixteenth-century estimates of the native population of Española before 1492 vary greatly. Las Casas put the figure at more than three million; Oviedo and Lopez de Gomara gave one million as their estimate. The works of Carl Sauer, Sherburne F. Cook, and Woodrow Borah allow us to analyze and understand these estimates more meaningfully, though the issue is still mired in controversy.[19] As early as the second voyage, Columbus introduced the system of allocating Indians to colonists for labor and tribute. Evidently a count and assignment were made in 1496 by Bartholomew Colon and was passed to the archbishop of Seville. This was obviously the source used by Las Casas. The figure of 1,100,000 did not include children under 14, the aged and the sick. In addition, as Sauer has demonstrated, the Spaniards in 1496 had occupied only a half of Española. Cook and Borah argued that the Indian population in 1496 was closer to Las Casas's estimate, between 2,5000,000 and 5 million. After all, colonization and its human consequences began in 1493. The native population then must have been larger than in 1496. Whatever the number was, all sixteenth-century writers agreed that Española was densely populated. This should not be surprising. With the availability of maize, cassava, and fish, the native peoples of the Caribbean had a good supply of food.

The population counts after 1496 are simply overwhelming.[20] Statistics are often too abstract to move the emotions. In this case, they elicit profound sadness in revealing the enormity of the tragedy:

1496	3,770,000
1508	92,000
1509	61,600
1510	65,800
1512	26,700
1514	27,800
1518	15,600
1540	250
1570	125

In the face of the decline in population, Indians from the Bahamas and other islands were forced to migrate to Española between 1510 and 1520. Las Casas's statement that there were no more Indians in the Bahamas in 1542 provides another illustration of the deadly consequences of the conquest of the Caribbean. A similar human catastrophe occurred in Puerto Rico, Jamaica, and Cuba. The destruction of the native peoples of the Caribbean would be the prelude to disasters in Mexico and Peru. On the eve of the conquest of Mexico, the estimated population was 25 million; in 1600 the Indian population had declined to one million. Of an estimated population in Peru of 32 million in 1520, the number dropped to 5 million by 1548. Undeniably, the data from which these figures are based are imprecise, but the scholarship on native American demography has been careful. Few scholars take seriously today the statement of George Bancroft that before Europeans came to the United States the area was "an unproductive waste...its only inhabitants a few scattered tribes of feeble barbarians, destitute of commerce and political connection."[21]

What were the causes of this catastrophe? The introduction of old world diseases - small pox, measles, whooping cough, bubonic plague, typhoid, influenza, malaria, and yellow fever - wreaked havoc among the Indians who had no immunity against these diseases.[22] After the outbreak of the small-pox epidemic in Española in Dec. 1518, one third of the native population died in a few weeks. Disease was then a major cause of the decline in population. But the decline occurred also in years when there was no epidemic. The Spanish obsession for gold and the establishment of the encomienda destroyed the native social structure and the rhythm of their lives. Las Casas and Judge Zuazo, a member of the first Audiencia of Santo Domingo, felt that this was the reason for the decline. Columbus himself had set the stage for this in 1496 in Española by allocating to his military leaders groups of native peoples who were expected to provide labor and tribute. This system of forced labor meant that Indians were sent all over the island to work in the mines; they had to adjust the purpose of their lives to that of their masters. Zuazo was convinced that this shifting from their homes to unknown surroundings caused the death of large numbers. Their community life was gradually destroyed and they even attended to fishing less frequently. The result was the development of malnutrition from protein deficiency and overwork. In the *Relacion de Texcoco* (1582), Juan Bautista Pomar reflected on the decline of the population in Mexico and concluded that Mexican Indians were vulnerable to disease because they were exhausted by hard labor and had lost the will to live. They suffered from an "affliction and fatigue of their spirits because they had lost the liberty God had given them; for the Spaniards treat them worse than slaves."[23]

African Slavery

The picture of the discovery and conquest of America would be incomplete without mentioning the part Africans played in the early clash of cultures in the Americas generally and the Caribbean in particular.[24] The shortage of labor caused by the decline in the native American population forced the colonial government to recommend the importation of slave labor from Africa. African slaves were brought to Portugal since the middle of the thirteenth century, but much more so in the fifteenth century as Portuguese exploration of the west coast of Africa advanced. By the 1460s there were large numbers of African slaves in both Portugal and Spain. The first group of African slaves were Spanish-speaking (Ladinos) and reached Española in 1505. Cardinal Cisneros banned the importation of Ladinos because he felt that they were prone to labor disturbances. The shipment of slaves resumed after his death in 1518. The license to ship 4,000 slaves over eight years was sold to a Genoese company.

One cannot ignore the fact that, during the three and a half centuries that African slavery lasted, between ten and twenty million Africans were taken from their homes in Africa to work in the plantations, factories, and mines of the Americas.[25] In addition to "social death" as slaves, Africans died in large numbers. A merchant in 1569 recorded that Africans died in such large numbers in the Indies that slavery would never lack a market. One description of a slave was: "The slave is a thing that may die."[26] The ideological justification for such cruelty was the alleged improvement in the condition of Africans through exposure to European civilization and evangelization. The sixteenth-century Jesuit theologian, Luis de Molina, explained it this way. Conversion to Christianity and improved material conditions were "much better than what they had [in Africa] where they went about naked and had to content themselves with a miserable existence." Carlos Esteban Deive commented with sharp irony on the paradox of Christianization and oppression: "the slave's body was chained so that, as recompense, his soul could be saved."[27]

Native Americans and African slaves suffered greatly in the Americas. Death ravaged both peoples. Why then did such sensitive and sensible persons like Bartolome de Las Casas, Pedro de Cordoba, and Judge Zuazo, among others, recommend the introduction of African slavery to relieve the plight of the native people? In memorials of 1516, 1518, and 1542, Las Casas, who had struggled more than anyone to improve and advance the cause of the native American, recommended the use of African slaves to Española both to mitigate the suffering of the Indians and solve the labor crisis. Fellow Dominican, Pedro de Cordoba (1516), the Jeronymite friars (1518), the Franciscan Pedro Mexia (1518) also urged the introduction of African slavery. The recommendation of Judge Zuazo in 1510 hit the nail on the head: "General license should be given to bring negroes, a race strong for work the opposite of the natives, so weak who can work only in undemanding tasks."

The Caribbean faced two related crises in the first half of the sixteenth century: the decline of the native population and the economic viability of the colonies. The myth of the strong African ran counter to the reality of their suffering and death. But it remained as another justification for the steady rise in African slavery. Bishop Sebastian Ramirez de Fuenleal noted in 1531 the increase in the demand for African slaves: "The entire population...of Española, San Juan and even Cuba are demanding that they should have negroes to mine gold and work on other plantations."[28] Slavery of course was not then considered immoral. It was legitimate to make captives in a just war slaves. Arguments from the law of nations, the Bible (Deut.20:14), and Aristotle (Pol.1:3-8) were drawn to defend slavery. It is ironic that such tireless defenders of Indians should advocate that the labor that crushed one people should be done by another. They had never imagined that the African slave population would rise to countless millions or that African slave labor was soon to become the labor base for the economies of all the European colonies. Las Casas for example had recommended the introduction of 4,000 African slaves, but the trade expanded beyond belief.

The charge that Las Casas was responsible for the introduction of African slavery in America was false because there were African slaves in Española before his recommendation.[29] Yet, it was not until 1546 that there was a change of heart. He confessed that he was wrong: "He came to realize that negro slavery was as unjust as Indian slavery and was no remedy at all, even though he had acted on good faith, and he was not sure that his ignorance and good faith would excuse him in the eyes of God." In *History of the Indies*, Las Casas included a long account condemning the slave raids in Africa: "In the past...we held the opinion in this island that if they did not hang a negro, he would never die, because we had never seen a negro die of disease...but after they put them in the factories, owing to the awful work that they had to do...they found death and disease, and so many of them die every day."

Reflection on the Conquest of the Caribbean

Men and women make history, but not in isolation from their context. The voyages of Columbus and his encounter with America set in motion a dynamic that would lead to the colonization of all parts of the Americas, impose European culture and institutions, and exploit the resources of Europe's new world primarily for the benefit of Europe and its peoples. In the process, between 80 and 90 percent of native Americans died; African people were brought as slaves to the Americas

in large numbers and very many died. Although attempts were made
to convert the Indians to Christianity after the second voyage of
Columbus in 1493, serious efforts began with the Franciscans in 1503
and the Dominicans in 1510.   By 1510 the native population had
declined so dramatically that the issue of preventing their extermination
was at least as important as conversion. This fact set in motion another
dynamic movement, namely, the defense of Indian rights to liberty and
property. Las Casas was the eminent spokesman for this movement.

How did native Americans comprehend their fate at the hands of
European conquerors and clerics?   The resistance to conquest and
domination speaks for their anger. Although they were tagged with the
image of cannibals, the remarkable figures of queen Anacaona and
Enriquillo showed them to be gracious, intelligent, and courageous. The
narrative of Enriquillos's rebellion demonstrated that though they
resisted domination native Americans were willing to share their
resources and land.

What did they think of the attempt to convert them to Christianity?
The refusal of Hatuey to convert to Christianity as he was readied for
execution in Cuba serves as an illustration that some native Americans
saw a correspondence between colonization and Christianity.   There
were few conversions in the Caribbean.   Though written after the
conquest of the Yucatan and embellished with nostalgia for the past, the
sentiments of the Book of Chilam Balam of Chumayel describing their
condition before Columbus and the Europeans came must have been
similar to those of the native peoples of the Caribbean: "There was then
no sin; in the holy faith their lives were passed. There was then no
sickness; there was then no aching bones; they had then no high fever;
they had then no small-pox; they had then no burning chest; they had
then no abdominal pains; they had then no consumption; they had then
no headache. At that time the course of humanity was orderly."[30]

NOTES

Chapter 3

1 Michelle de Cuneo, *Journal and Other Documents*, 214-215,226.

2 Las Casas, *History*, bk. 1, 48-52.

3 Oviedo, *Historia General y Natural de las Indias*, ed. by J. Natalicio Gonzalez and Jose Amador de los Rios, (Paraguay, 1959) 121-123.

4 Las Casas, *History*, p. 53

5 Oviedo, 123-127; Antonio de Herrera y Tordesillas, *General History of the West Indies* in *Two Worlds: The Indian Encounter with the European*, ed. by S. Lyman Tyler, (Salt Lake City, Utah, 1988) 195-198; see Samuel M. Wilson, "Columbus, My Enemy," *Natural History*, 12 (1990) 45-50.

6 Las Casas, *History*, bk. 3, 246-256; Oviedo, 253-283; see Manuel Galvan, *Enriquillo*, (Santo Domingo, 1882).

7 Las Casas, *History*, p. 251.

8 *Ibid.*, pp. 183-184; Miguel León-Portilla, *Fray Antón de Montesinos*, (Mexico City, 1982) p. 12.

9 Las Casas, *History*, p. 182, 187.

10 Cesar Sepúlveda, "Fray Anton de Montesinos y Los Derechos Humanos en el Hemisferio Americano," in *Fray Anton de Montesinos*, 57-62.

11 See Henry Raup Wagner, *The Life and Writings of Bartolome de Las Casas*, (Albuquerque, 1967) 1-13.

12 Las Casas, *History*, bk. 3, 208-211.

13 Wagner, *op. cit.*, 20-24.

14 Las Casas, *History, bk.3, 256-259.*

15 The Jeronymite order was chosen because of the existing conflict between the Dominicans and the Franciscans.

16 Las Casas, *History*, bk.3, 212-218.

17 *Ibid.*, 270-284.

18 *Ibid.*, 274.

19 Sherburne F. Cook and Woodrow Borah, *Essays in Population History: Mexico and the Caribbean*, (Berkeley, 1971) 376-410.

20 *Ibid.*, p.410.

21 Alfred W. Crosby, Jr., *The Columbian Voyages, the Columbian Exchange and their Historians*, (Washington,D.C., 1987)V.

22 Alfred W. Crosby,Jr., *The Columbian Exchange: Biological and Cultural Consequences of 1492*, (Westport, Conn.,1972); Carl Sauer, *op. cit.*, p. 202.

23 Quoted in Todorov, p.135.

24 J.H. Elliott, "The Spanish Conquest," in *Colonial Spanish America*, ed. by Leslie Bethell (Cambridge, 1987) p.20.

25 Carlos Esteban Deive, *La Esclavitud del Negro en Santo Domingo (1492-1844)*, 2 vols. (Santo Domingo, 1975); Ricardo Alegria, "Los Origenes de la Esclavitud Negra," en *Descubrimiento, Conquista, y Colonización de Puerto Rico, 1493-1599*, (Barcelona, 1969) 98-114; Manuel Moreno Fraginales, *Africa en América Latina*, (Mexico City, 1977); Herbert S. Klein, "The Establishment of African Slavery in Latin America in the 16th Century," in *African Slavery in Latin America and the Caribbean*, (New York, 1986) 21-43.

26 Joseph Miller, *The Way of Death. Merchant Capitalism and the Angolan Slave Trade, 1730-1830*, (Wisconsin, 1988) p. 666. This is how he saw the effect of capitalism on African society: "Whereas Africans attributed ultimate value to claims on human life, the world capitalist economy increasingly ...freed individuals to pursue private material gain without formal regard for the lives and welfare of others. As Africans expressed it, men who bought and sold people merely in order to hold goods had gone dead in their hearts...": *ibid.*,

673-674.

27 Deive, *op. cit.*, p. 377; see Luis N. Rivera Pagan, *Evangelización y Violencia: La Conquista de America*, (San Juan, P.R., 1990) 305-327.

28 Deive, *op. cit.*, 84-85.

29 See Silvio A. Zavala, "Las Casas Esclavista?," *Cuadernos Americanos*, 2(1944) 149-154; Robert L Brady, "The Role of Las Casas in the Emergence of Negro Slavery in the New World." *Revista de Historia de América*, 61-62(1966) 43-55.

30 *The Book of Chilam Balam of Chumayel*, ed. by R.L. Roys, (Norman, Oklahoma, 1967).

Chapter 4

THE VOYAGES, EUROPEAN HEGEMONY, AND WORLD HISTORY

The search for wealth by rulers, explorers, and conquistadors played the most important role in the drama of the enterprise of the Indies. At times it was nothing less than greed. Whatever opinion we may have about Columbus's spirituality, there is no denying that the desire for gold was almost an obsession. One can even argue that it was essentially the unrestrained pursuit of wealth that was responsible for the human destructiveness in the Indies. Both the Portuguese and Spanish maritime enterprises were part of the dynamic commercial civilization that was emerging in Europe in the late fifteenth century. From the 12th century, merchant capitalism was already undermining the feudal order of Europe. The resurgence of commerce and the rise of towns, especially in Italy and the Netherlands, were among the major factors that made Western European societies dynamic.[1] This development could be traced back to the eleventh century when merchants organized themselves into guilds. Some cities expanded their markets to include all of Europe and the Near East. Bank notes, credit systems, book-keeping, and trade fairs facilitated this expanded market. Increasing amounts of capital were placed in the hands of merchants. Capital accumulation was encouraged by the substitution of money rents for customary services and the rise of commodity production. Peasants were dispossessed and by the 13th century restrictions on the pursuit of profit were being lifted, leading to a more aggressive capitalism.[2]

The city-states of Italy vied with each other for control of Mediterranean trade. Banking families in Genoa, Venice, and Florence curried favor with kings and popes to expand their business. The Bardis of Florence collected papal taxes for pope Boniface VIII from England to Poland. They had trading posts in Syria, Greece, Spain, Bruges, Ghent, Antwerp, and Poland. During the 100 years war, they were the bankers to the English monarchy. Overextending their enterprise, the Bardi bank collapsed when England defaulted on its loan. The Medici bank came into its own from 1434 under Cosimo de Medici and expanded throughout Europe.[3]   There were eight branches in Europe linked to the main branch in Florence. They were engaged in banking as well as trade. In Florence, production in the two woolen and one silk textile factories was organized according to a "putting-out" system. Finished products were then sold to local exporters or to foreign branches of the Medici bank. The branch in Bruges bought and sold certain commodities like spices, olive oil, alum, currants, nuts, and citrus fruits like any merchant.   Banking families and merchant capitalists were able to gain control of their city-states or influence policy.

In northern Europe, merchant capitalists organized themselves into an international organization called the Hanse. Trading activity ranged from the Atlantic to the Baltic. They took products like cloth and fine goods from the more advanced Western European cities to the less developed ones of Eastern Europe where they received in exchange Swedish iron, lumber, herring, and furs. Bruges was the center of the Hanse.   Hanseatic merchants established trade missions as far as Konigsberg, Riga, and Novgorod.   The political weakness of the Hohenstaufen emperors allowed merchants from German cities to move wherever they were given privileges. Merchants from Cologne, like the Easterlings, went to London where they were allowed to participate in the guilds and even the city government. During their heyday in the fourteenth century, merchants of the Hanse met in Lubeck to plan their activities and military defense.   Their fortune declined in the 15th century when larger states like England, the Netherlands, and Scandinavia began to impose restrictions.

Merchant capitalism was already at an advanced stage in German city-states. Southern German states carried on a lively trade in Italian cities, like Venice which offered them incentives to conduct banking and trade operations in Italy.   German merchants linked the trade between Italy and the Netherlands. The Fugger and Welser families of Augsburg had amassed large fortunes and were deeply involved in the emerging international trade in the sixteenth century in the Atlantic and Asia.   The Welsers were given permission to establish a colony in Venezuela and the Spanish Hapsburgs were dependent on loans from the Fuggers.   They were both family partnerships which initially had invested in trade with Venice. In the middle of the 15th century, they directed their interests to silver mining in the Tyrol and Saxony regions where they accumulated profits which they invested in world-wide ventures.[4]

Spain had participated too in the dynamic commercial capitalist system of the late middle ages and early modern Europe. Situated in the Catalan-Aragonese empire, Catalan merchants plied the trade routes to the Near East, North Africa, and Flanders.[5] They competed with merchants from Genoa and Venice for mediterranean trade, and brought prosperity to Aragon. The wealth and beauty of Barcelona was a testament to the vital commercial activity and prosperity of the Catalans. The Black Plague of 1347 and later epidemics devastated the population and sent the economy into a tailspin although commercial activity was still significant in the late fourteenth and fifteenth centuries.

This commercial capitalist civilization was for the most part a general European experience. Development was of course uneven. Eastern European communities were dependent on developed sectors. In addition, the centers of this civilization kept shifting. The prosperity of Genoa, for example, declined in the 15th century, to be replaced by Florence as one of the centers of merchant capitalism. Antwerp replaced Bruges as the financial center. Textile industries which constituted the core of industrial activity in the late middle ages gave way to printing, mining, metallurgical, and silk industries. After John Gutenberg of Mainz pioneered the invention of the printing press in Europe around 1450, publishing industries were established throughout Europe. Important technical knowledge was discovered about mining. Soon, copper, silver, and iron mining activity expanded. The mining of Alum, used to fix dyes, was intensified in Italy from 1458. One of the major mining centers at Tolfa in the papal states employed some ten thousand workers. The pope had hoped to use the profits to finance a crusade against the Turks.

How did Europeans reconcile the pursuit of profit with the traditional moral condemnation of usury? When it was suggested that he was wealthy enough to retire, Jakob Fugger declared that he would continue to seek money "as long as I am able." The merchant families endowed churches and hospitals, and contributed funds to beautify their cities. Jakob Fugger II built a settlement for the indigent, dedicating it to the praise of God. Their piety was possibly pretentious. In the face of criticism from humanists, the Fuggers hired a professor of theology, John Eck, to defend the thesis that, while usury was wrong, the charging of interest was permissible.[6] Franceso Marco Datini headed his account book: "To God and Profit." Merchant families either saw no conflict between profit and conscience or used piety as a mask to make their commercial enterprises acceptable. This then was the

commercial civilization that Columbus and Europeans brought to the
Americas.   Compared with the economies of American societies,
sixteenth century European commercial civilization was more vital. But
was it more dynamic than the commercial systems of Asia, the Near
East, and Africa?

In their attempt to comprehend the reasons for the persistence of
underdevelopment and the hegemony of Western Europe and North
America, many scholars have pointed to the emergence of an
international capitalist system around 1500.   The transition from
mercantile capitalism to industrial capitalism in the late eighteenth and
nineteenth centuries saw Western Europe, particularly Great Britain,
achieve hegemony over the global system.[7] Armed with surpluses of
capital and unchallenged in technological and scientific superiority, the
West conquered Asia and Africa. The Columbus and Da Gama voyages
were early attempts to impose the West on the world. While Europeans
were able to conquer and dominate the Americas, it would take at least
300 years from the conquest of America to develop the economic,
technological, and military ability to dominate Asia and Africa. These
scholars located the seeds of modern capitalism in early modern Europe.
The material superiority of Western Europe and North America for most
of modern history can hardly be denied. But such paradigms do not do
justice to the achievements of the peoples of the Americas, Africa, the
Near East, and Asia before western dominance.[8] In addition, the recent
prosperity of some Asian societies call into question western paradigms
for material progress.

The Americas

Between 1000 and 1500 A.D. the peoples of the Americas had
developed maize as their dominant staple. In Peru the people used the
mountainous Andean terrain to produce twenty four varieties of potato.
Impressive irrigation systems were constructed by the Mayans and
Incans. The Olmec city of Monte Alban (c.1100 B.,C.), Teotihuacan
(c.300 A.D.-900 A.D.), and Tenochtitlan, the capital city of the Aztecs,
were among the witnesses to the achievements of the peoples of the
Americas. Commodity production was not unknown. Mexicans from
the highlands came down to the plains to buy and sell in the markets;
the long canoe laden with merchandise that Columbus encountered on
his fourth voyage off the coast of Central America was evidence that
there was trade between Mexicans and South America. The letters of

Cortes and the narrative of Bernal Diaz del Castillo described their authors' amazement at the splendor of American civilizations before their destruction and reconstruction as Christian and European civilizations. For Hernan Cortes, Tenochtitlan was "the most beautiful thing in the world... It cannot be believed that any of the princes of this world...possesses any thing of such high quality." Their buildings were "so well-constructed in both stone and woodwork that there can be none better in any place."[9] Bernal was equally awed: "I say again that I stood looking at it and thought that no land like it would ever be discovered in the whole world."[10]

Africa

Africa was not the cultural wasteland that many depicted. Entering the Iron Age around 500 B.C., Africans used the knowledge of iron to develop complex kingdoms and agricultural systems that freed specialists to engage in manufacturing and trade.[11] The achievements of Ancient Egypt, Nubia, and Axum have been celebrated enough to put to rest the judgement of European historians like Hugh Trevor Roper who wrote in 1965: "Undergraduates...demand that they should be taught the history of Black Africa. Perhaps in the future there will be some African history to teach. But at the present there is none, or very little; There is only the history of Europeans in Africa. The rest is darkness."[12] Ancient African civilizations were never isolated, and had contacts with mediterranean and Indian ocean societies. Cultural diffusion flowed in both directions along the two seas of civilization.[13]

The African states of Ghana, Mali, and Songhay shared in the great age of Islamic Civilization from the ninth to the sixteenth centuries. From its establishment around 300 A.D. till its destruction in 1076, the empire of Ghana was an important center of trade. It exported gold from Senegal to Europe. Salt, textiles, and jewelry were other items of trade. The large capital city, Kumbi Saleh, was an important center of trade and scholarship, where Islamic law, theology, and history were studied. The ruling Islamic ideology permitted the practice of indigenous African culture.[14] Sundiata defeated the kingdom of Ghana in 1240 A.D. and expanded his empire to include almost the whole of West Africa from Gambia on the Atlantic coast to Nigeria in the west and northwest to the Sahara desert. It was with the ascension to the throne of Mansa Musa that Mali became a renowned intellectual center. The wealth and generosity of Mansa Musa were well-known. On his

return from his pilgrimage to Mecca in 1324, he brought back with him
the Moorish poet and architect, Es Saheli, who built the famous
mosques and learning academies at Timbuktu and Gao. Timbuktu
ranked with Alexandria, Fez, Seville, Cordoba, and Constantinople as
a center of learning.[15] It was linked to other parts of Africa by caravan
routes. The decline of the kingdom of Mali was followed by the rise
to prominence of Songhai whose founder, Sunni Ali, conquered
Timbuktu in 1468.

The Islamic World

Islamic societies of the Near East, North Africa, and Spain created
outstanding civilizations between 700 and 1100 A.D. Agriculture
flowered in Iraq and Egypt where large surpluses were produced. Arab
links to India enabled them to transplant Indian tropical plants like rice,
sugar, cotton, and citrus fruits to the Near East. Arab artisans worked
in shipyards, mills, and foundries. Agricultural and industrial progress
created the wealth that underpinned the civilizations that were
established in Cairo, Damascus, Baghdad, and Cordoba, and sustained
their intellectual, scientific, and cultural achievements. A comparison
between Europe and the Ottoman empire in the sixteenth century would
show that the world outside of Europe was not inferior in the material
condition of their respective societies. The conquest of Constantinople
in 1453 by the Ottoman Turks inspired fear in Christian Europe; it was
one of the reasons why Europeans were searching for alternative routes
to Asia rather than continue to depend upon the Red Sea and Persian
Gulf routes, then controlled by the Venetians and the Arabs. The
Ottoman sultans made Constantinople the hub of trade between Asia,
Europe, and Africa. Possessing a vast empire, the Ottoman Turks
pursued a policy of economic self sufficiency, focusing on the natural
and human resources of their empire.[16] The fertile plains of Hungary,
Romania, and Egypt produced agricultural products; the artisans of
Constantinople, Baghdad, Damascus, and Cairo turned out a variety a
manufactured items. Imports were restricted to luxury products like
textiles, spices, silk, and furs. Sixteenth-century travelers commented
upon the prosperity and happiness of Ottoman society. Christian
peasants in the conquered Balkan lands were not dispossessed of their
lands. Their rights and privileges were protected by Ottoman laws.

Asia

When Vasco da Gama reached Calicut, India, on May 27, 1498, it was the realization of old dreams. For it was the desire to utilize the fabled riches of Asia that drove Columbus and Da Gama to undertake their enterprises. The accounts of 13th century travelers had whetted the ambitions of Europeans.[17] The Islamic reconquest of Jerusalem by Saladin in 1187 and their dominance of the vital coasts of Syria and Egypt despite several European Christian crusades to defeat Islam exercised a powerful influence on the imagination of the west. But it was the spice trade that was the major attraction for merchants from Europe. Spices had become essential for European cooking and could not be obtained except from the Malabar coast of India and Indonesia by means of the trade routes through the Red Sea and the Persian Gulf. Venice and Genoa competed for the trade over these routes. By the 15th century Venice had come to monopolize this trade. The Portuguese and Spanish explorations were projects that were shaped by the desire to get around the Venetian and Arab monopoly of Asian trade.

The Indian ocean was a center of international commerce for thousands of years. In the ancient world Indian ships had sailed to the Red Sea ports and Indian merchants had established relations with Egypt and other countries of the Near East. To the East, they established colonies in Malaya, Indonesia, Cambodia, and Champa. Their ships sailed as far as South China. After the ninth century A.D., Arab shipping and merchants competed with Indian shipping. Arab merchants traded freely in all parts of India. Indeed, there was no attempt to control mercantile activity as Arab, Hindu, and Chinese merchants competed freely for the spice trade of India and Indonesia. Despite several foreign invasions, India achieved many periods of prosperity and civilization, like the Buddhist Maurya, the Hindu Gupta and the Muslim Moghul civilizations that influenced other Asian societies. By the Christian era, Indian agriculture had produced wheat, barley, rice, cotton, jute, hemp, and silk. Long before their use in Europe, heavy plows were used in India. Indian civilization went into decline after the collapse of the Gupta dynasty around 500 A.D. But by the 10th century, there was another flowering in the Chola kingdom of South India. From the eleventh century, there was a rapid development of towns, an expansion of trade, and the introduction of a monetary system. Chola merchants established extensive trade network with

Arabia and Persia to the West and China in the East.[18] The volume of
trade between India and China was at an unprecedented level in the
thirteenth century. South India exported textiles, spices, drugs, jewels,
ivory horn, ebony, and camphor to China, and perfumes, sandalwood,
and spices to the Persian Gulf. Merchant guilds were established in
most towns and had access to any region in India. Domestic and
foreign trade was encouraged by kings and high officials.

After spending some seventeen years (1276-1292) in the service of
the Mongol king Khubilai Khan, Marco Polo returned to Venice and
composed his *Description of the World*, narrating his experience of the
prosperity and stability of Chinese civilization. Translated into several
languages and copied in innumerable manuscripts, his work was to
inspire several Europeans, not least Christopher Columbus, who
possessed a copy. The book of another traveller, the Tunisian Muslim
Ibn Battuta, would confirm the picture of an advanced civilization
between 1325 and 1355. The Mongol conquest of China was followed
by a long period of peace. Trade along the silk route of Central Asia
brought Chinese products to the Near East and Europe. Among them
included gunpowder, paper money, printing, porcelain, textiles, medical
discoveries, and art. Chinese culture had a strong presence in Persia
and the Arab world. In return, Muslim culture took permanent root in
China.

This was not the first instance of international commercial activity in
China's history. Under the Han dynasty (202 B.C.-220 A.D.), there was
trade between China and the Roman empire. The travels of Chang
Chhien (c.138 B.C.) brought knowledge of the old silk route and areas
between China and Persia.[19] As the Han Chinese state achieved unity
and centralization, its leaders strengthened its bureaucracy by making
Confucianism the basis for the Chinese social and political order.
Schools were set up to provide candidates for government offices.
Although China's history is full of anti-mercantile laws, and Confucian
philosophy did not give merchants a high rank in the social hierarchy,
under Han Wu Ti (140 B.C.-87 B.C.), capable merchants and financiers
were brought into the government.[20] Important advances in science
were recorded.   The Han period was marked by significant
achievements in astronomy, botany, and zoology. Paper was invented
and advances in textiles and decorated bricks and tiles made. Since
agriculture was the economic basis of Chinese society, achievements in
hydraulic engineering and irrigation were outstanding. The Tang (618-

906 A.D.) and Sung (960-1279 A.D.) dynasties saw the transition from ancient to early modern China.[21]   The capital Chang-An was the meeting place of Indians, Arabs, Persians, Syrians, Koreans, Japanese, Tibetans, and South East Asians.   The life and work of the pilgrim, Hsuan-Chuang (629-645 A.D.), who journeyed to India in search of Buddhist sutras, illustrated the discourse between Chinese and Indian civilizations.   Indian Buddhism was to influence China to the extent that it would form one component of Chinese traditional philosophy.   Other religions touched China, too.   In the seventh century, Zoroastrianism and Manichaeism reached China from Persia; Nestorian Christianity was brought by Syrian missionaries to China; Islam and Judaism, under the Tang dynasty.   It was under the Sung dynasty that China achieved a level of prosperity unequalled in its history.   The Chinese economy expanded to such an extent that "it might not be inappropriate to call it the commercial revolution of China."[22]   The introduction of a quickly maturing strain of rice from Vietnam made double-cropping possible. Irrigation projects were expanded to bring more land under cultivation. Tea was grown on hillsides and cotton became a common crop. Gunpowder was used for explosive weapons.   The abacus was introduced and used widely in East Asia.   The invention and development of printing was perhaps China's greatest legacy to civilization.   During the Sung dynasty, printing was widespread. Printing reached Europe some three hundred years after by way of Central Asia and the Near East.   Great commercial cities were also centers of the arts and sciences.   Shops lined Chinese cities and trade guilds (Hong) were established to organize trade as well as banking. Under the Sung dynasty, maritime trade with India and Near East was intensified.   The techniques of shipbuilding and navigation improved; large vessels, using sails and oars, came into use.   By 1119 the magnetic compass was used.   The increase in oceanic commerce gave importance to eastern and southern coasts of China, especially Canton.   Muslim Arabs and Persians had dominated oceanic trade and established their presence in Canton and Yang-chou.   By the Sung dynasty, China had come to monopolize trade with Korea and Japan.   Its products were in demand throughout Asia as far as East Africa and the Persian Gulf. Accompanying this increase in commercial activity was the expansion of its currency.   Copper cash was used in ancient China but by 1085 A.D. a monied economy was beginning to be used more generally than grain or textile receipts.   The development of paper money to replace the cumbersome copper showed the advanced nature of China's monied

economy. The splendors of China under the Yuan dynasty described by Marco Polo were built by earlier Chinese civilizations.

The Ming dynasty (1368-1644) that succeeded the Mongol was inspired by a desire for order and stability. The political turmoil following the break-up of the Mongol empire disrupted the lively trade between east and west. This gave the upper hand to the Confucian fundamentalists to pursue an isolationist, self-sufficient economic policy. In Confucian theory, trade was considered inferior. But the rise of commerce since the Tang dynasty had left its influence on China. The attitude to commerce was mixed. The advantages of foreign trade, especially to the southern provinces, was considerable. From a practical point of view, the government's treasury benefitted from overseas commerce. To satisfy Confucian form, envoys were sent to foreign nations to induce them to come to China to bring tribute, after which they were allowed to trade.

Between 1405 and 1433, the Chinese made seven expeditions westward under the command of court eunuch, Cheng-Ho, a Muslim.[23] To illustrate the scale of this operation, the first expedition comprised 62 galleons and more than a hundred auxiliary vessels carrying "868 civil officers, 26,800 soldiers, 93 commanders...." They visited more than thirty countries, among which were Champa in South Vietnam, Java, Siam, Ceylon, Calicut and Cochin in India, Hormuz, Aden, Mogadishu and Malindi in Africa. An inscription erected by Cheng-Ho in the temple of the Celestial Spouse before his fleet set sail on their final voyage in Dec. 1431 captured the spirit of these Chinese voyages that seemed different from the European expeditions to America: "The Imperial Ming Dynasty, in unifying seas and continents...goes beyond the Han and Tang dynasties...Thus the barbarians from beyond the seas have come to audience bearing precious objects and presents. The emperor, approving of their loyalty and sincerity, has ordered us and others at the head of several tens of thousands of officers...to go and confer presents on them in order to make manifest the transforming power of the [imperial] virtue and to treat distant people with kindness." How remarkable that the Muslim Cheng-Ho should make this offering to the cult of the Celestial Goddess: "Protector of the Country and the Defender of the People, whose miraculous power manifestly answers [prayers] and whose vast Benevolence saves universally." After a visit to a Buddhist temple in Ceylon on his third voyage, Cheng-Ho had an inscription composed in Chinese, Tamil, and Persian in honor of the local Buddha as thanksgiving for his and his men's safety.

Cheng-Ho's voyages were different from those of Columbus in ways more fundamental than the scale of their respective voyages. The Chinese had already in their history known of the lands, sea-routes, peoples and cultures that they encountered. It was not chance that dictated their appointment of the Muslim Cheng-Ho as commander. It was expected that he would be familiar with the Islamic cultures of India, East Africa, the Red Sea, and the Persian Gulf. The fleet had as interpreters a mullah called Hassan and another Chinese Muslim, Ma Huan, whose memoirs provided the principal source of the voyages. Columbus's enterprise, though supported by Spain, was an individual project, not one organized by the state such as that by Cheng-Ho. Perhaps the greatest difference was that Columbus and his crew sailed into the unknown as they set sail west for Asia. Prestige and trade were the objectives of the Chinese voyages. Treasure ships carried Chinese products to exchange for luxury products of the countries they visited; Cheng-Ho probably had the task of finding markets for Chinese silk and porcelain. As early as the thirteenth century, East African ports were expanding their imports of chinaware. Fei Xin who traveled with the fleet wrote a memoir describing the voyage. In *Triumphant Tour of the Star Raft*, he revealed charming glimpses of life in East African towns. The rare spices and rare animals amazed the Chinese. They received ambergris, myrrh, and gum copal in addition to lions, rhinos, and oryxes in exchange for silks, chinaware, gold and silver, pepper, grain, and beans.

The voyages were discontinued after 1433 and no attempt was made to capitalize on the discoveries. It signalled the victory of the official Confucian classes over the palace eunuchs. The extravagance and expenses of the voyages seemed to be symptomatic of the departure from the traditional Confucian moderation and aversion to commerce. In addition, they felt that China's large empire was self-sufficient and that human activity should be consistent with its traditional values. Change was acceptable, but within China's traditions. China's leaders closed its doors to maritime activity. The capital was moved 600 miles to Beijing.

The Question of Western Commercial Dynamism

The Columbus voyages have been interpreted as reflecting and heralding an emerging world capitalist economy between the 13th and 15th centuries and centered in Western Europe. Institutions and attitudes unique to Western Europe were to prove to be dynamic in driving the creation of modern capitalism. As L.S. Stavrianos put it: "The West alone was free to strike out in new directions and to evolve during the medieval centuries a new technology, new institutions and new ideas - in short, the new capitalist civilization."[24] Walt Rostow in *How it All Began* argued that "the scientific revolution is the element in the equation of history that distinguishes early modern Europe...The decisive weakness in traditional societies was...in the lack of innovators."[25] For Nathan Rosenberg and L.E. Birdzel in *How the West Grew Rich,* the causes were the same - Western innovations in trade and technology. In *The Modern World System*, Immanuel Wallerstein also located the incipient capitalist world-economy in the European middle ages. For him, class war in a context of economic stagnation and adverse climatological conditions begged for a more efficient and expanded productivity. This need was realized through a global market and backed by state power.[26] Conquests and commercial penetration of territories gave rulers the power and wealth to secure their position. With the establishment of the world-economy, the division of labor was divided into a core, semi-periphery, and periphery. The core was located in England, Holland, and Northern France, and featured states strong enough to ensure political stability, economic growth, and development. Core states utilized wage labor, and encouraged skilled uses of labor and peasant proprietorship. In the semi-periphery (Iberian nations, among others), sharecropping was dominant. States in the periphery were little more than adjuncts of the core, benefitting narrow ruling classes and condemning most of their peoples to misery. Coerced labor was the basis of the economy of the periphery. Fernand Braudel's view of the rise of modern capitalism shared much with Wallerstein, though he claimed that capitalism arose in 13th century Italy.[27] In *Europe and the People Without History*, Eric Wolf took the line that Europe was saved by capitalism. Societies in the wider world were ruled by parasitic classes and did not develop beyond the tributary mode of production. For Wolf, capitalism was facilitated by overseas expansion which drew producers in the wider world into a common exchange.[28] Alan K. Smith argued that many of the scholarly analyses were too ethnocentric. He offered as his paradigm the argument that the key was the wider world's inability to resolve the social question of the distribution of resources. In England and the Netherlands, however, unique changes had taken place. A new dynamic class had toppled the forces of tradition and privilege.

One major criticism of all these interpretations is that they seem to start with the fact of Western hegemony over the modern world-economy and imply as a result that it was because of dynamic forces in Western Europe. The description of the commercial, scientific, and intellectual achievements of the wider world reveals that the qualities that were characterized as dynamic in Western Europe were present in societies outside of Europe. Between 1250 and 1350, for example, a world-economy was established, centered in China.

Why did Asia or the Arab world not come to dominate the modern world system? The definition of European dynamism in early modern history needs to be reassessed. The work of Joseph Needham has shown that it was China that was in the forefront of science and technology. There were dynamic commercial civilizations not only in the mediterranean and northern Europe, but also in other parts of the world. The world of Columbus and Da Gama was superior to the wider world only in the instruments of force, not commerce. Capitalism and Western hegemony over the world-economy are plausible keys to understand the condition of the modern world, characterized by persistent uneven development. But it was the industrial revolution that gave the West the means to establish its supremacy. Locating the causes of the industrial revolution in the unique history, institutions, and values of north-west Europe remains problematical in light of the impressive achievements in the Asian, Islamic, and African worlds.

In *Before European Hegemony: The World System A.D. 1250-1350*, Janet Abu-Lughod argued that "there was no inherent historical necessity that shifted the system to favor the West rather than the East, nor was there any inherent historical necessity that would have prevented cultures in the eastern region from becoming the progenitors of a modern world system."[29] Demographic and political factors played a greater role than "psychological or institutional factors." The fragmentation and insecurity of the silk route trade caused by the decline and fall of the Mongol empire, and the destruction by Tamerlane around 1400 A.D. caused the prosperity of Arab Asia to decline; the Portuguese successes in the Indian ocean in the 1500s enabled them to establish colonies in India and Malacca. These events played an enormous role in preventing the Asian and Arab world economy from sustaining its growth in the 13th and 14th centuries. The event that had greater significance, however, was the Black Death which, spreading from China to Europe between 1348 to 1351, "decimated most of the cities along the great sea-route of world trade, disturbing customary behavior, changing the terms of exchange because of differential demographic losses, and creating a fluidity in world conditions that facilitated radical transformations, benefitting some and harming others."

The Ideology of Reconquest

The most telling feature of the commercial civilization in the West at the time of Columbus and Da Gama was its willingness to use conquest as the means to achieve a monopoly of trade. The Spanish expeditions to the Americas and the Portuguese to Asia had the same origins in the early 15th century Portuguese maritime and crusading activity. Conquest, conversion to Christianity, and commerce were the major components of the ideology that inspired Western European voyages.

The theme of reconquest was pervasive in Spain and Portugal. Portugal had regained their land from the Muslims by the 13th century; Christian Spain had reconquered all of Spain except Granada. In the late 15th century, Ferdinand and Isabella were willing to use the idea of a crusade to unify Spain that had been torn by factional conflicts. They did not make a distinction between reconquest and conquest, of course. The Spanish reconquest of Granada from the Muslims, their expulsion of the Jews, the conquest of America, and the attempt of Da Gama to impose Portuguese rule in Asia were the consequences of this ideology of reconquest. The ideology of conquest was the means to pursue the objectives of commerce and conversion. In his papal bull "*Romanus Pontifex*" of Jan. 8, 1455, pope Nicholas V gave his support, encouragement, and authorization to the Portuguese king Dom Henrique: "The Pontiff grants to the king of Portugal and his successors all lands conquered from Cape Bojador to Guinea, and all the southern coast of Africa to its tip. They also receive the right of occupation of all lands, harbors, islands and seas which they might conquer, and authority to promulgate laws, impose taxes, and build churches and monasteries." The approval of the right to conquest was explicit. Pope Sixtus IV confirmed this right of dominion in his letter "*Aeterni Regis Clementia*" of June 21, 1481. The Canary Islands were recognized as the possession of the Spanish Crown. Following Columbus's successful first voyage, pope Alexander VI issued the bull "*Inter Caetera*" on May 4, 1493, granting to Ferdinand and Isabella all islands and mainland, discovered or to be discovered west of an imaginary line from pole to pole 100 leagues from the Azores and Cape Verde Islands.[30] In 1494 representatives of Spain and Portugal negotiated the Treaty of Tordesillas, defining their respective spheres of influence on a world level. They agreed to draw the line of demarcation 360 leagues west of the Cape Verde Islands. What these papal letters and treaty demonstrated was that colonization and domination were important objectives of the projects from the beginning.

Writing in 1508, the Italian Fracanzano Montalboddo had already intuited the creation of a new world order integrating the Spanish and Portuguese discoveries. In his *Countries Recently Discovered and the View of the World of the Florentine Amerigo Vespucci*, he divided his work in six parts and included the Portuguese voyages to Guinea, Brazil, and India; the Spanish voyages to the islands and lands they founded; the New World letter of Vespucci about his purported third voyage to Brazil; and letters of Italians in Lisbon about the Portuguese voyages to Asia and present-day Canada.[31] By including the New World letter in the larger context of the voyages to Asia and Canada, Montalboddo was giving a fresh insight into the meaning of European expansion. In the specific context of the Iberian expeditions, commerce cannot be separated from the politics of the period. The interests of commerce and Christianity were determined by the application of power.

The Iberian New World Order

We have followed the depredations of Columbus and the Spaniards in the Americas. But the spirit of Da Gama and his Portuguese successors was little different. When he arrived in Calicut, India, on May 27, 1498, little did he realize that that city and the Malabar region had been a vital center of trade for two thousand years. It had been the chief center for the spice trade, and its ships sailed to the Red Sea and the Persian Gulf carrying spices, textiles, and other products. Spices from the islands of the Pacific passed through Calicut to Europe. Malabar merchants had warehouses in Cairo, Alexandria, and Fez. A special relationship developed between its Hindu rulers and Muslim merchants who had contacts with Egypt, Arabia, and the Persian Gulf.

At the end of the exploratory first voyage, Da Gama was given permission to trade with Calicut. The second voyage, however, was a grander enterprise. With thirty three ships and 1500 men, Da Gama arrived in the Indian Ocean bent on enforcing his claim to supremacy of the seas. The Welsers and other great merchants of Antwerp provided financial backing for the enterprise. There were no shortages of supplies or reinforcements. Without warning Da Gama intercepted and destroyed any vessel he met. On encountering an unarmed vessel returning from Mecca, he emptied the ship of goods, prevented Muslim passengers from leaving the ship, and then set fire to it.[32] Da Gama had hoped that the threat of force would intimidate the native rulers who had befriended him on his first voyage.

But the rulers of Calicut resisted the Portuguese for ninety years. Indeed, Goa was the only place in India that was conquered and colonized by the Portuguese. It was Affonso Albuquerque who constructed the strategic system that would give the Portuguese the mastery of trade in the Indian ocean. Coming out to Asia in 1506, he seized Socotra and demanded tribute from the king of Hormuz, thereby giving the Portuguese control of trade in the Red Sea and Persian Gulf. They had already used force to establish ports at Mombasa and Mozambique, and points of access to the gold trade in the interior of Africa. With the conquest of Goa, they possessed a suitable base for naval operations. In 1511 Albuquerque conquered Malacca, a major commercial center of East Asia and the link between China and the countries of South and South-West Asia. Thanks in large part to Albuquerque's initiative, Portugal was able to control trade in the Indian ocean in the sixteenth century.

It was conquest initially, not commerce that gave Europe mastery over the new world order that was emerging. To return to the Chinese voyages under Cheng-Ho as illustration, Philip Snow compared the Chinese voyages to Africa with the Portuguese in this way: "..they stormed no cities and conquered no land...the Chinese were tactful, anxious to avoid disturbing the small coastal states any more than was necessary to achieve their basic ends. Unlike the Portuguese they refrained from plunder. Instead, they coaxed the coastal rulers into trading by presenting them with gifts of coloured silk. They did not burn, as the Portuguese would, with the urge to impose their religious convictions, to lay siege to African souls."[33]

NOTES

Chapter 4

1. See Henri Pirenne, *Medieval Cities: Their Origins and the Revival of Trade*, (Princeton, 1925).

2. Maurice Dobb, *Studies in the Development of Capitalism*, (London, 1946);- *Modern Capitalism: Its Origin and Growth*, (London, 1928).

3. Raymond de Roover, *The Medici Bank: Its Organization, Management, Operations, and Decline*, (New York, 1948); -, *The Rise and Decline of the Medici Bank, 1397-1494*, Camb., Mass., 1963).

4. Richard Ehrenberg, *Capital and Finance in the Age of the Renaissance*, (New York, 1963).

5. J.H. Elliott, *Imperial Spain, 1469-1716*, (New York, 1963).

6. See Lewis W. Spitz, *The Renaissance and Reformation Movements*, vol. 1, (St. Louis, 1971) 118-136.

7. For a critique of the capitalist world-system paradigm, see Robert S. DuPlessis, "The Partial Transition to World-Systems Analysis in Early Modern European History," *Radical History Review*, 39(1987) 11-27.

8. Alan K. Smith, *Creating a World Economy. Merchant Capital, Colonialism, and World Trade 1400-1825*, (Colorado, 1991) 1-93.

9. A. Pagden, ed., *The Letters of Hernan Cortes*, (Oxford, 1972) second letter.

10. Bernal Diaz del Castillo, *The True History of the Conquest of New Spain*, 87-92.

11. Herbert J. Foster, *From the African Slave Trade to Emancipation: Readings in Black History 1450-1860*, (NJ, 1974) 5-9.

12. H. Trevor Roper, *The Rise of Christian Europe*, (New York, 1974), p. 6.

13. H.J. Foster, "The Ethnicity of Ancient Egyptians," *Journal of Black Studies*, 5((1978) 175-191.

14. George O. Cox, *African Empires and Civilizations*, (New York, 1974) 127-130.

15. *Ibid.*, p. 161.

16. L.S. Stavrianos, *The Global Rift*, (New York, 1981) p. 125.

17. K.M. Pannikar, *Asia and Western Dominance*, (London, 1959) pp. 21, 54.

18. R. Thapar, *A History of India*, I, (London, 1966) p. 207.

19. Joseph Needham, *Science and Civilization in China*, vol. 1 (London, 1954) 107-108.

20. *Ibid.*, p. 107.

21. *Ibid.*, 124-131

22. *Ibid.*, 132-139

23. See Phillip Snow, *The Star Raft: China's Encounter with Africa*, (New York, 1988) 1-36; J.L. Duyvendak, *China's Discovery of Africa*, (London, 1949) p.26.

24. Stavrianos, *op.cit.*, p.45.

25. Alan K. Smith, *op.cit.*, p. 3.

26. Immanuel Wallerstein, *The Modern World System*, I (New York, 1974) II (1980).

27. Fernand Braudel, *Civilization and Capitalism: The Fifteenth to the Eighteenth Centuries*, (New York, 1984) p. 28.

28. Eric Wolf, *Europe and the Peoples without History*, (Berkeley, Cal., 1982).

29. Janet Abu-Lughod, *Before European Hegemony: The World System A.D. 1250-1350*, (New York, 1989) 12-19; see also Anthony Reid, *Southeast Asia in the Age of Commerce, 1450-1680*, (New Haven, Conn., 1983) 63-119. For the specific commercial relationship between Spain and America, see Earl J. Hamilton, *American Treasure and the Price Revolution in Spain, 1501-1650*, (Cambridge., Mass., 1934); Juan Friede, *Los Welser en la Conquista de Venezuela*, (Caracas, 1961); Kenneth R. Andrews, *The Spanish Caribbean: Trade and Plunder, 1530-1630*, (New Haven, Conn., 1978).

30. For the papal bulls, see F.J. Hernáez, *Colección de bulas, breves, y otros documentos relativos a la Iglesia y Filipinas*, 2 vols, (Brussels, 1879); see also Fernandez Navarrete, *Colección de los viages*, vol. 2, 34-49.

31. *Portugal/Brazil*, p. 242.

32. Pannikar, *op.cit.*, p. 35.

33. Snow, p. 29.

Chapter 5

THE MISSION TO CHRISTIANIZE

The 13th Century Precedent: Pope Innocent IV (1243-54)

The mission to Christianize native Americans left no less an indelible a mark on the culture produced by the clash of indigenous and European civilizations than the exploitation of the material resources of Europe's new world. The earlier conquest of the Canary Islands and the conversion of the Guanches to Christianity gave a good reference point for the evangelization, or, as Robert Ricard put it, the spiritual conquest of America.[1] However, a look at the relations between Christians and non-Christians in the 13th century would illuminate more clearly evangelization as a political and historical force. On the one hand, in an increasingly assertive and expansionist Europe, popes sought to define the relations between Christians and non-Christians; on the other hand, major victories by Christian armies in Spain and the Mongol threat to Eastern Europe created new challenges and opportunities for relations between Christians and Muslims.

It was the noted scholar of canon law, pope Innocent IV, who developed the legal theory of relations between Christians and non-Christians.[2] In a commentary to the question whether Christians could seize lands occupied by Muslims other than the holy land, Innocent IV argued that all men possessed the right to private property and self-government.[3] Therefore, the Christian responsibility for the salvation of all men was not a just cause of war against peoples who were not Christian. Yet, this statement was not as simple as it seemed. Innocent maintained, nevertheless, that the pope had a spiritual responsibility for all men. It was this responsibility that authorized the pope to send missionaries to preach Christianity to non-Christians and, if obstructed, to call upon Christian armies to invade those lands. The significance of this was that, while non-Christians possessed natural rights to lordship and property, Innocent IV was declaring that only the pope, not the emperor nor the leader of a Christian state, could intervene in the affairs of non-Christians, and then only for a spiritual purpose. But, did

Muslim missionaries have a similar right to preach in Christian lands? Innocent IV's answer was a categorical no because in his judgement they were "in error and we are on the righteous path." Henry of Segusio, known as Hostiensis, a student of Innocent IV, disagreed with his master's line of argument.[4] For him, Christ's coming had effectively ended the authority and jurisdiction of infidels and their sovereignty and property could legally and justly be transferred to Christians. Hostiensis cautioned, however, that although Christians had the right to universal dominion, intervention in the lands of non-Christians should preferably be by peaceful means by missionaries. Notwithstanding their differences, both Innocent IV and Hostiensis agreed that it was the pope who possessed the right of intervention.

Their arguments served as the framework for ideas about the relations between Christians and non-Christians within European society and outside. Innocent IV's defense of the natural rights of all people to self-government and property was in the mainstream of the opinion of canon lawyers. This set of ideas emerged initially out of deliberations on relations between Christians and Jews in Europe. In the letter, *Impia Judaeorum* (1244), Innocent IV defined the ambiguous tolerance to Jews that served as an alternative to persecution. He maintained that Christians should live in peace with Jews and not seek to force them to convert. Reiterating that they were still wicked and ungrateful, he insisted that the pope, not Jewish leaders, was the ultimate arbiter of Jewish doctrine. That was why he had ordered the public burning of copies of the Talmud, he explained.

The successful campaigns of James I of Aragon (1213-1276) in conquering large sections of Muslim Spain made discussions about policy towards Muslims urgent. Writing in the fourteenth century, Oldratus de Ponte (d.1335) sided with Hostiensis in arguing that after the birth of Christ non-Christians did not have the right to sovereignty and property according to natural law. Muslims in Spain were to be treated with tolerance, but he warned that Christians must always be on guard. As long as they posed no threat, non-Christians should not be expelled from Christian lands without reason. Still, Oldratus could not hide his historical bias against Muslims. He said that it was permissible to wage war against the descendants of Ishmael because, as people of the desert, they were by nature uncivilized and needed the heavy hand of Christian armies before they could be pacified and be prepared for Christianization and civilization. Contrary to the beliefs of Oldratus,

Christian rulers in Spain found Muslims and Jews valuable and ignored papal decrees prohibiting resettlement of conquered lands by Muslims.

The prospect of a bountiful harvest in Lithuania and other indigenous peoples of Northeast Europe following the conversion in 1250 of Mindowe, king of the Lithuanians, caused Innocent IV to send letters to the bishop urging gentle treatment of the new Christians since they were passing from the law of nature to the higher law of Christianity. The pope's solicitude for the Lithuanians did little to restrain the rapacity of the Christian Teutonic knights and the kingdom of Poland who were intent on conquering Lithuanian lands. The Teutonic knights ignored also the pope's appeal to assist the prince of Galicia in his defense against the imminent Mongol threat. Responding to stories about Mongol interest in Christianity and the growing belief that non-Christians could be converted by persuasion and rational argument, Innocent IV sent a Franciscan mission to the Mongol khan: Lawrence of Portugal and John of Piano Carpini, by way of Russia; and another by way of the Near East, comprising the Dominicans Ascelinus and Andrew of Longjumeau. In the letters sent to the khan, the pope blamed the Mongols for shattering the peaceful order of the world. He urged them to live in peace with their neighbors or invite God's punishment. Guyuk, the great khan and grandson of Genghis Khan, replied by calling on the princes and people of Europe to submit themselves to him and asked why the pope considered himself the agent of God and not him.

In one sense, the pope's definition of relations with non-Christians and his diplomatic initiatives emerged from the recognition of his political power in Europe in the middle of the thirteenth century with the defeat of the emperor Frederick II. But it was more the conviction that the pope was responsible for the souls of all peoples that motivated the missionary movements. During the late fifteenth century when the secular interests of royal dynasties had become more powerful than the papacy, the Portuguese and Spanish Crowns still appealed to the pope for the spiritual jurisdiction over their conquests. The rising tide of missionary activity in the Canary Islands, the Americas, and Asia following conquests sprang up in part from the implications of the responsibility the pope and by extension Christianity shouldered for the spiritual welfare of all men. The urgency of this mission was articulated in the bull of Gregory IX, *Cum Hora Undecima* (1235), and reissued several times from the thirteenth century to the fifteenth

century.   In it, Gregory IX urged missionaries to preach Christ's
message to all men with the hope of converting non-Christians and also
correcting the beliefs of schismatics.   The apocalyptic character of the
papal message explained in part the inspiration of the missionary
movement: "Since the eleventh hour has come in the day given to
mankind...it is necessary that spiritual men [possessing] purity of life
and the gift of intelligence should go forth with John [the Baptist] again
to all men and all peoples of every tongue and in every kingdom to
prophesy..."[5]

In the middle of the thirteenth century, the idea of armed crusades
was giving way to a preoccupation with the conversion of non-
Christians. Peter the Venerable in the twelfth century had already urged
the winning over of Muslims "not by force but by reason, not by hate
but by love."   There were many like Roger Bacon who doubted that
armed crusades were effective. Increasing knowledge of Mongols and
Buddhists, in addition to Muslims offered a fertile field for missionary
endeavors to convert non-Christians by persuasion. Widespread belief
in the millennial prophesy of Joachim of Fiore also contributed to the
strength of the missionary movement. According to Joachim, Islam, the
seventh head of the beast mentioned in the apocalypse, would be
conquered less by fighting than by preaching. The desire for conversion
by argument became almost an obsession. Even in conquered Valencia,
where James I had initially discouraged conversion of conquered
Muslims, there was a change of policy and an aggressive conversion
movement began.

Ramon Llull

Majorca was conquered by James I in 1229.   Held by Islam for
almost three centuries, its population was a mix of cultures - Muslim,
Jewish, and Christian. After a conversion experience in 1263, Ramon
Llull conceived and pursued his project of conversion of Muslims and
Jews by rational persuasion.[6] He went on missions to the pope and
Christian rulers to ask them to found institutions to train missionaries
in Arabic and Eastern languages. Shaped by his knowledge of Islam as
a living faith, he was influenced by the Catalan Dominican, Ramon de
Penyafort, who had suggested that missionaries learn oriental languages.
He encouraged and participated in disputations between learned
representatives of different religions.   In 1263 in Barcelona, for
example, there was a debate between the Jewish rabbi, Moses ben

Nahman, and the Dominican friar, Pau Christia, presided over by King James I. The dream of converting Jews and Muslims was focused on Spain and North Africa. Treatises that became significant in later missionary work in the Americas and Asia were inspired and written during the late 13th century. It was Penyafort (d.1275) who requested from Thomas Aquinas in 1269 a work to help missionaries and so inspired the masterpiece, the *Summa Contra Gentiles*; the Dominican Catalan, Ramon Marti, wrote his influential *Pugio Fidei Adversus Mauros et Iudaeos* for this mission. Llull's *Book of the Gentile* was composed at this time.

For Llull, conversion of Muslims was extremely important because Islam was the major obstacle to conversion of the world, especially the Mongols. His disputations with Muslim scholars showed that he was familiar with the Islamic scholastic tradition. But it was the neo-platonism of Al Ghazzali (d.1111) and the Jewish Cabalists that was the most significant influence on his work. The spirit of Llull's evangelization could be seen at the conclusion of his *Book of the Gentile*. After listening to the presentation of arguments by a Christian, a Jew, and a Muslim, the gentile left without saying which religious philosophy he accepted. Conversion, then, was to be matter of free choice, not force. It was to be based on the serious study of non-Christian peoples and cultures. Llull's model for missionary work was the peaceful method of the early apostles. He appreciated the beauty of the liturgy of Islam and the depth of the religious spirit of Muslims. Yet, it was the same Llull who supported in 1291 the policy of an armed crusade. That his support was motivated by the intention to secure for missionaries the right of preaching the gospel still detracted from Llull's vaunted tolerance. It was probably the fall of Acre in 1291 that prompted him to support armed action to recover the holy land, and then only as the means for making the missionary enterprise effective. Llull and fellow Franciscan, Roger Bacon (b.1214), were as committed to the idea of the conversion of Muslims by rational argument as the Dominicans under Ramon de Penyafort. As Robert I. Burns put it: "Academic Spanish Islam, heir of Averroes and Avempace, wrestled with the sons of Albert, Aquinas, and all the array of the thirteenth-century scholastic genius."[7]

Why did the dream of converting Muslims and Jews fail? By the early fourteenth century, the schools of Valencia that were established to train missionaries were already in decline. The number of converts was dwindling. Though the schools and philosophical disputations achieved for a brief period the bridging of languages and mentalities of different cultures, at heart the missionaries did not show sympathy for Muslim and Jewish beliefs. To understand the other, it is necessary to display sympathy for the other. Explanation of beliefs is not enough. The dreams of thirteenth-century missionaries to Muslim lands were based on false assumptions - that the conversion of Muslims was imminent and that Muslim philosophers did not have a high regard for Islamic religious beliefs. It was nevertheless no small achievement that Christians could sit and engage in debate with their historic enemy with the hope of finding common ground, following the bloody early crusades. But, thirteenth-century missionary activity in its aggressiveness contained the seeds of intolerance that would ripen two hundred years later in America: "Paradoxically, however, its aggressive rationalism and polemical proselytism, like some virus introduced in Christendom's bloodstream, heralded a new age of self-righteous harassment and discrimination. By the end of the century Christendom had put on an armor of inquisition and was entering an era of primitive harshness."[8]

The Patronato

On July 28, 1508, pope Julius II issued a papal bull establishing the *Patronato* whereby the Spanish Crown was given the right to name bishops and other religious officials of the Americas. This meant that the Spanish monarchy was entrusted with the responsibility of the mission to convert native Americans to Christianity. The obligation to found parishes, churches, and cathedrals fell on their shoulders. They themselves had maneuvered to receive this privilege. For it was part of their political objective of making the new world conform to the culture and traditions of Spain. At best, the *Patronato* offered the ideal of a paternalistic and benevolent state that would use its sword to advance the claims of religion. Native Americans could expect to be protected by a just Crown; at worst, religion served at times the interests of the sword. In effect, this is precisely what a crusade meant, namely, the union of religious and political power in support of an ideological objective.

Earlier, Ferdinand and Isabella had been able to obtain the *Patronato* of Granada in 1486, enabling them to appoint bishops and all religious positions in Granada and to receive the tithes that normally would go to the Church. In granting the *Patronato*, the pope wanted to show his gratitude to the Crown for undertaking a crusade to reconquer Granada. Pope Sixtus IV had sent a representative to preach the crusade that launched the battle of Granada in 1483. On assuming office in 1492, pope Alexander VI widened the privileges of the *Patronato* by granting the Crown a third of all tithes collected in Spain, not just Granada. The *Patronato* was an important institution of Spanish colonial administration and, through this system, they were able to shape colonial culture. The institution was appropriate for a crusade and it must be borne in mind that arguments for it were couched in terms of a crusade. Both the battle of Granada and the conquest of America were conceived in part as a crusade. The *Patronato* is another piece of evidence of this. Through the *Patronato*, the reforming zeal of Queen Isabella and Ferdinand's centralizing policies were combined. The Jesuit historian Pedro de Leturia saw the *Patronato* as encouraging "national expansion and the strengthening of royal power with the spiritual and missionary dream of the propagation of the gospel and the Church; the crusade of Granada is extended in the Indies."

The important papal bulls of Alexander VI in 1493, *Inter Caetera* and *Eximiae Devotionis*, were part of this political maneuvering. The division of spheres of influence between Spain and Portugal was motivated essentially to resolve differences between the two Iberian nations and to advance the evangelizing as well as the commercial interests of the Spanish Crown. Before Columbus departed on his fourth voyage in 1502, the Spanish monarchs received another papal bull from Alexander VI conceding to the Crown the right to Church tithes which they would receive from the natives and inhabitants of the Indies. The system of the *Patronato* was one of the reasons why Spanish Christianity came to dominate the culture of Latin America. The Crown's direction of the missionary interests gave the evangelical purpose a greater importance than if it were an independent movement. The danger the movement faced in this situation, however, was that purely religious concerns had to make concessions to national and secular interests.[9]

NOTES

Chapter 5

1. Antonio Rumeu de Armas, *La Política Indigenista de Isabella*, (Valladolid, 1969) 29-88.

2. See James Muldoon, *Popes, Lawyers, and Infidels: The Church and the non-Christian World 1250-1550*, (Phil., 1979) VII-XI; Pedro de Leturia, "Las Grandes Bulas Misionales de Alejandro VI, 1493," in *Relaciones entre la Santa Sede e HispanoAmérica*, (Caracas, 1959), 155-204; James Muldoon, "The Contribution of the Medieval Canon Lawyers to the Formation of International Law," *Traditio*, 28(1972) 483-497; Kenneth J. Pennington, Jr., "Bartolomé de Las Casas and the Tradition of Medieval Law," *Church History*, 39(1970) 149-161; James T. Johnson, *Ideology, Reason and the Limitations of War Religion and Secular Concepts, 1200-1740*, (Princeton, 1975).

3. For the the standard life of Innocent IV, see Horace K. Mann, *Lives of the Popes in the Early Middle Ages*, (London, 1902-32) vol. 14.

4.Muldoon, *Popes, Lawyers, Infidels...*, p. 16.

5. *Ibid.*, p. 37.

6. *Ibid.*, p. 37.

7. Robert I. Burns, *Muslims, Christians and Jews in the Crusader Kingdom of Valencia*, (Cambridge, 1984) p. 103.

8. *Ibid.*, p. 108.

9. See Pedro de Leturia, *op.cit.*, 4-258; a critical edition of the text of pope Julius II's bull is on pp. 252-258; see also William E. Shiels, *King and Church: The Rise and Fall of the Patronato Real*, (Chicago, 1961).

Chapter 6

SIXTEENTH CENTURY SCHOLASTICISM AND THE COLONIZATION OF AMERICA: FRANCISCO DE VITORIA AND HIS INFLUENCE

The ideas of Francisco de Vitoria exercised a powerful influence over those who advocated a more humane colonization of Spanish America. His students and colleagues were in the forefront of the struggle against the oppressive trends of the conquest. Vitoria's humanism was rooted in the general humanistic movement of the early sixteenth century and in the resurgence of Thomistic studies. His contact with both trends was made while he was a student at Paris between 1507 and 1523.[1] It was there that he met the humanist Lefebre and Jerome Alexander whose knowledge of Greek attracted many students. But, the most enduring influence was the revival of Thomism which arose out of both the general dissatisfaction with the prevailing character of scholastic philosophy and the reform of the Dominican college at Paris.

Nominalism, which had arisen in the fourteenth century as a reaction against the excessive formality of scholastic philosophy, itself evolved into sophistry and mere argumentation, as the Spanish humanist, Luis Vives, so aptly described it. The intellectual preoccupation with logic made its adherents seem out of touch with the reality of the late fifteenth and early sixteenth century, a period that witnessed greater interest in moral questions. Thanks to the reforming zeal of John Standonck, the college of Montaigu, which numbered among its students Erasmus, Vives, and Calvin, and had been the center of Nominalism, was now shaped by this new orientation.[2] The scholarly community was subjected to a more disciplined life. They had to attend to religious devotion more scrupulously, sweep floors and mend their own clothes. As for the curriculum, emphasis was placed on the *Ethics* and *Politics* of Aristotle. The spirit of reform was taken to the Dominican college at Paris by Peter Crockaert, who had studied under his countryman, Standonck, at the college of Montaigu.[3] Crockaert infused his students, among whom was Francisco de Vitoria, with enthusiasm for the philosophy of Aquinas by using the *Summa Theologica* as the basis of his teaching and training them to edit the texts of Aquinas. In 1512, Crockaert, with the assistance of Vitoria, published the *Secunda Secundae*, an essentially moralistic work of Aquinas. In the prologue, Vitoria accused the opponents of Thomism of abandoning the best authors and reminded them that, in following Aquinas, they were not surrendering freedom of opinion.[4] There was to be no return to a fundamentalist approach to the works of Aquinas. Rather, the new Thomists found in his works certain key ideas that they found useful in understanding the troubled, transitional world of Western Europe at that time. This revival of Thomism was not a reaction against the general humanistic tendencies of the age, but a part of it. There was little that was rigid or obscurantist about these Thomists. In emphasizing the publication of texts, they were simply utilizing the invention of printing in the West to reach a larger scholarly audience. Their objective was no different from those humanists who became editors and printers, like Aldo Manutius and Beatus Rhenanus, the editor of the works of Erasmus. Crockaert thus succeeded in establishing a significant school of Thomistic studies at the Dominican college of Paris, an intellectual focus which Vitoria would take to the university of Salamanca. Paris was, of course, not the only center of Thomism. The classic commentator of Thomism, Cajetan, lectured on the *Summa* at Pavia as early as 1497 and, in 1508, was the first to publish a complete commentary on the *Prima Secundae*.[5] The revival of Thomism in Paris was therefore a part of the general resurgence of Thomism in Europe in the early sixteenth century.

Vitoria returned to Spain in 1523 to become professor of theology at Valladolid and then Salamanca, where, among those students who attended his classes, were several who went to America. At Salamanca, he replaced the *Sentences* of Peter Lombard with the *Summa Theologica* of Aquinas as the major text for his course. He found the Dominican convent of San Esteban in Salamanca, his residence for the last twenty years of his life, already involved in a spirit of reform. Due to the zeal of Fr. Hurtado de Mendoza, a burning commitment to the ideal Christian life and scholarship was beginning to shape the direction of Salamanca.[6] Vitoria's reputation was so highly regarded that the king of Spain consulted him on a variety of pressing issues of the day, such as matters relating to the conquest of America, the papal or conciliar supremacy of the church, and the king of England's divorce from his Spanish wife. These questions were seriously debated in Europe and formed the topics for his courses at Salamanca.

The colonization of America had raised considerable discussion since Fray Anton de Montesinos charged the colonists in Española with the oppression of the native population.[7] Of course, the indefatigable Las Casas had left no political stone unturned to bring the issue on the stage of Spanish politics. Nurtured in the climate of renewed ethical considerations at Paris and Salamanca, Vitoria presented his view of Spanish colonization in his lectures in 1538. In formulating his idea of human liberty, he "opened the paths of a new thought that would definitively dominate Spanish culture and policy."[8] More, from his deliberations on the conquest of America sprang a theory of international law, which Grotius would later develop.

In his treatise, *De Indis*, he set out to analyze the complex question of the conquest, and to define what the relationship between Spaniards and Indians of America ought to be. Earlier treatises had, of course, been written on Spain's legal title to the newly-discovered lands. The Scottish theologian, John Major, professor at Paris, had given his thoughts on the question of the relations between Christians and the Indians of America in 1510. Military conquest was necessary, he said, because the Indians, in their inability to understand Spanish, would not allow Christians to teach them. A defender of the Spanish Conquest, he recommended that fortifications be established so that the Spaniards would gradually have time to build an understanding with the native people.[9] For Major, the object of conquest was the establishment of Christianity. The first systematic treatise, however, was written by Palacios Rubios (1450-1524) between 1512 and 1514.[10]

Professor of canon law at the universities of Salamanca and Valladolid, and adviser to the Crown for some twenty years, he was asked to give his opinion on the question of the government of the Indies. Not surprisingly, he defended the Spanish right of conquest of America. Basing his argument on the extensive power of the pope, he declared that "the supreme dominion, power, and jurisdiction over the islands in question pertains to the Church, which the entire world and everyone, including infidels, must recognize as their lord and master." [11]

The church was within its right when it transferred this power to the Spanish Crown. He left no doubt that he believed that Spanish dominion over America was implicit in the donation of Pope Alexander VI who "conceded and granted those islands with all their dominions, cities, castles, places, villages, rights, jurisdictions, and all that pertained to them, to you and your heirs and successors, the monarchs of Castille and Leon, in perpetuity."[12] By virtue of this right, the Crown could exact tribute and services from the inhabitants. In his attempt to justify the virtual enslavement of the Indians, Palacios Rubios had to reconcile a condition that was tantamount to slavery with the notion of Christian liberty. He admitted that "nature created, in a certain way, all men equal and free," but, historically, slavery was "approved or confirmed by the law of nations, and canon and civil law."[13] That some men should rule and others obey was, as far as he was concerned, both necessary and useful. For example, he said, it was natural that men should rule women because the former were endowed with reason, the latter deprived of it. Those men who were more rational should rule; those who seemed to lack rationality were by nature slaves. Slavery, then, was defended on both natural and legal grounds.

He was quick to make the point, however, that if the natives consented to become Christian, they would retain their primitive liberty. Moreover, the Indian nobility would retain their status, liberty, and dominion over their property, once they were Christianized. Indeed, they had every right to defend themselves in a just war against the Spaniards if they were threatened with the confiscation of their lands and property simply because they were not Christian. However, were they not to recognize the Christian church as their lord and master, and refuse to accept its teachers, the Crown could justly make war against them and wrest dominion from them, "to remove them from infidelity, heresy, or their cruel rites and ceremonies." Palacios Rubios indicated that a similar justification was behind the expulsion of the Jews in 1492: "For this reason, in my opinion, the Jews were expelled from these kingdoms by your Majesty and his dear wife, pious queen Isabel, since Jewish perfidy, with their perverse will, stubbornness, and raging hatred, persecuted the Christian religion; contact with them, for many reasons, was dangerous for the faithful, especially since it was learnt that Jews had attracted many Christians to their depraved customs, rites and ceremonies, and, since the strong suspicion existed that they would continue to do so in the future, they were deservedly expelled."[14] In this way, Palacios Rubios defended the highhanded and cruel treatment of the Indians of America and Jews by the Spanish Crown. The Church, which possessed the authority of God, could deprive non-Christian rulers of their dominion or jurisdiction because, by virtue of infidelity, they could not claim power in their own right but by the will of the Church: "God is the lord of the whole world, and so he who seeks to separate another from his dominion, as infidels do, who disturb the faithful, ought justly to lose the right that they exercise over them."[15] The main lines of the treatise of Palacios Rubios represented one of the many ideological positions the roots of which went back to the disputes over papal supremacy in the middle ages.[16] Its main defenders were pope Innocent IV, Hostiensis, and Durandus. Innocent IV (+1254) held that Christ, as lord of the world, had the power to depose rulers, a power that was transferred to the pope. Hostiensis (+1271) distinguished between the temporal/spiritual jurisdictions of Christendom, both of which came from God. For him, the spiritual was greater. Indeed, the emperor received his dominion by the authority of the Church, which could depose him. Durandus (1237-1296) claimed that the pope had both spiritual and temporal power. What formed the ideological content of the early formations of Spanish colonial policy was clearly the notion that the pope had broad temporal and spiritual powers to order Christendom in accordance with Christian values. Interestingly, the idea of Christendom was extended to include America. For Palacios Rubios, papal supremacy was an important principle in upholding the idea of the unity of Christendom. His views certainly influenced the regulations that were given to Pedrarias Davila when he set out for Darien in 1513 to the effect that he had to explain to the Indians that "God created the heavens and the earth and the first human beings....that Christ entrusted to Peter that he should be the lord and master of all the peoples of the world, and that he should be the head of every human lineage, wherever men should live, and over every law, sect, religion."[17] This practice was widely used as late as 1526, as the Spanish conquest extended to Mexico and Peru.

A similar defense of Spanish political dominion was articulated in 1512 by Matias de Paz, professor of theology at the universities of Salamanca and Valladolid.[18] He stated unequivocally that the king, armed with the authority of the pope, "could make war on infidels and submit their lands to the yoke of the redeemer because the entire world was given to Jesus Christ."[19] However, he urged that the Indians be told about Christianity before commencing war against them. If they rejected the teaching and returned to their own cults, it was permissible to reduce them to slavery. Paz distinguished between "Jews, Sarracens, Turks," and the Indians of America. He admitted that he had heard that in America there were "generous people, in no way greedy or evil, but to a great extent docile who would be easily directed to the faith, if treated with charity." Despite exalting the power of the king to make war to expand Christian influence, he counselled that propagation of the faith be done by other means, if possible. He reiterated that Spanish dominion was legitimate only on religious grounds, "not for the caprice of dominating nor the desire to get rich."[20]   Certainly, the Indians should be ruled under royal jurisdiction, but never despotically. Once converted, their freedom should be restored, although it was permissible to demand some services from them, provided those services were consistent with Christian values and reason.

In his response to the question of the proper conduct towards those Indians who lived peacefully without molesting Christians, he declared that the Church could justly dispossess all infidel rulers from their dominion because "the Catholic Church has dominion over the whole world." Since no one could be saved outside the Church after the coming of Christ, the principal right of dominion rested with the Church. Yet, infidel rulers could be permitted to retain their dominion, if the Church or its representative recognized that dispossession through war would not advance the cause of Christianity. Paz subtly made a distinction between dominion "for possession" and dominion for the teaching of Christianity.[21]   He conceded that the Church could not expropriate the temporal possessions of the Indians because infidelity did not nullify what they possessed by natural right. As for dominion to spread Christianity, infidelity was a legitimate cause of depriving Indian communities of power. As a consequence of this, the Christian ruler or priest should look after the welfare of his subjects, not for his own interests. His Indian subjects were to be converted to Christianity by persuasion, not by threats. Paz felt that infidelity of the Indians was different from that of Moslems and Jews who, in his opinion, had historically resisted or attacked Christianity. The Indians, though they were ignorant of Christianity, did not attack Christians. For Paz, Christian dominion was quite compatible with Indian liberty. Enslavement and the harsh services they had to perform were the factors that caused them to abandon Christianity. They were reduced to such dire straits that Indian mothers aborted their babies rather than have them enslaved. "In the name of charity," he pleaded, "even if they were justly enslaved, they should be given their freedom...since their faith diminished further under slavery, but with liberty would grow."[22] He recorded that the evidence of missionaries confirmed the truth of his conclusion that Christian influence would be stronger among the Indians if they were treated humanely and kindly, as free human beings living under the grace of Christ and not subjected to the weight of slavery.

Paz used Innocent IV and Hostiensis as the major sources for his treatise, as Palacios Rubios had done. But he also took pains to explain the views of Peter Lombard, St. Thomas, Durandus, and Thomas of Strassburg on relations between Christians and non-Christians. Their defense of Christian imperialism and Indian liberty must have influenced the clarification of the laws of Burgos, promulgated in 1513, which stipulated that those Indians who were desirous of becoming Christians and were politically mature should be set free.

The abortive experiments in the Caribbean to determine whether the Indians could use liberty responsibly between 1516 and 1535 filled the pro-Indian advocates with despair.[23] The conquest of Mexico and Peru and the consequent enlargement of Indian servitude made their concern for the Indians far more urgent. Under the prodding of Las Casas, the halls of the universities of Salamanca and Alcalá de Henares bristled with the colonial issue. Not surprisingly, the Indian problem was a burning question for the most celebrated theologian in Spain, Francisco de Vitoria. His condemnation of the war in Peru in 1534, and his declaration that the native people were "not foreigners, but true vassals of the king" indicated his growing interest in colonial matters. His contribution to the intellectual life of Spain was generally widespread and, on the Indian question, of crucial significance.

Domingo de Soto, Vitoria's student and, later, colleague at the Dominican college of San Esteban, lectured in 1534 on the question of Spanish dominion in America.[24] One could detect in his line of argumentation some differences from the earlier position of Palacios Rubios and Matias de Paz on the colonial question. For Soto, neither the pope nor the emperor had direct temporal dominion over the world.[25] Sure, Christians had every right to preach everywhere and could defend themselves by force, if prevented. But, in no way was this right of defense to be used to confiscate the property of the Indians or subject them as slaves to Christian rule. Christianity was to be taught, and persuasion used, in complete liberty.

Vitoria's *relectio* on the Indian question was believed to have been given at the end of 1538.[26] In his treatise, he proposed to discuss the legal and moral titles by which Spain came to dominate the inhabitants of America. He did not dispute the claim that the Crown had acted in good conscience in matters relating to the conquest. But, he felt that the frequent reports of "so many massacres, so many plunderings of otherwise innocent men, so many princes evicted from their possessions and stripped from their rule" justified doubts entertained over Spanish policy.[27]   It was his sensitivity to the deteriorating conditions in America that prompted his inquiry into the legal and moral foundations of the indigenous peoples' rights to property and the colonists' seizure of it. The colonists had used as their defense Aristotle's statement that some people were by nature slaves and better suited to serve than rule. They argued that the natives did not have "sufficient reason to govern even themselves" and were little different "from brute animals and are utterly incapable of governing." Vitoria contended that the natives were in peaceable possession of their goods, both publicly and privately, and "must be treated as owners and not be disturbed in their possession unless cause be shown."

Vitoria then turned his attention to those who justified the conquest and dispossession on religious grounds. Their proponents argued that since it was God's grace that conferred dominion, the native people could not exercise dominion because they "were in mortal sin." Vitoria rejected this line of argumentation which he traced back to the Waldenses, John Wycliffe, and Armachanus. For him, sin was not an impediment to true dominion. Recalling biblical history, he pointed out that David did not lose his kingdom because he had sinned. From a spiritual point of view, natural dominion represented the gift of "reasoning powers" to man, and sin did not abrogate these powers. In addition, civil dominion pertained more to civil law, and its rights most assuredly could not be nullified by sin.   Neither could unbelief constitute a just cause for loss of dominion. Vitoria cited Aquinas to support his conclusion that ownership was based on either natural or civil law and could not be removed by lack of faith.[28] Consequently, Christians were not entitled to seize the lands and goods of the native population.

Turning to the argument whether irrationality or unsoundness of mind vitiated the right of ownership. Vitoria reasoned that it did. He armed himself with the argument advanced by Aquinas that only rational beings possessed true dominion because only they had the right of choice. If power alone was sufficient, a thief would have dominion over his victim because he had the power to kill him.   But, he contended, Indians were neither irrational nor of unsound mind because they had the use of reason. This was apparent from the study of their social and political customs. It was not their fault that they seemed unintelligent; it was only because they were uneducated like the peasantry in Christendom. Therefore, Spaniards had no right to take lands from Indian princes and private persons alike.[29]

Referring to those who cited Aristotle to propound that the Indians were by nature slaves and therefore incapable of self-government, Vitoria questioned their interpretation of Aristotle. What Aristotle meant, he insisted, was that it was better for the more intelligent in a society to rule over the weakminded. In no way did this mean that those who ruled had the right to confiscate the possessions of the ruled. Even if it could be proved that the Indians were inept, dominion could not be denied them. In any case, nature had endowed them as human beings with the capacity for self-government.

Having established that the indigenous population had true dominion over their lands, Vitoria went on to discuss the illegitimate grounds on which they could be dispossessed. To the rationalization that the Christian emperor superseded in jurisdiction the native rulers in that he was the ruler of the world, he argued that the emperor was not the ruler of the whole earth.[30] According to natural law, man was free and so no one had dominion over the world. The matter of dominion was the province of human law. Nor could it be proved that emperors received this title by divine law. While Aquinas had stated that the Romans were entrusted with empire by God because of their justice and laws, their sovereignty was not derived by divine grant but from wars. Although the argument could be made after the coming of Christ, it was still inadmissable. The kingdom referred to was a spiritual one. Vitoria reiterated that the emperor was never the lord of the world. But, even if he were the lord of the world, as some insisted, he could not "seize the provinces of the Indian natives, establish new lords there, and remove the former ones, or take taxes." The proponents of imperial supremacy did not claim that "he was lord in ownership, but only in jurisdiction." Vitoria argued that this right did not give him the power to convert provinces for his own use or to give away towns and even states, at his pleasure.

To those who based the Spanish conquest on the authority of the pope, Vitoria insisted that the pope was not the temporal ruler of the world.[31] In the medieval struggle between pope and emperor over jurisdiction of Christendom, papal defenders like Hostiensis and Anconitanus had defended the supremacy of the pope. Palacios Rubios and Matias de Paz had cleverly used the authority of these writers to assert the power of the pope to make the king of Spain ruler over the

Indians. In their minds, refusal to accept Christianity constituted justification for waging war against the Indians and seizing their lands. Vitoria argued that the pope's temporal power was never fully accepted. Among those who held contrary opinions were Torquemada, Joannes Andreae, and S. Bernard. It also seemed contrary to the teachings of the Scriptures. For Vitoria, the power of the apostles was not to be "lords over God's heritage, but examples to the flock." Clearly, the power given to popes was spiritual. Even if Christ had spiritual power over the whole world, such power was not transferred to popes. Consequently, popes did not have such power over non-Christians as to excommunicate them or invalidate their marriages. Of course, the pope had temporal power only to advance spiritual matters. But, he had no spiritual power over the Indians. Indian rejection of papal jurisdiction did not constitute grounds for making war on them and seizing their property. Moreover, they could not be compelled to accept Christianity. After all, Moslems living among Christians did not have to give up their property. Therefore, Christians did not have a just cause of war and, at the time of the first voyages to America, "they took with them no right to occupy the lands of the indigenous population."

Equally illegitimate was the title of right of discovery. Indeed, the law of nations allowed those who discovered and occupied deserted lands to claim them as their own. But, this claim was ill-founded because the Indians were "true owners, both from the public and the private standpoint."

Next, Vitoria took up the matter of Indian refusal to accept Christianity.[32] His opponents had argued that the pope in his spiritual capacity had the power to compel the Indians to accept Christianity and, in the last resort, to make war on them because of their unbelief and blasphemy. Vitoria reasoned that the natives could in no way be accused of unbelief if they had not heard of Christ. Ignorance was simply not a sin. If they lived a good life in accordance with the law of nature, "God will illuminate them regarding the name of Christ." Neither could the natives be condemned for not accepting Christianity simply because it was announced to them that Christianity was the true religion "without miracle or any other proof or persuasion." Citing Cajetan, Vitoria felt it would be rash to expect them to accept Christianity unless it was taught by men worthy of belief, "a thing which the indigenous Indians do not know." In no way should war be waged against them. Since no wrong had been done by the Indians, there was no just cause of war. However, Vitoria admitted that the

Indians would be guilty of mortal sin if they rejected Christianity presented to them "with demonstrable and reasonable arguments" by men who lived an "upright life, well ordered according to the law of nature." He hastened to add that these criteria had not yet been met. On the contrary, he had heard that the "scandals, crimes, and acts of impiety" were the order of the day, despite the efforts of many who had approached their civilizing task diligently and sincerely. Given the manner in which the conquest proceeded, the Indians were not bound to accept Christianity. Even if Christianity had been presented to the people appropriately, it still was not permissible to make war against them. Aquinas himself had argued against compulsory conversion. Faith was an operation of the will; freedom, not fear, was, in his opinion, the precondition for the acceptance of Christianity. Citing arguments drawn from canon law, the council of Toledo, and history, Vitoria concluded that war was "no argument for the truth of the Christian faith." In the case of the indigenous people of America, then, the conditions for a just war and the seizure of their lands simply did not exist.

Vitoria also opposed the apologists for the military conquest of America who based their justification on certain Indian practices like cannibalism, incest, and sodomy.[33] They had argued that these acts contradicted the natural order and consequently Indians could be forced by war to desist from them. The implication was that the pope exercised universal punitive jurisdiction in moral matters. Vitoria responded that such a right, if accepted, could be expanded to include fornication, theft, and homicide. True, S. Paul had inveighed against fornication and idolatry, but both he and Aquinas believed that the right of moral correction was to be exercised "over those only who have submitted themselves to the faith." He added that it was obviously not easy to determine what sins were contrary to the laws of nature. Further, the pope could not make war against nor seize the lands of Christian fornicators and sodomites. If he could, "there would be daily changes of kingdoms." Indeed, those acts were more objectionable among Christians who accepted them as sins than among those who did not. Referring to the Old Testament, he cited the example of Israel which never seized the land of unbelievers "because they were unbelievers or idolaters... or guilty of other sins of nature."

To those who claimed that Spain's sovereignty was based on the title given them by some Indian rulers, Vitoria was skeptical. Free choice was the indispensable condition for the transfer of a title. Confronted by the Spanish army in battle array, Indian rulers more than likely made the offer under fear. For him, then, this argument was "utterly inadequate and unlawful for seizing and retaining the provinces in question." He could not accept the reasoning of those who took a prophetic view that God in his judgement had condemned all Indians and delivered them into the hands of the Spaniards as the Canaanites to the Jews. Even if it were true, the perpetrators would not escape blame "anymore than the kings of Babylon who led their army against Jerusalem and carried away the children of Israel into captivity were blameless." To those who used Christian moral values to judge the native people, Vitoria retorted: "Would...that there might be no greater sins in morals among certain Christians than there are among those barbarians."

Turning his attention to the conditions for legitimate relations between Spain and America, he believed firmly that Spaniards had every right to travel to America according to international law.[34] Defining international law as "what natural reason has established among all nations," he argued that international law gave one the right to travel to and even stay in a foreign country, provided he did not mistreat the local population. Indians therefore did not have the right to prevent Spaniards from traveling to their country any more than the French had to prevent Spaniards from traveling to or living in France. Citing biblical, classical, and church texts, Vitoria stressed magnificently the common nature of all human beings, whatever their religion, nationality, or race, and argued for the naturalness and rationality of interdependence and mutual respect. Friendship and hospitality were rooted in the law of nature, and the seas were common to all. So, freedom to travel and to use what was common property was implicit in nature. What Vitoria was suggesting was that international law was derived from the law of nature. This rational and humane conception was well illustrated by his reference to a text by S. Augustine: "When it is said 'love thy neighbor', it is clear that every man is our neighbor."

For Vitoria, international law also established the right of individuals and nations to trade freely with each other. No ruler, be he Indian or Spaniard, could prevent his subjects from trading with other peoples. Spaniards then could lawfully carry on trade with the natives provided they did them no harm. Mutual benefit could be derived in that scarce commodities could be imported to America in exchange for gold and silver which they had in abundance. Vitoria obviously considered free trade as operating under just economic laws. It must be pointed out also that the benefits of trade with Spain were in his opinion to accrue to the Indians. This statement was clearly made to criticize the economic system which was then benefiting Spain and the colonists in America. The basis of his argument was the notion of the brotherhood of all men. It was against natural law for one man to disassociate himself from another without good reason. He quoted Ovid: "Man is not a wolf to his fellow man, but a man." Vitoria continually stressed that these rights of trade and even digging for gold or fishing for pearls should not bring injury to the native population.

On the question of citizenship, he insisted that Spaniards born in America automatically became citizens of that Indian state while those who sought naturalization were entitled to this provided they submitted to the same responsibilities as Indians.[35] If these rights were challenged by the Indians, the Spaniards should first try to persuade them rationally that they intended no harm, but wanted to live in peace with them. If the Indians rejected this appeal and prepared to make war against them, the colonists could then use force to defend themselves. Citing Aquinas, Vitoria asserted that "warding off and avenging a wrong" was a just cause of war because the Indians would be denying the Spaniards their rights under international law.

Mindful of the cultural differences between Indians and Spaniards, Vitoria conceded that the Indians could have been motivated by their understandable fear of such awesome strangers to expel the Spaniards. However, while the Spaniards were justified in defending themselves by war, it was not right for them to enforce other rights of war as confiscating their goods or seizing their cities. In such a case, war was just on both sides: "The rights of war may not be invoked against the innocent and the ignorant." When the means of rational persuasion were exhausted to no avail, it was permissible for Spaniards to seize their lands and reduce the natives to subjection to enjoy the rights sanctioned by international law.[36] For this statement, he cited S. Augustine that "peace and safety are the end and aim of war." It was lawful then to wage both a defensive and offensive war to secure the ends of peace. To add to this controversial point, he felt that international law permitted victors to seize as their own what was captured in war. To be sure, the argument of free trade and travel as a justification of war was somewhat weak. Vitoria in a subtle way tied it to another idea that had deep roots in the history of civilization.

Ambassadors, he said, were inviolable in international law; the Spaniards were the ambassadors of Christian civilization. Therefore, the Indians were bound to receive them hospitably. Moreover, Christians possessed the right to preach the Gospel: "If the Spaniards have a right to travel and trade among the Indians, they can teach the truth to those willing to hear them." There is little doubt that for Vitoria Christianity was the path to truth for everyone. If the Indians could be excused before the European discovery, they were not after it. Spaniards, therefore, had the moral responsibility to teach Christian values to the native population. Removal of the barriers to this was implicit in this responsibility. If recourse to war had to be taken to advance this cause, so be it, he seemed to imply. Brotherly correction, he said, was as important in natural law as brotherly love.

But why should the Spaniards be the teachers of Christian civilization in America? Vitoria supported their claim on the grounds that it was granted to them by the pope and, further, by the fact that it was the Spanish Crown which financed the voyages. He had, however, to explain this position in view of his earlier statement that the pope was not the temporal ruler of the world. His reasoning was that although the pope's juridical power was in the domain of spiritual affairs, he nevertheless possessed temporal power in matters that had a spiritual objective. Twisting almost painfully between arguments derived from international, natural, and religious law, Vitoria supported the pope's power to grant to Spain the exclusive right to colonize America. The conquest was to be spiritual; hence, the pope's power and Spain's right of colonization were defensible. Replying to the possible question why Spain alone, and not other Christian nations, should be entrusted with this mission, he contended that such an action would prevent the development of quarrels that would undermine the process of conversion to Christianity. Clearly, the religious turmoil that was dividing European Christendom was the background for this apparently self-serving conclusion. Spain, then, possessed the right to colonize America. But, this right meant the responsibility to create and sustain political order and peace necessary for the teaching of Christianity. Vitoria emphasized that, while they did not have the right to prevent the teaching of Christianity, the indigenous peoples were free to accept or reject it. The coercive power of Spain was therefore limited to providing the conditions for the propagation of Christianity. This power could also be justifiably used again Indian rulers who prevented their subjects from converting to Christianity or who inflicted punishments on those who were converted. For Vitoria, coercion must be balanced by "moderation and proportion, so as to go no further than necessity demands." Vitoria urged his students to be mindful particularly of the paramountcy of the spiritual objectives of colonization. Although wars might be justified in international law, they sometimes led to massacres and inhumane acts which soured relations between peoples of different cultures and made the values of Christianity unacceptable. Persuasion, restraint, and moderation were more often better methods of achieving a spiritual goal than coercion and war. He confessed that, in his understanding of the events in America, the Spaniards "were bound to employ force and arms" to continue their work there, but these measures were undertaken "in excess of what is allowed by human and divine law." Vitoria was in no doubt about the value of the spiritual ends of Spanish colonization, but he was equally insistent on the proper means of advancing those ends. Admitting that the means were often dictated by the particular circumstances of events, he urged as an operating principle alongside legal rights the reference to the mission of teaching Christian civilization in deciding what means were to be used in specific situations, "lest what in itself is lawful be made in the circumstances wrong."

As Vitoria used the argument of expediency in imploring the Spanish authorities to be wary of waging war when they had the legal right to do so, so he urged a similar expediency in suggesting that, in areas where large numbers of Indians were converted, the native rulers could be deposed and the Christian Indian community brought under the jurisdiction of a Christian ruler to protect their new way of life. By giving the pope the ultimate responsibility for such an action, he hoped to forestall the capricious interpretation of this by secular rulers whose primary interest might be graspingly materialistic.

Returning to the question of the ritual of human sacrifice practiced by some native cultures, he stated that Spaniards did not need papal authority to intervene to stop the practice. Everyone had the right to rescue innocent people from an unjust death. It did not matter whether all the Indians accepted this ritual and rejected the Spaniard's offer of assistance to put an end to it. The right of intervention to protect human rights was rooted in the universal moral order. How did he square this justification of intervention with his earlier condemnation of it? Intervention was to be condemned if it led to the seizure of Indian territory, but approved if motivated by the consideration of safeguarding the human rights of individuals.

Spanish political supremacy was permissible if the majority of inhabitants freely chose a Spanish ruler over a native one. This political conception was in keeping with the development of political thought in Western Europe from the Middle Ages. Aquinas had held that the principle of political authority was derived from the community. A ruler must use this power for the good of the community and, if he used it tyrannically, he could be deposed. Vitoria cited the example of the Franks who deposed Childeric and put in his place Pepin, the father of Charlemagne. The final formal title by which the Spaniards could establish sovereignty over America was by virtue of their support for Indian allies. Drawing on the precedent of the case of the Tlaxcaltecs who had allied themselves with the Spaniards against the Aztecs, Vitoria asserted that it was lawful for Spaniards to offer their support as an ally in a civil war to the side that had suffered a wrong in return for the promise of sharing the fruits of victory. The cause of allies and friends was, in his opinion, a just cause of war. He saw the legal grounds of the expansion of the ancient Roman empire, approved by S. Augustine and Aquinas, as being on this principle.

There was left only one title for Vitoria to treat, namely, imperial trusteeship. Some had argued that since the Indians were incapable of conducting the business of government properly, Spain should undertake to administer their country for them: "Accordingly, they have no proper laws nor magistrates, and are not even capable of controlling their family affairs; they are without any literature or arts, not only the liberal arts, but the mechanical arts also; they have no careful agriculture and no artisans; and they lack any other conveniences, yea necessaries, of human life."[37] Vitoria neither affirmed nor denied it. He contended, however, that the argument would have merit if the claims were true. Whatever its merits, he added, prime consideration must be given to the welfare and interests of the Indians, not merely the profit of the Spaniards.

Finally, he stated that if Spain's supremacy could not be justified in any of the legal titles he had enunciated, it did not mean that Spain should withdraw from America, thereby suffering economic losses. Trade could continue, despite the loss of political hegemony, and the government in Spain could recover its revenue by a tax on imports from America. He cited the example of Portugal which had benefitted economically from trade in Asia without reducing the native peoples to subjection. Further, there were so many Christian converts among the

American Indians that "it would be neither expedient nor lawful for our sovereign to wash his hands entirely of the administration of the lands."

The doctrine of Indian liberty so majestically initiated by Vitoria was elaborated in the lectures given in 1539 by Bartolome Carranza at the college of San Gregorio in Valladolid.[38] He rejected the notion of papal or imperial power over the Indians and stated that, though they could not prevent the preaching of Christianity, the Indians could not be forced to accept it. To the question whether Spaniards had the right to enslave Indians after the conquest, he replied that they did not have the right to retain them just as they had no right to conquer and place them in subjection in the first place. The pope could appoint a Christian ruler to look after the spiritual life of those Indians who were converted to Christianity, but in no way could he keep them as his subjects. The Indians had the right to life and human dignity given to people of all races and they could not be deprived of this right either by the king or church. Moreover, if the Indian community agreed not to listen to the ideas of another religion or follow laws which were different from their own, they could not be forced to do so. What Carranza was arguing for was the acceptance of the idea that Indians had the right to form their own society. This right was based, he thought, in natural law which operated equally for all people. Acceptance of this principle led him to the radical assertion that in America it was not illegal for Christians to be subjects of non-Christian rulers because Indian dominion over their lands was legitimate. In this respect, he went beyond the position of Vitoria who, in accordance with the view of Aquinas, had argued against such a position because it would constitute a danger to Christianity. More, if Christians waged an unjust war against the Indians, Carranza concluded that Indians could make Christians their prisoners and acquire true dominion over them in accordance with international law. Faithful to the vision of both scholastic and humanistic trends of the sixteenth century, Carranza conceived of the Indian communities of America within the general international community, bound by the same ideals.

The general theological support of the most important theologians for the pro-Indian cause as well as the political and diplomatic triumphs of Bartolome de las Casas prodded the emperor Charles V to issue the momentous New Laws in 1542. These laws revealed the spirit of the ideas of Las Casas, Vitoria, Soto, and Carranza; the Indians were vassals of the Crown and had the right to life, safety, and self-preservation; they could freely dispose themselves and their property; they should be educated and instructed in Christian values; and they had the right to demand justice against the injuries done to them by the Spaniards.[39]

It was, however, too much to expect that such a remarkably humane piece of legislation would be accepted. Resentment among the colonists in America and critics in Spain found an able spokesman in the Spanish humanist, Gines de Sepulveda.[40] His treatise, *Democrates alter*, composed in 1544 sparked an intense controversy in Spain for several years. To be sure, his militant imperialism was a restatement of earlier ideas on colonization, articulated by Palacios Rubios and Matias de Paz. But, the teaching of Vitoria and political activity by Las Casas had made too great an impact on the intellectual scene in Spain to allow Sepulveda's thesis to go unchallenged.[41]

Fray Melchor Cano, who had succeeded his master Vitoria in the prime chair of theology at Salamanca upon his death in 1546, then took up his intellectual cudgels against Sepulveda.[42] In 1546, he gave a series of lectures on the question of Spain's sovereignty in America which must have carried not a little weight in the refusal to have Sepulveda's treatise published. In response to the argument of Sepulveda, he affirmed that, in accordance with international law, the Indians possessed true dominion over their land, a right that could not be nullified by their infidelity or alleged backwardness. No one was by nature a slave or subject of another human being. In natural law, there was no "difference between human beings because all were born equal." Sure, the Aristotelian notion of the hierarchy based upon intelligence had some merit. But, this was a matter of personal choice. Greater wisdom and a superior political system did not give any state the authority to conquer another state. He criticized the defense of conquest as operating for the greater usefulness of the natives. The desire to improve the conditions of other people was a matter of charity, not of justice, and could not, therefore, be accompanied by coercion. To Sepulveda's claim that the superior political system of the Roman empire was the historical precedent for Spain's militant imperialism, Cano contended that while the Romans conquered some provinces justly, they gained others because of greed and ambition, just as "Spain conquered for the gold that they took" from America. Judea, he recalled, was not invaded because they did not have a political system. Indeed, theirs was superior to the Romans because they received it from

God.

Neither was idolatry a cause for enslavement. As for crimes against nature, it was permissible to defend the innocent, whether they were practiced by Indians or by Christians. This did not mean that it constituted grounds for making war against the Indians. The right of intervention to protect the innocent was defensive: "Consequently, we should not go further than is necessary for this end. If, therefore, we can remove them from these crimes by persuasion, in no way should we do it by force or coercion."[43] Most certainly, this did not justify the excessive tribute that the Spaniards levied on the Indians. This practice was nothing less than "shameful robbery."

For Cano,the variety of sovereign kingdoms in history was proof that the emperor was not the ruler of the world. He could not have possessed this power by natural law because there would obviously be a contradiction between that idea and another notion, also rooted in natural law, that no one was by nature the political subject of another. Like Vitoria, Cano rejected the notion that the pope had dominion over the world by virtue of the superiority of his spiritual power. True, he had a certain spiritual jurisdiction over Christians and could ask Christian rulers to defend the rights of Christians. But, the pope did not possess any power over the Indians. To be sure, he had the responsibility to protect the preaching of Christian culture, but this authority pertained to the domain of charity. The idea of charity in international politics was the central theme of Cano's treatise. Continuing, he said that the obligation of charity did not carry with it any coercive force, unlike justice, which was acquired by force. The dynamic of charity and other spiritual virtues pointed towards equality, and were more hindered by violence than helped by it.

What then were the legitimate bases for the intervention in America? Cano argued that all nations shared a natural kinship and right of communication. International law permitted every man to travel wherever he wanted, provided he did not do any harm. However, if the Indians seemed to resent the Spaniards, it was because the Spaniards had gone to America "not as pilgrims, but as invaders, unless one can call Alexander a pilgrim." Secondly, one could intervene to preach Christianity. However, the Indians were free to accept it or reject it. If tyrannical rulers tried to prevent their people from being exposed to Christian teaching, theoretically force could be used. But, Cano pointed out that it was to be used solely to defend the innocent, not to convert them to Christianity. The desire of the majority of Indian communities to have the emperor as their ruler and support for the group that had justice on its side in a civil war were other grounds for Spanish intervention. No sooner had Cano formulated the titles for intervention than he reprimanded those who plundered the wealth of America for the good of Spain and the colonists, as if to say that the actual conquest was not motivated by the ideas he had elaborated.

Diego de Covarrubias was another member of the commission to decide upon Sepulveda's book.[44] In 1548, he presented his lectures on the colonial issue. Structuring his thesis in such a way as to refute Sepulveda's ideas, he articulated his own thesis defending the liberty of the American Indians. He first tried to reconcile the contradiction between the natural liberty of all human beings with the historical existence of slavery. Using texts drawn from Greek philosophy, Roman law, sacred scriptures, Aquinas, and Torquemada, he asserted that the principle of natural liberty was incontrovertible. By natural law all men were born equally free. The imperative of liberty was at the heart of existence. From the beginning of time, nature had as its objective the good of the cosmos, the human race, and the state. However, as history developed, some men abused this liberty, disturbing the general order. Through the consent of all nations, wars were introduced to preserve justice by punishing the wicked. Prisoners were made slaves to save them from a deserved death. Slavery then was the law imposed by history to repress collective crimes and preserve peace. There was no such thing, then, as natural slavery. He admitted the idea that civilized nations could intervene in communities where the people were more like animals than men. But, he doubted that this was the character of the American Indians. The principle of intervention was the general good of all humanity by assisting those who did not have the means for dignified self-preservation.

Focusing the light of these principles on the Indian communities, he boldly asserted the natural law of liberty. They had the right of sovereignty and independence; their rulers possessed true dominion over their towns, and could demand respect for their basic rights. Not only could they justly prohibit Spaniards from extracting gold from their territory and fishing for pearls in their public rivers, but they could also deny them entry to their lands. Extending the concept of sovereignty further than Vitoria, he declared that the Indians had the right to prohibit the immigration of Spaniards who were interested only in commerce because, once admitted, those Spaniards, more clever, stronger, and better armed, would only bring ruin to their lands. Neither the pope nor the emperor could authorize a war to compel the Indians to accept Christianity because the Indians possessed justly their property and territory. Wars of religion, then, must be condemned. He added that such a holy cause did not justify the enormous cruelty and barbarity that took place.

Yet, he felt that there were legitimate reasons for intervention. Spaniards had the right to preach Christianity in America, a right, he stressed, that should have been pursued by means of persuasion and an enthusiasm characterized by respect for Indian rights, unattended by the desire for dominion. More specifically, armed intervention was justifiable in certain situations to assist and protect the innocent who were sacrificed every year. All people belonged to one international community and were brothers. The same reasoning justified intervention to assist an oppressed party in its war against tyrannical rulers. In addition, as Christians, they had the responsibility to intervene to protect those Christians whose lives were threatened by non-Christians.

Covarrubias sought a synthesis of the idea of the individual rights of the Indians on the one hand and the rights of the international and Christian community on the other. Theoretically, they were not incompatible. As long as peaceful means were used, conflicts and differences could be resolved. In practice, however, force was the order of the day. That was why Covarrubias emphasized the importance of Indian rights and the sovereignty of Indian communities. Where violence was perpetrated unjustly by the Indians, he likewise did not hesitate to state those situations in which Spaniards could justly intervene, not to enslave, but to defend and protect the liberty of the oppressed.

The support of the Sepulveda thesis by an influential sector of the Spanish intellectual community was obviously the stimulus for the lectures on the conquest of America given by Juan de la Peña between 1559 and 1563. A student of Cano and Carranza and a friend of Las Casas, Juan de la Peña had observed the course of the debate on the conquest from the beginning of its new turn under Vitoria in the 1530's. As an advocate of Vitoria's position, he viewed with alarm the influence of Sepulveda. What was at stake, in his opinion, was Spain's civilizing mission. On the question of the origin of Spain's dominion in America, he restated the position of the theologians that neither the pope nor the emperor possessed temporal power over the Indians. He insisted that the right of intervention given by Pope Alexander VI to the Spanish Crown did not constitute the right of conquest, but the right to oversee the Christianization of America by peaceful means. He disputed Sepulveda's contention that the Spaniards waged a just war against the Indians because of idolatry. Since faith was a supernatural gift, no one could be forced to receive it. To do this was tantamount to tyranny. Christ was the head of all human beings. If Christians were already members of his body, those who were not Christian were potential members who, endowed with free will, must freely be persuaded of the truth of Christianity.

Peña then analyzed with some depth the notion of barbarism. It was the magical term used by men like Sepulveda to define the nature of the American Indian and to justify war against them. Sepulveda found his source in Aristotle's statement that it was natural that the intelligent should rule over the unintelligent. For him, Spanish dominion and Indian subjection were the natural conditions for the advancement of Christian civilization in America. Referring to the Portuguese enslavement of Africans, Sepulveda wrote that the condition of Africans was better under slavery, to prove his point about his recommendations for the American Indian. Peña understood the term to mean a cultural situation in which the laws of a society were not rational and where all kinds of unnatural crimes were practiced, or where there was not even a rudimentary semblance of a political system. In such cases, a case could conceivably be made for armed intervention. But, he contended, he did not know of any society that fitted that definition. Certainly not the Indians of America. Peña rejected the use of the notion of superior and inferior civilizations, as he sought to demystify the politically charged term, barbarism. To accept this principle, in his opinion, would mean that any society that thought itself superior had the right to wage war against those nations it considered inferior. He could not accept Sepulveda's citation of the conquests of the Roman empire as being motivated by this principle. For him, greed, ambition, and force of arms were the motives in most cases. To illustrate his point, he asked whether the king of Spain had the right to intervene in France if he felt that Spaniards were superior in intelligence.

In his treatment of those situations where Spain had the right to intervene militarily, he followed the analytical line drawn by Vitoria, Carranza, Cano, and Covarrubias. The most serious cause was the defense of innocent sacrificial victims. War was, of course, to be the last resort, and one must take into consideration whether the war would cause a greater loss of life than the religious rituals. He recalled the story told by Plutarch of a Roman general who was sent to a city to punish its citizens for human sacrifice. On learning that it was an ancient custom, the general "pardoned the past and prohibited the practice in the future." Wars that were undertaken justly were defensive, and once the objectives were achieved, Spaniards were to restore to the native people all that they had taken.

The theoretical underpinning of Spanish imperialism in America took on a different character in the 1530's, thanks to the influence of Francisco de Vitoria. The early militant imperialism, defended by Palacios Rubios and Matias de Paz, was superseded by a conception that sought to give the colonization the foundation of justice. Nurtured by men like Las Casas, Anton de Montesinos, and Alonso de Zorita, and the religious orders, this concept was defined brilliantly by Vitoria and developed by his students and followers. In truth, its genesis occurred in the late fifteenth century, a period that brought a general tendency towards institutional reform. In that turbulent century, when European feudalism was giving way to commercial capitalism, Europeans on the one hand were more assertive and adventurous; on the other hand, their anxiety prodded them to seek reform in institutions that had become frozen in old practices and abuses. What was surprising was that some would go back to the scholastic philosophy of Aquinas as they sought humane solutions to new problems. But, intellectual life in the fifteenth century was characterized by a certain sterility. The breakdown of the medieval synthesis of reason and revelation had left Christendom intellectually adrift. The Protestant Reformation offered one solution to the ensuing spiritual vacuum. Scholasticism, especially the ideas of Aquinas, provided the foundation for those who desired modernization and reform within the traditional structure of Christendom, a trend that led to the council of Trent.

The conquest of America began the process of the European domination of the world, certainly one of the most significant aspects of modern history. The problems that it raised, like the right of domination and the rights of subject peoples, brought answers that still raise controversy today. In the sixteenth century, in the face of increasing dependence on the wealth of the Indies, despite encountering a native population whose culture was markedly different from theirs, some Spaniards in America and in Spain struggled to make the defense of the American Indian the official policy of their government. The value of their support for Indian human rights and the sovereignty of Indian communities, their belief in the equality of all communities, regardless of race, culture, and religion, within an international community, sharing similar ideals, surely transcends their historical context. One can question their implicit belief in the superiority of Christianity and European culture. But, in this, they were rooted in their own times. This presumption of superiority, one must hasten to add, has been held by other religions and cultures. Did Vitoria's view of the mission of Spain triumph over Sepulveda's? On the official governmental level, the influence of Vitoria and his followers was instrumental in getting considerable legislation passed to protect the Indians. The peaceful conquest of northern Mexico and the Philippines must be credited to the pro-Indian movement. But Sepulveda's position was more in tune with those in Spain and Europe, not to mention the colonists in America, who had benefitted economically from the conquest, especially after the opening up of the silver mines in Mexico and Peru in 1546. The reconciliation of the theme of the struggle to win human and civil rights for the American Indians with that of their social and cultural catastrophe remains elusive.

NOTES

Chapter 6

1. Born around 1486, Francisco de Vitoria entered the Dominican convent of San Esteban in Burgos while still young. He left for Paris in 1507 for his arts course, later graduating to the study of theology in 1513. He commenced lecturing at Paris in 1516. In 1522 he received his licentiate and doctorate in theology, returning to Spain the following year. See Ricardo G. Villoslada, *La Universidad de Paris durante los estudios de Francisco de Vitoria*, (Rome, 1938); Heinz-Gerhard Justenhoven, *Francisco de Vitoria zu Krieg und Frieden*, (Köln, 1991).

2. Standonck (1443-1504) studied at Gouda with the Brethren of the Common Life. A. Renaudet, "Jean Standonck, un reformateur catholique avant la Réforme," *Bulletin de la Soc. de l'Histoire du Protestantisme Français*, LVII(1908) 5-18.

3. See Villoslada, p. 230.

4. *Ibid.*, p. 279.

5. *Ibid.*, 291-301.

6. V. Beltran de Heredia, *Historia de la Reforma de la Provincia de España (1450-1550)*, (Rome, 1939) p. 143ff.

7. Las Casas, *Historia Apologética*, (Madrid, 1909).

8. Luciano Pereña Vicente, *Misión de España en América*, *(Madrid*,1956) 7-10.

9. Pedro de Leturia, "Maior y Vitoria ante la Conquista de America," in *Analecta Gregoriana*, 101(Rome, 1959) 259-298.

10. For some twenty years Palacios Rubios was adviser to the Crown of Spain and president of the council of the Mesta. A lawyer of considerable reputation, he took an active part in the preparation of the laws of Toro (1505). His *De Iustitia de Iure obtentionis ac retentionis regni Navarrae*, published in 1514 or 1515 gave an important clue to his position on the Spanish conquest. He argued that the Spanish conquest of Navarre by pope Julius II was a holy war and thus justified. E. Bullon, *Un Colaborador de los Reyes Católicos. El Doctor Palacios Rubios y sus Obras*, (Madrid, 1927).

11. Palacios Rubios, *De las islas del mar océano*, ed. by Silvio Zavala, (Mexico City, 1954) p. 128.

12. *Ibid.*, p. 128

13. *Ibid.*, p. 27.

14. *Ibid.*, p. 57.

15. *Ibid.*, p. 117.

16. See J.N. Figgis, *Studies of Political Thought from Gerson to Grotius, 1414-1625*, (Cambridge, 1931).

17. M. Serrano Sanz, *Orígenes de la Dominación Española en America*, (Madrid, 1918) p. 279.

18. Born between 1460 and 1470, Matías de Paz studied in Paris from 1490 to 1496. He was professor of theology at the university of Valladolid and in 1513 obtained the chair of sacred scripture at the university of Salamanca. He died in 1519. See Beltran de Heredia, "Un precursor del maestro Vitoria, el P. Matias de Paz y su tratado De Dominio Regum Hispaniae super indos," *La Ciencia Tomista*, XI(1929) 173-190.

19. Matías de Paz, *De Dominio*, ed. by S. Zavala, (Mexico city, 1954) p. 215.

20. *Ibid.*, p. 222.

21. *Ibid.*, p. 222.

22. *Ibid.*, p. 255.

23. See S. Zavala, *La Encomienda Indiana*, (Madrid, 1935); L.B. Simpson, *The Encomienda in New Spain*, (Cal., 1929).

24. Born in 1495, Domingo de Soto was a student at the university of Alcala before continuing his studies at the university of Paris where he was influenced by Vitoria. He returned to Alcala as a professor in 1519-20, developing a reputation as an outstanding theologian. He was a firm defender of the Vitorian vision of the colonization of America. See Beltran de Heredia, *Domingo de Soto. Estudio Biográfico Documentado*, (Madrid, 1961).

25. *Ibid.*, p. 252ff.

26. See J. Baumel, *Leçons de Francisco de Vitoria sur les problémes de la colonisation et de la guerre*, (Montpellier, 1936) 57-88.

27. Francisco de Vitoria, *Relectio de Indis et de Iure Belli*, ed. by Ernest Nys, (Washington, D.C., 1917) p. 119.

28. L. Getino, *El Maestro Fray Francisco de Vitoria y el Renacimiento Filosófico-Teológico del siglo XVI*, (Madrid, 1914).

29. *De Indis*, p. 126.

30. See the several studies of C. Barcia Trelles on Vitoria and international law; see Justenhoven, p. 189.

31. *De Indis*, p. 139.

32. *Ibid.*, p. 146.

33. *Ibid.*, 146.

34. *Ibid.*, p. 151. See James Brown Scott, *Francisco de Vitoria and his law of Nations*, (New York, 1939).

35. *Ibid.*, p. 154.

36. Vitoria discussed the notion in a separate series of lectures, *Relectiones de Iure Belli, ibid., 165-187.*

37. *Ibid.*, p. 161.

38. Professor at the college of San Gregorio in Valladolid, Bartolome de Carranza was invited by the emperor to attend the council of Trent in 1545 and was one of Phillip II's closest advisers. His influence later waned and in 1559 he was placed in the Inquisition's jail in Valladolid on charges of heresy. In 1576 he was formally condemned by pope Gregory XIII and ordered to recant sixteen heretical opinions in his catechism. He died shortly afterwards. See Pereña Vicente, *Misión de España en América*, 27-37.

39. Pereña Vicente, 38-57.

40. See T. Andres Marcos, *Los Imperialismos de Juan Ginés de Sepulveda*, (Oxford, 1925).

41. Bell, *op.cit.*, 90-91, n. 69.

42. Born in 1509 in Cuenca, Melchor Cano was a student at the university of Salamanca and joined the Dominican convent in 1523. From 1527 to 1531, he was a student of Vitoria. He then went to the college of San Gregorio where he was also a student of Carranza. He became a professor of theology at the university of Alcala from 1543. He gave a course on the Indies in 1539-1540. See Pereña Vicente, 61-89; see Beltran de Heredia, "Melchor Cano en la Universidad de Salamanca," *La Ciencia Tomista*, 143(1933) 178-268.

43. Pereña Vicente, p. 109.

44. Born in 1512, Diego de Covarrubias went to the university of Salamanca in 1522. He received his doctorate in 1539 and received the chair of canon law the following year. In 1547 he was named to the commission to investigate the propriety of Sepúlveda's book. Pereña Vicente, 151-182.

Chapter 7

ALONSO DE LA VERA CRUZ, COLONIAL UNIVERSITIES, AND THE DEFENSE OF NATIVE AMERICANS

In the dialogue on the university of Mexico at its opening of Jan. 25, 1553, the humanist Francisco Cervantes de Salazar must have captured the vitality, excitement, and significance of that moment. To the question: "Can there be a place left for wisdom in this land of greed?" He answered: "Those who teach so far from their homeland as well as those who study in the midst of the pleasures and opulence of their families deserve more and greater privileges...with the light of wisdom they have dissipated the darkness of ignorance."[1] Continuing the dialogue with brilliant portraits of the first professors of the university, he wrote:

"To whose class are those Augustinian friars going?"
"They are going to the lectures in theology of Fray Alonso de la Vera Cruz, the most eminent professor of arts and theology...He is the first professor of this divine and sacred science, a man of wide erudition, in whom outstanding virtue competes with the most outstanding teaching."

Faced with the near destruction of the peoples and cultures of the Americas, the Spanish Crown and the Church attempted to construct a new Christian culture, often though not always with European institutions. The transplantation of the medieval European university to the Americas was of momentous importance in that the universities were to play a major role in the creation of Spanish American colonial culture.[2] Persuaded to leave his position as professor at the prestigious university of Salamanca in 1536 and join the Augustinian missionaries in Mexico, Alonso de la Vera Cruz was arguably one of the outstanding scholars and intellectuals in sixteenth-century Mexico.[3] The first professor of the chairs of sacred scriptures and theology, he published several commentaries on Aristotle for his students in the faculty of arts. So important was his influence that some claimed that he was the founder of the university of Mexico.

Following the heels of the conquistadors, the religious and to a lesser extent the secular clergy were also the agents of the Crown's policy to capture the "hearts and minds" of the native peoples. The Franciscans (1523), Dominicans (1528), and Augustinians (1533), who spearheaded missionary activity in Mexico before the coming of the Jesuits to Mexico in 1572, were quick to establish primary schools for the moral and technical education of Indian boys.[4] There were also schools for Indian girls by 1530. The Franciscan Pedro de Gante set up the first primary schools, but the Dominicans and Augustinians also had active, successful schools of their own.[5]   Indian students learned the fundamentals of Christian doctrine; they were also trained to become blacksmiths, carpenters, painters, sculptors, and jewelers; they learned the arts of embroidery, quarrying, and stonecutting, mosaics and inlays. All instruction was in the native languages which meant that knowledge of native languages was of paramount importance to missionary teachers. The ideological significance of this was that the religious were going to encourage the Indians to live according to their native customs in matters that were not religious. This indigenous approach to the question of culture was not simply strategic; many were generally disturbed by the excesses of the Spanish colonists. In addition, this "nativist" approach to the Christianization of the Indians was meant also to preserve the authority of the missionaries.

The establishment of the college of Tlatelolco in 1536, a school for the advanced education for Indians, deserves mention among the early educational institutions in Mexico. Here Indian students studied the liberal arts.[6] Founded with the objective of being a center for Mexican studies and to produce native clergy, its fortunes rose and fell. It certainly failed to produce a cadre of native priests and was the object of envy and contempt of many colonists. The remarks of the outstanding scholar, Bernardino de Sahagun, who taught Grammar at the college, illustrate this well: "When the [Spanish] laymen and clergy were convinced that the Indians were making progress and were capable of progressing still more, they began to raise objections and oppose the enterprise."[7] Yet, there remains a significant testament to the success of the college. Many of its Indian students, like Antonio Valeriano and Pablo Nazareo, were expert in Nahuatl, Latin, and Spanish and became translators.[8] Their most outstanding legacy was their collaboration in the research and writing of Sahagun's monumental work, *The General History of the Things of New Spain*.[9]

This work by Sahagun has had great appeal for scholars and is a major source of knowledge of pre-conquest Aztec society. From his arrival in Mexico in 1529 to his death in 1590, he occupied himself in a life of teaching and writing. Having mastered the native Nahuatl language, he set out to compile and organize knowledge about Aztec culture. It took forty years and he was assisted by his Indian students at Tlatelolco, native dignitaries, and native experts. The work was written in Nahuatl and illustrated with paintings. Sahagun later added a Spanish translation. To this day scholars marvel at his methodology and consider him the father of modern ethnography. Jorge Klor de Alva suggested that there was mutual familiarity and respect for each other's ideas and methods between Vera Cruz and Sahagun. Both emphasized logical and empirical methods in their inquiry. The purpose of Sahagun's work was originally to assist in the missionary enterprise. But, in the course of his research, he came to appreciate Aztec culture. He did not have a high regard for Aztec religion, but his admiration for their moral teaching and wisdom was great. Impressed in particular by their civic virtues, the nurturing of their children, and their sense of responsibility, he was curious why a virtuous people had followed such a demonic religion. In matters of religion, Sahagun was unable to transcend his Christian beliefs; in all other aspects, he was able to understand and value the culture of the native people.

It was the Franciscan, Juan de Zumarraga, first bishop of Mexico, who initiated the idea of establishing a university in Mexico. In 1537 he informed the Crown that Mexico needed an institution of higher learning and reminded the king that he permitted the foundation of a university in Granada to facilitate the conversion of Muslims to Christianity. This was an interesting precedent because in the clash of cultures between Europeans and native Americans there existed the experience of the encounter with Islam as an important example. It ought not to be surprising that the works of Thomas Aquinas were popular in the schools of Spanish America. His *Summa contra Gentiles* was designed as a handbook for missionaries to Muslim lands to demonstrate the truth of Christianity and refute the "*Mahumetistae et pagani.*"[10] For the most part, however, the missionaries preferred not to see similarities between Muslims and native Americans. Rather, they sought to show that native Americans were different from them. It was not until 1553 that the university of Mexico opened.

The idea of founding a university in the Americas did not originate in Mexico. Not long after the conquest of the Caribbean, initiatives to establish a university in Española were started. The Dominicans established a school of higher education in 1518 and in 1538 pope Paul III granted the charter of foundation making the *Studium* in the Dominican convent a university: "...a community of masters and students with...the customary liberties, exemptions, and immunities, so that the city of Santo Domingo gain a great reputation. Its inhabitants as well as those from the neighboring islands will be better instructed in the Christian faith and it will serve as an incentive to continue the works of charity."[11]

It was the Dominicans also who were instrumental in getting a university established in Peru. At a meeting of the provincial chapter in Cuzco on May 6, 1548, a resolution was passed to request the necessary authorization for a university. In 1533 the inauguration of the university of San Marcos took place in the Dominican convent.[12] Like the medieval universities of Europe, the first universities of America arose from ecclesiastical institutions and purposes. Moreover, higher education was now on its way to becoming the monopoly of the universities.

The university of Mexico structured its academic organization and curriculum in imitation of the university of Salamanca.[13] Its curriculum which shaped the intellectual formation of Spanish America was little different from European universities. Students were expected to take courses in the faculty of arts before entering the higher faculties of theology, law, and medicine. There were three chairs of arts; the *Summulae Logicales* of Peter of Spain, logic, and philosophy. After taking courses for two years, students took an examination on nine questions: three on the *Summulae*, three on logic, and three on philosophy. What was remarkable was the continuing emphasis on the logical works of Aristotle which had revolutionized university learning in the thirteenth century and was still the core of the curriculum in sixteenth century Europe. Its establishment at the universities in America was the first time that this curriculum was used outside of Europe. Lest we lament unduly over this cultural imperialism, we should remember that European academic culture was not purely European and Christian. The classical Greco-Roman world and the great Muslim and Jewish commentators had helped to shape this academic tradition. Take, for example, Peter of Spain, the author of the widely used *Summulae Logicales*. In a later work, the *Science of the Soul*, he combined elements borrowed   from Plotinus, Boethius,

Alfarabi, and Avicenna.[14] It was Vera Cruz who wrote the first texts on the logical works of Aristotle for his students in the faculty of arts: the *Recognitio Summularum* (1554), the *Dialectica Resolutio cum Textu Aristotelis* (1554), and the *Physica, Speculatio* (1557).[15] The importance of dialectics can be seen in his preface to the *Recognitio Summularum*: "It is a matter of great urgency to instruct students in the essentials of dialectics, to point out to them the way to sacred theology so that they would not grow old on the shores of the Sirens and be discouraged in their anxiety over the magnitude of their difficulty."[16] Dialectics was "the art of arts", the indispensable method for the study of theology, law, and medicine.

As for the higher faculties, theology consisted mainly of the study of the bible, the theological questions systematized in the *Sentences* of Peter Lombard and the works of Thomas Aquinas.[17] In the faculty of law, the texts used in the courses on canon and civil law were the traditional ones - the *Decretum*, the *Decretales*, and the *Corpus Iuris Civilis*, consisting of the *Digest*, the *Codex,* the *Institutes*, and the *Novellae*. The study of the law was very popular in Spanish America. For it was the *Letrados* or men of law who conducted the affairs of the Indies. The Audiencia, the major political and administrative body in Spanish America, was comprised almost entirely of *Letrados*.[18] The first chair of medicine in Mexico was not established until 1582; the texts used were drawn from the Greco-Arabic tradition, that is, the works of Hippocrates, Galen, and Avicenna. This did not mean that there was no research in medical matters until late in the sixteenth century. In 1527 the office of *Protomedico* was created. This official was a naturalist who collected information on plants, trees, and herbs and sent back reports to Spain. He acted as controller of the practice of medicine, examining candidates for medical practice, testing drugs, and disciplining violators of medical regulations.[19]

These texts in the arts and higher faculties constituted the core of academic learning. Traditional European academic culture arose and developed in a world that had for the most part a single vision of reality. How ironical it was that Europeans were trying to impose this reality and culture on peoples who had such a radically different culture precisely at that moment when the unity of Christian culture was shattered by the emergence of Protestantism. One can even speak of multiple ironies. In 1492, with the defeat of Spanish Muslims and the expulsion of Spanish Jews, Spain abandoned its pluralistic cultural traditions and visions in favor of a single and, in their minds, purer Christian tradition. It was one thing, however, to seek to impose a pure Christian culture; it was something else to make it effective. Native Americans and missionaries, certainly those in the sixteenth century, found ways to keep native traditions and beliefs alive.

The texts and philosophy of Thomas Aquinas were enormously popular in America. It is no exaggeration to say that Thomism was the heart of the curriculum during the colonial period. The advice Vera Cruz gave to his students is a good illustration of the significance of Thomism in the academic culture of Spanish America: "No day should go by without reading an article by S. Thomas. In reading any book, they should note whatever was novel and useful, comparing it with what S. Thomas had said on that subject...Whatever was not clear, they were to jot it down and then consult S. Thomas."[20]

The transplantation of the European university and its scholastic system to America would tend to support the argument that it was just another institution whose objective was to consolidate the Christianization and Europeanization of America. It is difficult to deny that the purpose of the Church, the missionaries, and the university was to assist in the spiritual conquest of the Americas. But the history of these institutions during the first century after the conquest was not predictable and showed that some Spaniards were critical of the victors and their actions and struggled to present the point of view of the vanquished as the Crown began to formalize its system of justice. That Vera Cruz selected the defense of Indian rights as the topic for his course in theology in 1553 illustrates the seriousness of the reform movement in Mexico and also the exciting intellectual culture of the middle of the sixteenth century.[21] This course, entitled *De Dominio*, at the university of Mexico and Las Casas's defense of native American peoples and cultures at Valladolid must rank highly as witnesses to the struggle for human rights.[22]

Born around 1507 in Caspueñas, a town in the diocese of Toledo, Vera Cruz received his bachelor of arts degree from the university of Alcala and then went to Salamanca to study theology where one of his masters was Francisco de Vitoria. When the Augustinian procurator, Francisco de la Cruz, went to Salamanca in 1535 to recruit missionaries for Mexico, Vera Cruz already had the reputation of being an outstanding scholar and teacher. He was also tutor to the children of the Duque del Infantado, an important Spanish nobleman. What would motivate a young scholar to leave such a promising career to undertake a new life as a missionary in a strange land among such diverse peoples and cultures? One cannot discount Francisco de la Cruz's idealistic appeal to his sense of a mission to civilize, but the intellectual climate at Salamanca that was inspired by Vitoria must have been the significant influence in his decision. Having professed as an Augustinian in 1537 shortly after his arrival in Mexico, he was named master of novices of his order. Before receiving his appointment as a professor of sacred scripture and theology, Vera Cruz had achieved several distinctions. He mastered the Tarascan language of the peoples of Michoacan and founded several colleges. In 1542 he substituted for Vasco de Quiroga as Bishop of Michoacan. This acquaintance with Bishop Quiroga must have been an important influence on his life and work.[23]

Vasco de Quiroga was another of those outstanding humanists who came to the Americas in the first half of the sixteenth century. The native people had great respect and love for Quiroga and Vera Cruz. The Augustinians helped out Quiroga with teaching in his village-hospitals. As Vera Cruz was mastering knowledge of the Indian cultures of Michoacan, he must surely have shared insights with Quiroga. A member of the second Audiencia of Mexico that arrived from Spain in 1530, Vasco de Quiroga immediately undertook the reorganization of Indian society hoping to prevent the recurrence of the injustice done during the first Audiencia. He was interested in creating a system that was based on the reality of the conditions of Indian life. Harsh rule since the conquest in 1521 had so undermined the rhythm of native Mexican life that large numbers of children and women were left without the means to look after themselves. Indian poverty had become widespread. Quiroga said that he found many Indian children roaming the streets and markets looking for food left by the pigs and dogs. In a letter to the council of the Indies in 1531, he proposed establishing Indian village-hospitals to care for the needy and to teach them the Christian way of life. He felt that an ordered life in these villages would also help continue the development of children of the Indian elite who were trained in the schools of the religious orders. They had shown ability in reading and writing in Nahuatl, Latin, and Spanish. He was moved by their simplicity and humility, but feared that the chaos of Mexican social life would demoralize them.

Village-hospitals were established in Mexico city and Michoacan.

Inspired by Lucian's *Saturnalia* and the *Utopia* of the English humanist Thomas More, Quiroga organized his village- hospitals by following in close detail the framework of More's *Utopia*. Among the measures were: Each village-hospital was to comprise six thousand families; the family was an extended one of sixteen married couples; property was held in common; work in the town and countryside was alternated; judges were elected; administration of the villages was in the hands of native Americans. There were regulations even about dress. Order and a Christian way of life were the central values of these communities. But, training in policía or civilized life was as important. Very much influenced by their experience of the significance of urban life in Spain, almost all the reformers and educators could not accept the scattered character of native communities and sought to congregate them in towns as in Spain. The first village-hospital, Santa Fe de Mexico, was founded in Mexico city in 1532 as a refuge for "poor Indians, desperate persons, widows, orphans, and twins." The hospitals were more villages than places to heal the sick, though a building was constructed in the villages to care for the sick.

Indians from other communities fled to the village-hospitals hoping to escape the heavy tribute burden. By all accounts, the hospitals in Mexico city and Michoacan flourished. Criticism was of course raised against the village-hospitals; some colonists argued that the lands might more profitably be distributed among the Spaniards to establish farms. Martin Cortes, son of the conqueror of Mexico, brought a lawsuit challenging Indian ownership and jurisdiction of the village-hospitals. In decisions in 1563, the Audiencia of Mexico commanded that the ownership and jurisdiction of the villages remain in the possession of the Indians. When Quiroga made his will in 1565, there was evidence that the village-hospitals were active.

When Vera Cruz came to give his course in 1553, he already had considerable experience of life in Mexico. The ideas contained in the *De Dominio* must have seemed to him urgent in the early 1550s.[24] We know that during the next academic year (1554-55) he chose as his topic the *De Decimis*, the question of the church tithes that native Americans had to pay. The controversy over the New Laws of 1542, the first severe epidemic between 1545 and 1548, major silver strikes in Zacatecas in 1546 and Guanajuato in 1550, and the labor legislation in 1549 (*Repartimiento*) made the 1540s in Mexico turbulent. The content of the *De Dominio* followed two main lines of argument: a criticism of the encomienda, expanding the discussion to include the question of land; and the question of the legitimacy of the Spanish conquest.

For Vera Cruz, Indians had the right to dominion over their land, labor, and tribute. This right resided in their communities and could not be expropriated by force. If the seizure of property took place in a just war, expropriation might be defensible. But that was certainly not the nature of the Spanish conquests: "From an unjust cause of war dominion cannot originate, since it is characteristic of tyranny to exert unjust oppression." Consent of the ruler or community was necessary for the transference of dominion from Native Americans to Spaniards. He charged that encomenderos did not have proper title to their encomiendas. They were therefore "maintaining their possessions through force and violence."[25] They were "robbers", "thieves", and "kidnappers". Vera Cruz kept insisting that religion was not a factor in determining ownership. Indians could not be deprived of their land and other property because they were not Christian. If given the opportunity, "they would protest against the tyranny and oppression they are suffering, not from the emperor but from some of those to whom the custody of the natives was committed who devour them [in the same way] as they eat bread, who plunder, and torture them...of all this I am an eyewitness."[26] Vera Cruz admitted that the payment of tribute was not of itself unjust, provided that the ruler had just dominion and used tribute for the welfare of the community. That, too, was not the case. Spanish colonists kept demanding tribute in the form of "gold or silver, precious stones, vases or other objects, and the more so those who demanded slaves or servants or even free men." With what passion he pleaded: "I beg you, good reader, to put aside all prejudice and reflect by what law, by what right did the Spaniards who came to these regions armed to the teeth, attack these people subduing them as though they were enemies and occupying lands not their own, seeking out arbitrarily with force and violence all their valuable possessions, and robbing the people." It was force, not freedom that was the operating principle at work in the exaction of tribute. He was moved by the suffering of the native people: "Their cup of suffering was filled to the brim when the Spaniards gave clear evidence of their intention by cruelly killing and greedily plundering." Referring to the encomendero practice of increasing the quota of tribute even when the Indians were too poor to pay, he wrote: "My heart bleeds at the thought of how inhumanly such tribute is exacted with the consequence that the native leaders...are thrown into prison and are coerced with such punishment to plunder other Indians ...until they make up the excessive tribute."[27] He recalled another horrible illustration of women being coerced to weave cotton shawls as tribute: "I saw more than once the following take place: women worked day and night at these tasks. They were violently forced into one place and locked up there with the children they nourish as if condemned to a prison, and from such seclusion it follows that if they are pregnant, an abortion results from the excessive exertion, and if they are nursing mothers, because of too much work, wretched food, and the irregular schedule, the milk they give their young is poor and thus the children die." Or, take the example of the Spanish colonists whose Indians had completed their term of work in the mines. Wishing to have then continue to work for him, he flattered the Indian leader by embracing him and showering him with gifts. Instead of hearing the usual: "You dirty dog," he now hears: "O, Sir John, do honor me with your company." To demand tribute, the consent of the people was necessary. Tribute was to be levied in accordance with their ability to pay it "easily". He remarked that poor farmers in Spain were better off than the Indians. The exorbitant and unjust exaction of tribute made it impossible for the native people to look after their own needs and interests.

On the question of the Spanish purchase of Indian lands, he was convinced that it was illegal because Indians sold their lands out of fear. Vera Cruz acknowledged that private property existed among Mexican Indians. But this applied only to a small number of individuals. Vera Cruz focused on their communal lands. Native rulers could not sell these lands because communal lands, even untilled lands, did not belong to the rulers but to the entire community. To sell communal land was to destroy the integrity of the community: "Neither the governor nor the viceroy nor the entire community has the power to work for the destruction of the common good, but had only the power to work for its advancement and promotion."

Vera Cruz linked the issue of land to that of labor and tribute. Strictly speaking, the encomienda meant the allocation of labor and tribute, but not land. Vera Cruz strongly upheld the traditional view. Individuals and communities retained ownership of their lands. Land was not tribute but the source from which they paid the tribute.[28] Vera Cruz did not mince his words. If land was taken "to plant his crops or to set up grapevines or mulberry trees or other fruit trees or to pasture his herds for his own profit, such a Spaniard...is a robber." No one should "take over the otherwise cultivated lands of the natives either to plant or to graze cattle or for any other purpose." This was how he explained his position. Lands were not really abandoned because Indians changed the area of planting every year. By allowing their herds to graze there, in effect the colonists were ruining the land. Vera Cruz concluded this question on the seizure of Indian lands with the reminder that the Indians suffered great losses and continued to do so. Not only were the Indians robbed of their lands, but their crops were destroyed causing shortages of food and hunger. Where tribute, labor, and land had been excessively and unjustly obtained, Vera Cruz insisted that restitution had to be made to the native people. The call for restitution was given to urge his students who might have been confessors to colonists to demand restitution as the price of forgiveness. This was the way to provide moral bite to the laws that already existed to protect Indians but which were honored more in their breach than in their observance.

Was this attack on the encomienda justified? It was the preeminent Spanish institution used from the second voyage of Columbus in 1493. Legally, it was the allocation of groups of Indians to privileged colonists. These encomenderos were to receive tribute and labor from their designated Indians. In return, they were responsible for the Christian welfare of the Indians. The encomienda was therefore many things; it was a system of social relations, a cultural system, and a labor system. It was different from Indian slavery in that the Indians held in encomienda were legally free. In the Caribbean, however, there was little difference as the Indians were coerced into providing labor, food, and their women for the encomenderos. The history of the encomienda is but the history of the tension between laws passed to regulate and control the institution and compromises with the laws. The fact was that the Spanish Crown and individual Spaniards had expected to profit materially from the conquest of the Americas. Simply put, they needed Indian labor. While the importance of the encomienda was replaced by the repartimiento in Mexico and the mita in Peru, systems of rotated labor drafts in the 1550's, no really viable alternative to these essentially forced labor systems was found. The increasing realism of some of the religious demonstrated the importance of the labor system to the production of wealth. The need for labor would be made even more dramatic by the drastic decline of the native population caused by the waves of epidemics. The response of the twelve Dominicans of the Mexican chapter in 1544 to the inquiry of Tello de Sandoval as to the impact of the New Laws was revealing. In stating that the stability of the Spanish presence in Mexico depended on the continuation of the encomienda, they showed a remarkable change of attitude. They made a specious argument that there could not be stability without rich men nor rich men without encomiendas. But their last statement was the most telling: "...because without Indians, all trade and profit cease."[29] Even moderate religious like Domingo de Betanzos, a friend and supporter of Las Casas, came to accept rather than challenge the system.

But how does one reconcile what is essentially an oppressive economic system with the Christian purpose of the encounter? While Vera Cruz adopted a radical position against Spanish economic institutions and practices, his political position seemed moderate with respect to European military intervention in America. Having defended Indian rights to dominion, property, and their own communities, Vera Cruz inquired whether the Spanish conquest and presence in America were just. He was trying to establish an argument that would form the basis of a new vision of America, a new world which Spaniards and Indians would construct in a cooperative spirit.

To those who built their arguments for conquest on imperial or papal supremacy, Vera Cruz argued that neither possessed universal temporal jurisdiction over the whole world and so could not wage war against non-Christians simply because they were not Christian. The emperor therefore did not possess ownership of Indian lands and neither he nor his representatives could arbitrarily grant large tracts of land or communal property to Spaniards without the consent of the native people. Vera Cruz, however, did leave open the possibility of intervention "through a concession of the supreme pontiff, whose duty it is to provide the remedy for the spiritual purpose, namely, that the gospel of Christ be preached throughout the whole world." He agreed that the pope possessed spiritual power which carried with it the responsibility to teach Christianity everywhere. By virtue of this mission, the pope had the "right of disposing of the temporal insofar as it is related to the spiritual."[30] Vera Cruz argued that the pope could authorize the use of force to persuade non-Christians to receive missionaries. At the same time he insisted that no one should be coerced to become a Christian. More relevant to his topic was his rejection of any notion that force was permissible to seize the lands of native Americans. For Vera Cruz, then, the spiritual purpose was the only acceptable justification for European intervention in America.

In the final two questions, Vera Cruz analyzed the just and unjust motives for conquest, but they were related to the point he had established earlier, namely, the propagation of Christianity as the motive of colonization.[31]   Repeating his theoretical argument that should the right of Spanish missionaries to preach Christianity be denied, the Indians could be coerced to open their society to them, he quickly asserted that this was not what actually took place: "From the beginning, armed soldiers came who frightened and plundered and slew the natives of the new world."   There was no justification for the conquests. The accusations that native Americans were intellectually deficient whose lives were immoral were not valid motives for conquest. In the first place, he said that they were not true. Not only were they not simple-minded like children, but in their own ways they were eminent: "Before the arrival of the Spaniards...they had officials, orderly government, and most appropriate enactments; they had their own laws."

In the long eleventh question he developed arguments for the valid motives for dominion. Following the lines of argument of Francisco de Vitoria, he suggested that, in addition to the right to preach the gospel, Europeans had the right to travel in America, engage in commerce with the native peoples, and even the right of access to the mineral wealth of America, provided Europeans did no harm to Indians and their societies. Vera Cruz was proposing a new basis for the encounter, one that was characterized by mutual respect and freedom. If this seemed unrealistic, it was because the history of the Americas had already been too firmly gripped by force and power to offer hope for a reversal. In criticizing the encomienda so vehemently, he was pleading for the freedom of the Indians, a freedom that was based on economic justice; in presenting the possibility of valid motives for European intervention, he was justifying the European presence in America, but in a different role - that of civilizers, not destroyers. This was his vision of America, a dynamic mix of the two civilizations.

What were the influences on the thought of Vera Cruz? His treatise, *De Dominio*, bore many similarities with the *De Indis* of his master, Francisco de Vitoria.[32]   Vitoria had given his lectures on the subject in the 1537-38 academic year, after Vera Cruz had left for Mexico. Still, the views of Vitoria on the colonial question were well-known by the late 1520's. His *De Potestate Civili* was given in 1527-28 when he discussed the valid and unjust motives of the conquest.   Vitoria's condemnation of the war in Peru in 1534 and his declaration that the native people were not "foreigners but true vassals of the king" indicated his interest in American affairs. Vera Cruz could have been acquainted with the *De Dominio* of Domingo de Soto, another student and colleague of Vitoria, which was presented at Salamanca in 1534. Vitoria exercised great influence on the intellectual climate of Spain, especially on the colonial issue.[33] His students explained his perspective whenever they were given the opportunity.[34] Thanks to Vera Cruz, the university of Mexico participated in this intellectual movement.[35] The outlines of this movement remain clear, whether defended in Europe by Vitoria and his students or in Mexico by Vera Cruz. They supported the principle of human rights for Indians and the sovereignty of their communities. At the same time they proposed a more benevolent and cooperative European presence in America. In formulating these rights, they came up with the principles of an incipient international law. Vera Cruz and the university of Mexico must receive credit for their contribution to these international principles.

Was Vera Cruz also influenced by Bartolome de Las Casas? Many of the advocates of reform in Spain and America were inspired by Las Casas. The friendship between Vera Cruz and Las Casas during the last years of Las Casas's life is well-known and moving.[36] When Vera Cruz returned to Spain in 1562, he worked closely with Las Casas and recorded his last writings and activities. It was Vera Cruz who presented to the council of the Indies the final petition of Las Casas, urging to the very end another commission to investigate the suffering inflicted on the Indians. Vera Cruz also recorded his death on July 20, 1566, and his farewell words in his last will and testament: "God....saw fit to choose me as his minister, though unworthy, to plead for all the people of the Indies against the oppressions and injuries suffered from our Spaniards...and to restore them to the primitive liberty unjustly taken from them."

There were differences between Vera Cruz and Las Casas. Vera Cruz was more moderate in his discussion of the rights of conquest, a moderation, motivated strategically, to be sure, but also by the vision of the possibility of cooperation between native Americans and Europeans. But in his treatment of the other major question on the evils of the encomienda and the Spanish system of land, labor, and tribute, he was extremely critical of the colonists. Vera Cruz was vicar provincial between 1543 and 1546 and it was likely that he was either present at or at least acquainted with the proceedings of the conference of representatives of the religious orders that Las Casas called in Mexico City in 1546, where Las Casas presented his *Confesionario*. Was this the source for Vera Cruz's insistence on the doctrine of restitution that was so notable a feature of his *De Dominio*?[37] The notion of restitution was not of course an original idea. It was a part theoretically of the medieval Christian moral system. Vitoria, too, had enjoined restitution in his treatise. How significant this imperative was is difficult to measure. However, in the concrete situation of America from the 1540s to the 1560s, it played a central role in the Lascasian moral system.

During the 1554-1555 academic year, Vera Cruz lectured on the question of ecclesiastical tithes (*De Decimis*).[38] He argued that Indians should be exempted from this inasmuch as they were already burdened by tribute and labor service. This angered the archbishop of Mexico, Alonso de Montufar, who left no stone unturned in his efforts to prevent the publication of Vera Cruz's work. He sent a copy of the *De Decimis* to the Spanish Inquisition and recommended that the Inquisition be established in Mexico to root out heresy. Neither the Inquisition nor the council of the Indies prohibited the publication of his works. But contrary winds were already blowing by the end of the 1550's. Archbishop Montufar was one of those who became obsessed with heresy. Unable to silence Vera Cruz, he was responsible for the formal introduction of the Inquisition in Mexico in 1569. A different spirit was in the air.[39]

The great debate over the natural rights of native Americans was in large part a response to the traumatic context of post-conquest America in the sixteenth century. One marvels at the courage of Vera Cruz and others in shaping the struggle for a more just society. They remind us that in a context of oppression the promotion of justice and truth are integral to evangelization. Christianity entered the Americas accompanied by a colonial power. That some saw as their duty the responsibility of supporting the powerless, and holding the powerful accountable to moral laws remains an important legacy of this clash between European and native American civilizations.

NOTES

Chapter 7

1. Francisco Cervantes de Salazar, *Mexico en 1554. Tres Diálogos Latinos*, ed. by J. Garcia Icazbalceta, (Mexico, 1875) 19-37.

2. A.M. Carreño, *La Real y Pontificia Universidad de Mexico*, (Mexico city, 1961) p. 13; John Tate Lanning, *Reales Cédulas de la Real y Pontificia de Mexico de 1551 a 1816*, (Mexico city, 1914); A. Abadie-Aicardi, "La Tradición Institucional Salmantina de la Universidad de Mexico (1551-1821) en la Tradición Universitaria," *Jahrbuch für Geschichte von Staat, Wirtschaft und Gesellschaft Latein Amerika*, 12(1975) 1-66.

3. M. Beuchot,et al., *Homenaje a Fray Alonso de la Vera Cruz en el Cuarto Centenario de su Muerte (1584-1984)*, (Mexico city, 1986); E.J. Burrus, "Alonso de la Vera Cruz, Pioneer Defender of the American Indians," *The Catholic Historical Review*, 70, no. 4(1984); Arthur Ennis, "Fray Alonso de la Vera Cruz," in *Augustiniana*, V-VII, (New York, 1955-57); J.A. Almandoz Garmendia, *Fray Alonso de la Vera Cruz y la encomienda Indiana*, (Rome, 1967); see my article "Scholastic in the Wilderness: Alonso de la Vera Cruz," *Zeitschrift für Missionswissenschaft und Religionswissenschaft, 4*(1974) 273-278

4. R. Ricard, *The Spiritual Conquest of Mexico*, English trans. by L.B. Simpson, (Berkeley, Cal., 1982) 1-38.

5. *Ibid.*, 207-216; see E.A. Chavez, *Fray Pedro de Gante. El Primero de los Grandes Educadores de la America*, (Mexico city, 1934).

6. F. Borgia Steck, *El Primer Colegio de America, Santa Cruz de Tlatelolco*, (Mexico city, 1944); Juan Estarellas, "The College of Tlatelolco and the Problem of Higher Education for Indians in 16th Century Mexico," *History of Education Quarterly*, 2(1962) 234-243.

7. Ricard, *op.cit.*, p. 226.

8. Pablo Nazareo translated the gospels and the epistles of St. Paul into Nahuatl. His wife Doña María was the daughter of the brother of Moctezuma. Antonio Valeriano was one of the best latinists at the college. According to Fray Juan Bautista, he seemed another Cicero or Quintilian. See J. Garcia Icazbalceta, *Bibliografía Mexicana del Siglo XVI*, ed. by A. Millares Carlo, (Mexico city, 1954) p. 474.

9. J. Jorge Klor de Alva, H.B. Nicholson, E.Q. Keber, eds., *The Work of Bernardino de Sahagún*, (New York, 1988) 31-63; Munro S. Edmonson, ed., *Sixteenth-Century Mexico: The Work of Sahagún*, (New Mexico, 1974) 1-75; T. Todorov, *The Conquest of America*, English trans. (New York, 1984) 219-241.

10. M. Chenu, *Introduction a l'etude de St. Thomas d'Aquin*, (Paris, 1950) p. 254.

11. V. Beltran de Heredia, *La Autenticidad de la Bula*, (Santo Domingo, 1955) p. 17.

12. L.A. Eguiguren, *Alma Mater: Orígenes de la Universidad de San Marcos, 1551-1579*, (Lima, 1939) p. 98.

13. E. Esperabe Arteaga, *Historia Pragmática e Interna de la Universidad de Salamanca*, (Salamanca, 1914-1916) 139-356.

14. E. Gilson, *History of Christian Philosophy in the Middle Ages*, (New York, 1955) 319-322.

15. *Recognitio summularum* and the *Dialectica resolutio* were published in 1554; the *Physica, Speculatio* in 1557.

16. *Recognitio summularum*, 2v.

17. J. Jimenez Rueda, *Las Constituciones de la Antigua Universidad de Mexico*, (Mexico city, 1951) tit. VI; see O. Robles, "El Movimiento Neo-escolástico en Mexico," *Filosofia y Letras*, 23(1946) p.108.

18. J. Malagon Barcelo, "The Role of the Letrado in the Colonization of America," *The Americas*, 18(1961) 1-72.

19. F. Ocaranza, *Historia de la Medicina en Mexico*, (Mexico city, 1934); John Tate Lanning, *Academic Culture in the Spanish Colonies*, (Oxford, 1940) p. 102.

20. J. Grijalva, *Crónica de la Orden de San Agustin en las provicias de la Nueva España*, (Mexico city, 1624) 492-496.

21. E.J. Burrus, "Alonso de la Vera Cruz's Defense of the American Indians, 1553-1554," *The Heythrop Journal*, IV(1963) 225-253).

22. E.J. Burrus, "Las Casas and Vera Cruz: Their Defense of the American Indians Compared," *Neue Zeitschrift für Missionswissenschaft*,XXII(1966) 201-212.

23. Fintan B. Warren, *Vasco de Quiroga and his Pueblo Hospitals of Santa Fe*, (Washington, D.C., 1963) 26-72. See Silvio Zavala, "The American Utopia of the Sixteenth Century," *The Huntington Library Quarterly*, 10(1947) 337-347.

24. For the history of the text of the *De Dominio* and *De Decimis*, see the introduction of E.J. Burrus to *The Writings of Alonso de la Vera Cruz*: II, (St. Louis, 1968) 56-60.

25. Alonso de la Vera Cruz, *De Dominio*, ed. and trans. by E.J. Burrus, 103-105.

26. *Ibid.*, p. 109.

27. *Ibid.*, p. 175.

28. *Ibid.*, pp. 139, 225. See Charles Gibson, *The Aztecs Under Spanish Rule*, (Stanford, 1964) 58-97, 194-299.

29. L.B. Simpson, *The Encomienda in New Spain*, (Berkeley, Cal., 1950) p. 170.

30. *De Dominio*, p. 317.

31. *Ibid.*, p. 337-467. See Bernice Hamilton, *Political Thought in Sixteenth-Century Spain*, (Oxford, 1963) 110-134.

32. Francisco de Vitoria, *Relectio de Indis et de Iure Belli*, ed. by E. Nys, (Washington, D.C., 1917) 9-100.

33. See the recent work of Heinz-Gerhard Justenhoven, *Francisco de Vitoria zu Krieg und Frieden*, (Koln, 1991).

34. Henry Raup Wagner argued that Vitoria's *De Indis* could have been given as early as 1532 because in the introduction to the work, Vitoria speaks of "Indians who came forty years into the power of Spaniards." Wagner, *op.cit.*, p. 227 n. 3.

35. David Traboulay, *"Sixteenth century Scholasticism and the Colonization of America,"* *ZMR*, 4(1986) 15-37.

36. Wagner, *op.cit.*, 226-240.

37. All transcripts of the *Confesionario* were officially destroyed. *The Twelve Rules* later published by Las Casas might have been identical. See Wagner, 167-174.

38. Alonso de la Vera Cruz, *De Decimis*, in *The Writings of Alonso de la Vera Cruz*, ed. by E.J. Burrus, IV.

39. Ricard, *op.cit.*, 57-58.

Chapter 8

ALONSO DE ZORITA AND THE RATIONALITY OF NATIVE AMERICAN SOCIETY

It is ironical that the Spanish colonization of Mexico, which was characterized by excessive suffering on the part of the native population, witnessed the expression of some of the humanistic trends that arose in Europe at the turn of the sixteenth century. The educational, social, and political activities of the Franciscans, Dominicans, Augustinians, and Jesuits were the fruit of reforms that were taking place in Europe prior to the conquest. A resurgence of studies on the works of Thomas Aquinas, the influence of Erasmus in Spain, and the reforms of the religious orders formed the ideological basis of the pro-Indian movement in its struggle with the colonists.[1] Alonso de Zorita, a layman, was a member of this movement that was conducted for the most part by religious orders. His work is especially significant in that it provides the analytical framework by which one can understand more clearly the struggle of the pro-Indian movement.

Alonso de Zorita was a tireless worker for the pro-Indian cause. A graduate in law from the university of Salamanca in 1540, he must surely have been exposed to the humanistic ideas of Vitoria. He came to Santo Domingo in 1548 and spent some nineteen years in the New World, serving in the audiencias of Santo Domingo, Guatemala, and Mexico before retiring to Spain in 1566. His *Brief and Summary Relation of The Lords Of New Spain*, written in his retirement, contained his observations on the customs of the native population and the effects of Spanish colonization on it.[2] Trenchant in his criticism of the Spaniards, he minced no words in describing the catastrophic consequences of the Spanish conquest. Yet, in his sensitive portrayal of the social relationships of the native Mexicans, he implicitly revealed his own humanistic vision and spirit that must without doubt have been the inspiration for his well-known integrity and commitment to justice. This spirit was forged, at least in part, by his acquaintance with Las Casas, Bernardino de Sahagun, Geronimo de Mendieta, Toribio de Motolinia, Andres de Olmos and Francisco de Las Navas, among the friars, and Pablo Nazareo, the Indian rector of the college of Santa Cruz de Tlaltelolco, whose humanistic writing Zorita said he used in writing his book.[3]

In his treatment of the government of pre-conquest Mexico, Zorita labored to show that the rulers were not tyrants but men of sterling character whose concern for the welfare of their people was of paramount importance.[4] Generally the eldest son succeeded his father but if he were incapable of ruling the choice fell to another son or grandson. If no worthy successor could be found, the nobility then selected the successor. In this way "like the great Alexander, the rulers were more concerned with leaving a successor capable of governing their lands and vassals than with leaving inheritance to sons or grandsons".[5] The sacred character of the ruler was demonstrated in the ritual he had to undergo. The ruler-elect spent a year or two in a temple performing penance. At night he slept on a mat, getting up at appointed times to burn incense before the altar. During the day he sat on the ground. The point behind this exercise was to remind him that he should be always vigilant for his people. After this preparation, he was invested at the temple. Zorita was anxious to show the king of Spain that the religious underpinning of Indian government paralleled that in Spain. Of course, he was quick to point out that though they performed many commendable religious acts like giving thanks to their idols and distributing alms, "their works were like bodies without heads because they had no knowledge of the true God."[6]   Yet, Zorita was mindful that his political opponents had used Indian religious practices as the justification for their dominion over the natives. So, he emphasized that the natives attended to their religious devotion with seriousness, dignity, and humanity. In its exhortation to fasting and discipline, he seemed to imply that Indian religion was in some respects similar to Christianity. He did not mention the rituals where human sacrifice was offered, as other writers had done, particularly those opposed to better conditions for the Indians. But that was because the polarization of political life on the Indian question was so extreme that it was difficult to present a more balanced treatment of this question. It was sufficient for him to show the humane and civilized aspects.

The ruler was reminded that he was the instrument of God's justice to punish the wicked and help the weak. He was to be "a great shelter and protection to all", to listen to the advice of the aged, and encouraged to follow in the footsteps of his predecessors: "Consider that your forbears knew hardship and care in ruling over their realm and did not sleep free of care; they strove to increase their realm and leave a memory of themselves. The order of things that they left was not established in a single day. They took care to console the poor and afflicted, the people of small means. They honored the aged because they found good counsel in them. They willingly assisted the needy."[7] Contrary to charges that the natives were ignorant and ungrateful, Zorita firmly and sincerely stressed their generosity and the rationality of their society. It was fear for the cruelty of the Spaniards, he remarked, that caused this natural and spontaneous kindness to turn to distrust. The underlying philosophical idea Zorita was endeavoring to communicate was that in the matter of succession and election of rulers the natives were following the principles of Natural Law and, in a sense, "Canon and Civil Law, although they were ignorant of this".

The Thomist interpretation of Natural Law was in vogue in Spanish universities in the sixteenth century and formed the basis of the development of the theory of the dignity of all human beings.[8] For Aquinas, the Natural Law was the rational creature's participation in the eternal law, an imprint of the dictates of Divine providence.[9] They constituted commandments of reason that were required for the common good. By the correct use of his intellect, man was therefore capable of living a moral life because morality derived its goodness from the rule of reason. The Salamancan theologians sought to clarify this notion. Obviously, it was relevant to the development of their own positions on the colonization of America. For them, respect and dignity should be extended to Indians no less than Spaniards because they were rational beings. In his analysis of Indian customs, Zorita clearly wanted to confirm the rationality of the native peoples. Indian political and social relationships merely supported the conclusions of the theologians. Francisco de Vitoria and Domingo de Soto had argued that such precepts as justice, worship of God, and temperance were natural and self-evident. They could be grasped by the intelligence and generally supported by experience. As Soto put it, natural law was common to all humanity: "For there can never be any men, however incoherent and barbarous, so long as they are in their right minds, to whom this kind of truth is not obvious."[10] The imperative towards justice and morality did not then depend upon revelation nor conflicted with Christianity. What this association between 'natural', 'rational', and 'just' implied was that the commitment to rule justly and mutual social obligations were rooted in the nature of man. In the light of this principle, Zorita's picture of Indian society becomes clearer and more significant. Not only was it a historical document; it was also inspired politically. His firm commitment to the pro-Indian movement was a major factor in the composition of this work, to counteract the opposition who held the opinion that the Indians were irrational and barbaric and must be converted to Spanish ways and Christianity by force, if necessary.

Zorita placed the blame for the chaos of Mexican colonial society squarely on the Spanish destruction of the native political and social structure. Hierarchical though it was, he seemed to feel that the Indian system gave to the society peace and order, so foreign to the political and social relations of his own time.[11] The supreme lords or *tlatoques* had civil and criminal jurisdiction over the people. Subject to them were the *tectecutzin* and the *calpullec*. The former received the dignities of the nobility because of service to the state or exploits in war; the latter were the elders of barrios or villages. The *tectecutzin* had domain over the people attached to their place, who provided the lords with personal service in their households and brought them fuel and water. They worked certain fields for their lords and served them in times of war. In return, the lords were obliged to defend and protect them, providing them with lodgings, meals, and wages. The lords were therefore appointed to look after both the "general and their private good". The *calpullec* were the heads of barrios, a social unit that was fundamental to ancient Mexican society. Each province had several barrios and Zorita asserted that the lands were apportioned when the people originally came to that land.

His description of the clan or *calpulli* was of great significance because it was the heart of ancient Mexican society.[12] It was precisely the destruction of this that caused the failure of Spanish colonial policy. Members of a clan held their land communally, not individually. Although they could not alienate their land, they enjoyed its use for life and left it to their heirs. If a family died out, the land would be assigned to other members of his clan who did not have land according to their "needs, condition, and capacity to work it". If land that was already cultivated was vacated, it would be rented to someone from another clan for a part of the harvest. In no way could an elder take land away from a member of his clan if it was being cultivated. However, if it was not, through negligence, he was warned that it would be taken away. By virtue of their membership in the clan and their right to share in the communal lands, the members had to give a portion of their harvest as tribute to the lords. There were exceptions to this rule. Serfs or *mayeques* tilled the lands of nobility while some free peasants were assigned to provide services and goods instead of tribute.

The tribute did not depend upon the caprice of the lords but was agreed upon after a meeting between members of the clan and their lord, who kept records of the allotments of land and tribute. Zorita felt that the proper functioning of this system was the main reason for the harmony and unity of Indian society before the conquest. It was a different story after the conquest. Ignorant of the communal character of Indian land tenure, the Spaniards apportioned land individually. Through bribery and deceit the land of the natives was being constantly reduced and surrounded by the land held by Spaniards. Worse, cattle owned by Spanish ranchers were ever destroying the crops planted by the natives.

Sons, grandsons, and great-grandsons of the supreme lords formed the fourth class of the nobility and were called *pipiltzin*. They served as ambassadors, ministers and executors of justice. Exempted from the payment of tribute, they received a stipend and board from the ruler.

Stressing the autonomous growth of Indian communities, Zorita emphasized that not even their tribute-system militated against this. Each community paid tribute from the crops that were grown there and so did not have to leave their surroundings to find tribute elsewhere. There was therefore no rupture in the family relations as happened under Spanish colonial rule. Tribute was generally paid in maize, peppers, beans and cotton for which each town set aside certain fields. It was also given in the form of water, fuel, and domestic service for the ruler's household. The custom was for the ruler to assign to each town the tribute expected which then allotted to each family that portion of the collective tribute it had to provide. The rational character of the Indian economy was carried out harmoniously. As Zorita put it: "Thus the peasants worked the tribute fields and harvested and stored the crops; the artisans gave tribute from the things they made; and the merchants gave of their merchandise-clothing, feathers, jewels, stones-each giving of the commodities in which he dealt."[13] The various economic activities were rationally linked. Cotton, for example, was given when collected from cotton-producing towns to those that could not produce it to be worked into cloth. A small quantity of gold dust was exacted as tribute which was collected from river beds without difficulty. Indian society did not have a monied economy but a system of bartering certain things for others, a mode which Zorita found to be "most conformable to nature". For the most part the tribute was small and the paternalistic ruler took special care not to burden some towns more than others. The large population of pre-conquest Mexico, the well-planned economy, and a benevolent ruler concerned for the welfare of his people reduced the economic and social hardships to a minimum. When asked to compare the native system of taxation with that under the Spaniards, Zorita replied that "one Indian pays more tribute today than did six Indians of that time, and one town pays more in gold pesos today than did six towns".

Work was not the alienating experience it had become under the Spaniards. The Indians did their communal work in their own towns and so "did not have to leave their homes and families, and they ate food they were accustomed to eat and at the usual hours". They accepted their responsibilities for the construction of temples, homes for the lords, and public works. Rising early, they went to work after the morning chill had passed, worked without being hurried or harassed, and stopped before the evening chill had set in. When they returned home, they found their meals prepared, after which they enjoyed the company of their wives and children.

The self-reliance of the Indian contrasted markedly with the dependency of the Spaniard. The Indians knew all that was necessary to earn their livelihood. Familiar with both rural and urban tasks, they did not need others to build their homes nor did they have to search for materials for everywhere they "find the wherewithal to cut, tie, sew, and strike a light". They knew the names of all the birds, animals, trees, what herbs could be used for medicinal purposes, and what could be eaten. All knew "how to work stone, build a house, twine a cord, and where to find the materials they need".[14] They lived in small huts, some of which were thatched. Satisfied with a little food and simple dress and accustomed to sleeping on a mat on the floor, these meek and patient natives did not strive for wealth nor offices. Childbirth, with or without the help of a midwife, occurred without the comforts or attention accorded such an event in Spanish families. As for the upbringing of their children, great care was placed in making them "healthy and strong, cheerful, able and teachable".[15]

Parents instilled in the minds of their children the values of their society. Zorita insisted that these values did not contradict Christian values. On the contrary, they prepared the way for the acceptance of Christianity. He showed this by reporting a speech an Indian lord gave to his subjects in Texcoco just after the process of conversion had begun. The lord told his people that the missionary was "like a great spreading leafy tree under whose boughs we find shade and air, consolation and instruction". He urged his people to place themselves under God's protection for God was "like a very pretty, lovely bird under whose wings all find shelter and protection".[16] Faith, service, and good works were necessary for God's mercy and blessings, he reminded them. For Zorita, all this showed how wrong were those who denied the Indian "any intelligence and will allow them no human trait other than the shape of men". Both lords and commoners were vigilant in instructing their children to be virtuous.[17] At the age of five, a ruler's son was sent to the temple to be trained by priests until he married or went off to war. His daughter was constantly reminded to be discreet in speech and conduct. Often she never left her home until marriage or if she did, she had to be accompanied by elderly women. At the age of five, her nurses taught her to embroider, sew, and weave and urged her to be clean. Above all, she was taught to respect and obey her parents and teachers and to work diligently. The lower nobility and commoners also took their children to the temples to serve their gods. They saw to it that their children followed the occupation for which they showed the ability and inclination. But generally sons followed the occupation of their fathers. Mischievousness and lying were especially frowned upon. If a son were caught lying, his father punished him by pricking his lip with a thorn. When asked how the alleged Indian reputation for falsehood was started, old Indians replied that the Spaniards were so haughty and cruel that, in their fear of displeasing them, they assented to everything, however incredible. Fear and mistrust had made them wary of speaking out directly and openly.

There were separate schools for the sons of the nobility and commoners.[18] Sons of the nobility were sent to special temple schools or *calmecac*, commoners to village schools. Each school was headed by an elder who supervised the education of the students. The students cultivated the fields that were set aside for the support of their school and were expected to observe the rigorous discipline set up by their teachers. Their training was Spartan, "for they ate but a little hard bread, and they slept with little covering and half exposed to the night air in rooms and quarters like porches." Clearly their education was to prepare them for the responsibilities of adult life, be it family life or war. When they reached marriageable age, usually at the age of twenty, they were expected to ask permission from their teachers in addition to their parents' consent. An indigent student received aid from his school at the time of his marriage while the family of a rich student was expected to give gifts to his school and his teacher when he left school.

The graduate was encouraged to uphold the values he learned, to work hard to support his family, not to neglect his children, to be brave in war, to respect his parents, honor the aged, and follow their advice.

Parental advice confirmed the training at school. Quoting speeches a priest had translated for him, Zorita reported that fathers of the classes of nobles and merchants urged their sons to have reverence for God and serve him with love, to respect the old, console the poor and ill, and to love and honor all.[19] They were not to hurt others, engage in adultery, or be lewd. Restraint and humility were to be practiced in social relationships. A portion of their food should be given to the needy and if given something, however small, they should receive it with gratitude. Hard work and frugality were important attitudes: "Life in this world is filled with hardships; it is not easy to satisfy one's needs." To this his son replied that he was grateful for the great good that his father had given him and for the counsel "that issue from your bowels, the bowels of a father that loves me". Peasants and commoners advised their sons to serve their masters well and to be content with their lot: "Do what pertains to your office. Labor, sow and plant your trees, and live by the sweat of your brow. Do not cast off your burden, or grow faint, or be lazy; for if you are negligent and lazy, you will not be able to support yourself or your wife and children." Like the sons of the nobility and merchants, they too were encouraged to respect the old, parents and the afflicted, and warned against idleness. Mothers counselled their daughters at the time of their marriage. Daughters of upper class families were told to be modest and pleasing to their husbands. So too were those from the lower class but they were reminded that "hardship and suffering are our lot". They were to do their household work, weave and embroider dutifully. This picture of Indian education might seem idealistic but it corroborated the experience of the Dominican Fray Julian Garces, a student of the renowned Spanish humanist Antonio de Nebrija. As a teacher at the school of San Jose and the college of Tlaltelolco, he felt that his Indian students showed greater facility for learning than the Spaniards.[20] He found them neither boisterous nor unruly, neither stubborn nor mischievous, neither pretentious nor vain, neither harmful nor quarrelsome. They did not indulge in complaints, gossip, insults and other vices typical of Spanish boys. Drinking or eating inordinately was unthinkable for them and they did not ask for more than they received at the dinner table. When they were told to sit, stand, or kneel, they did so readily. He marvelled at the fertility of their minds for they were able to master every type of discipline, even

Latin. They could count, read, write, paint and performed every mechanical and liberal art clearly and quickly. As for being assigned difficult tasks, they did not utter a word of complaint. Their mastery of the organ and plain chant was so good that Spanish musicians were not needed. Unlike Spanish boys, they had such a sense of shame that they were careful how they appeared in public.

Zorita's opponents had condemned the bellicose nature of Indian society. He admitted that wars were frequent but mitigated this by showing that they understood the notion of a just war.[21] The killing of a merchant or an ambassador was considered a legitimate cause of war. The ruler would then convene a meeting of all the elders and warriors, and explain the reasons for his decision. If the assembly felt it was a just cause of war, they would give their consent. But if the reason was not of consequence, they advised against war. Zorita insisted that the ruler sometimes accepted their advice. They nevertheless supported the ruler if he continued to summon them on the same issue despite their disagreement out of respect. The decision to make war was sent to the enemy who then held deliberations whether to defend themselves or not. If they considered themselves too weak to resist, they offered gold ornaments, feathers and other ornaments as symbols of their surrender. Towns that had yielded peacefully gave less tribute than those which had surrendered after defeat. The question of laws of war was an important one for sixteenth century theologians. Undoubtedly, the horrors of the war in Granada during the closing years of the fifteenth century, the conquest of the New World, and the Turkish threat had exercised a profound impact on their imagination. In his description of the Indian process of war, Zorita seemed familiar with their positions and implied that the Indians had complied generally with the conditions necessary for a just war. Rejecting the non-violent tradition, the theologians held that in special cases the power to make war was necessary to protect the welfare of the community, and to provide the conditions for a just and secure peace.[22] The right of self-defense extended to avenging wrongs perpetrated against the community and could be claimed by a legitimate ruler as representative of the community. However, the only just cause of war was a wrong suffered, and a great one at that. For the effects of war were so catastrophic that vigilance should be taken lest war be declared over minor offences. That was why the ruler should assemble a council of the wise men of a community to examine carefully the cause and justice of the intended war. War should be declared only reluctantly and should be prosecuted "only as far as necessary to defend one's country, and obtain one's rights, and ultimately as a result of the war, to ensure peace and safety".

The Indian system of government and justice was an equitable one, respected and obeyed by the people. A minimum of conflicts occurred and harmony prevailed, Zorita contended. Theirs was a society of laws where justice was carried out wisely. Judges played an important part in dispensing justice. In each city, the ruler was represented by two judges, whose salaries came from the produce of fields that were set aside for them. They heard cases from daybreak to two hours before sundown. Appeals were heard by the twelve superior judges, who collaborated with the ruler before passing sentence. Every twelve days the ruler convened a meeting of all the judges to discuss the more difficult cases. Judges were not permitted to receive a fee or gift from anyone, whether rich or poor. Failure to follow this would result in a stern reprimand and, after the third offence, his hair was cropped and he was stripped of his office. There were ordinary judges in each town to decide cases of less importance. They were empowered to arrest wrongdoers and did the preliminary investigative work on more complex cases which were later presented to the council for resolution. Laws were carried out firmly. Adultery, sodomy, creating a scandal were punishable by death, and no one was exempt. The married daughter of the wise ruler, Nezahualpilli, was put to death for adultery although her husband had pardoned her. Wine was prohibited except for the sick and those who were more than fifty years old. The hair of an offender was cropped publicly and his house razed. For the most part, however, litigation was held to a minimum in Mexican Indian society. As an Indian lord told Zorita:"When we were pagans, there were very few lawsuits, men told the truth, and cases were decided very quickly."[23] Zorita recalled two cases from his own experience to demonstrate the basic Indian sense of justice. Some Indians had come to him in Guatemala to reclaim land that was taken from them by other Indians. When the offenders were summoned before Zorita, their replies surprised him. One offered to return the land without further ado, and the other suggested that his land be divided because he had found it neglected and had planted cacao trees on it.

In recording the customs, institutions, and attitudes of the indigenous people Zorita hoped to show that they were a rational and intelligent people. He felt that those who said that the Indians were barbaric and uncivilized simply did not know at first hand Indian society. This fallacy could have been perpetuated by a dependence upon unreliable sources or by the fact that the Indians were not Christian or even because their customs and language were different from the Spaniards. How else could one explain the contradictory statements of Hernan Cortes when, in his letter to the Emperor, he called the natives uncivilized after praising their rationality and declaring that their mode of life "was almost the same as in Spain, with just as much harmony and order" earlier in the same letter.[24]

Zorita's treatise was therefore a defense of Indian civilization. But it was more than that. In describing and explaining the structure and values of native society, he sought to show the destructive effect that the political, social, and economic policies of Spanish imperialism was producing on that society.

Social relationships were of primary concern in the Indian value system. From early in his life, he was taught to respect his parents, elders, women and the sick. His worth as a human being depended upon how he carried out his responsibility to his family, and clan. Harmony in the collective was to be maintained and so willingness to compromise was stressed while aggressiveness and disputativeness were avoided. The spirit of individualism was absent. Rather, it was his family and clan that gave meaning to his life. Honor, kindness, and hospitality were the important moral values. Solidarity with one's family and clan helped to create an orderly world in which tensions were reduced to a minimum. Religion provided a context of ultimate meaning for the central value system. The deity was viewed as a benevolent one, bestowing infinite blessings on the collective. In return, social responsibilities were to be carried out with love. There was of course no political democracy in Indian society. It was believed that the hierarchical political order was somehow divinely ordained. Loyalty to one's father, the ruler of one's clan, and the supreme ruler was the important political value. The political authority had the obligation to bestow blessings on society. In return, the people considered it their responsibility to respect the demands of their rulers. Mutual trust fueled the reciprocal character of this political relationship. Economic values were not as important as the religious and cultural values of the society. The communal ownership of property and the self-sufficient nature of the economy precluded the development of the capitalistic spirit. Luxury was avoided and the Spartan training of the young obviously helped to develop a spirit of frugality which made the desire for material comforts superfluous. The lack of a monetary system also reinforced the self-sufficiency of the economy. These then were the values that cemented the structure of Indian traditional society. Zorita saw clearly and profoundly the incompatibility between the Indian system and that imposed by the Spaniards which gradually over the span of his experience in the New World would insensitively dismantle the traditional structure of Indian society.

The conquest brought America within the orb of the massive Spanish empire.[25] Its resources of precious metals, sugar, tobacco, and hides helped make Spain the greatest empire in the sixteenth century. Indeed, the economic rise of Europe was in part due to the gold and silver that flooded Europe from America.[26] Spain's extensive imperial commitments and wars were financed by it. In the first half of the sixteenth century treasure was exported to Antwerp which became the distribution center from where gold and silver from America passed to Germany, Northern Europe, and England. Spanish economic life grew to depend more and more on America. Demand in the Indies for foodstuffs and manufactured goods meant that these industries were intensified in Spain. The prosperity of the cities of Toledo, Seville, and Burgos, among others, was to a large degree due to the trade that developed with the Indies. It was then the demands of the structure and values of Empire that delivered the shattering blow to Indian society. The bitter criticism with which he would go on to describe Spanish colonial institutions and attitudes was motivated, to be sure, by his advocacy of the pro-Indian movement, but more by the clarity of his vision.

Before the colonial relationship between Mexico and Spain was defined, Cortes distributed the recently conquered land among his men who demanded of the Indian lords tribute, personal services, and slaves in excess of what was given before the conquest.[27] The portents of cruelties similar to those perpetrated against the natives in Española and Cuba earlier forced Charles V to write to Cortes, prohibiting the practice of encomienda.[28] Spaniards were to allow the Indians to live in liberty and it was urged that conversion should be effected peacefully and not by force. This remarkably humane instruction was of course the result of the struggle of Las Casas and his supporters who had singled the encomienda as the most significant reason for the destruction of the native population in the islands. Cortes, however, refused to comply with the emperor's wishes. He argued that the Spaniards had no other means of support than the Indians and, if they were freed, they would have to abandon Mexico. Moreover, he contended that if the encomienda were abolished the Indians would return to the slavery of their own system, the mere thought of which moved them to serve willingly the Spaniards. Still, he promised the emperor to mitigate the excesses that were practiced in the islands. An end to the encomienda would result in the loss of his new empire and the souls of the natives, Cortes added.

Zorita did not support such duplicity. He saw the encomienda as a pernicious system that operated throughout the Indies such that one might think that there was "one common directive". He charged unequivocally that the system was destroying the Indians everywhere and, if not stopped, would destroy them completely. Through forced labor for the construction of Spanish towns the Indians had to work far from their homes, disrupting "their whole tempo of life, the time and mode of work, of eating and sleeping". The demolition of the old Mexico city and the rebuilding of the new city was linked to the plague that beset ancient Egypt. Quoting the opinion of Fray Toribio de Motolinia, Zorita wrote: "The seventh plague was the building of the great city of Mexico. In this work, during the first years, more people were employed than in the building of the temple of Jerusalem in the time of Solomon. So great was the number of Indians in actual construction, in bringing food for the workers, and in providing food and service from their towns for the Spaniards, that a man could scarcely make his way through some streets and over the causeways, broad as they are. In the work of construction some were crushed by beams, others fell from heights, and others were caught beneath buildings that were being torn down in one place in order to erect others elsewhere. The Indians not only had to get the materials and pay the masons, carpenters, and stonecutters. What was more, they must bring their own food or go hungry."[29]

The system whereby the colonists received an allotment of Indians who had to give him labor services and tribute would gradually result in the decimation of the Indian population. Statistics showed that the population declined from 16,871,408 in 1532 to 2,649,573 in 1568.[30] To be sure, epidemics such as smallpox, typhoid, malaria, measles, and influenza were significant contributors to this. For Zorita, however, the principal reason lay in the insatiable demand for cheap Indian labor to work the mines, the sugar and cacao plantations, the cattle ranches, and the wheat farms. Reduced to servitude, countless Indians died in the mines or on their way to the mines loaded with heavy materials. Some fled to the surrounding woods, abandoning their families, and so Indian towns became depopulated. Work in the mines saw the enslavement of thousands of Indians. During the conquest, there was no shortage as Indian prisoners were legally enslaved. After it, the encomenderos resorted to the practice of purchasing slaves which invited all sorts of abuses. They would make preposterous demands of gold as tribute only to collect slaves as a substitute for money tribute because they knew well that Indian towns did not have money. Even women were taken from their families and sent to the mines.

Another oppressive colonial practice was the use of Indians as carriers or *tamemes*. Men, women, and children were forced to carry the merchandise and furniture of entire Spanish households to far away places. Trekking over the fields and mountains in different climates from their own communities, they spent most of the year on this type of work. Household service which some Indians were expected to give to Spaniards was also no bed of roses. To serve the allocated one week, they often had to set out from their homes two weeks before. So, one week's service occupied five weeks of their time. As Zorita put it, the roads were "filled with Indian men and women, exhausted, dying of hunger, weary and afflicted; and the roads were strewn with the bodies of men, women, and even their little ones, for they used them to carry food-something these people had never before done."[31]

Their life was further disrupted by having to work on Spanish farms. Not only had they to fence the sheep, cattle, and pig farms, but they also had to construct the farm buildings, roads, bridges, watercourses, stone walls, and sugar mills. More, they had to provide the materials at their own expense and bring them to the sites on their backs. They had to fetch water and wood, clean the stables, and remove the rubbish. It was no wonder that Spanish farms had increased while those of the Indians diminished. Zorita could not have been more explicit. The rise and prosperity of Spanish towns and fortunes were carried out at the expense of Indian lives and communities.

The resources of Indian communities were continuously being drained by the excessive tribute they had to pay.[32] Some were reduced to such straits that they were forced to sell their land and even their children. Thrown into jail when they were unable to pay, they were sometimes tortured to tell where their gold was. From a declaration of the tax paid to Cortes in 1533, it was learned that the province of Cuernavaca had to give every eighty days 4800 blankets, 20 shirts, 20 skirts, 20 bed-covers, and 4 cotton pillows. Besides providing field and house service, they had to cultivate every year 20 cotton fields and 8 of maize, as well as harvesting and storing the crops. Every thirty days they had to take 7000 pounds of maize, 300 of pepper, 200 of beans, to the mines in addition to supplying Indians for work in the mines. The Crown made an effort to remove the abuses of the tribute system and ordered new assessments be made. Zorita was critical of this new system of counts and felt that it did not in any way alleviate the wrongs done to the Indians. In the first place, the encomenderos found a way to use the system to their advantage by appointing their favorites as assessors or offering bribes; secondly, if the Indian community asked for a re-assessment, they had to bear the cost of the process which was an added burden. Thus, the Indians exhausted whatever little money they had in lawsuits while the tribute remained based on the first count. Despite the initial good intention behind the new system, the per capita assessment resulted in tribute being collected from "cripples, blind and maimed persons, and other wretches who cannot work and even lack food". Moreover, no attempt was made to consult the people in determining the extent of the tribute. Had they done this, they would have realized that the Indians possessed very little other than their labor and that the exorbitant tribute meant that they had almost nothing to spend on food and clothing, not to mention for expenses related to the marriage of their children.

Zorita drew attention to the increase of Spanish herds which were threatening to overrun the entire country, a tendency which he had also observed in Guatemala and Colombia. In spite of Indian vigilance, cattle herds roamed and destroyed their crops. The encomenderos seized Indian lands for cattle pasture, had the Indians build enclosures, but did not seriously try to refrain from encroaching upon the areas where the Indians planted their crops. To compound the matter, they drove their herds prematurely to summer pasture at the time when the harvest from the grain and tuna fruit fields remained to be gathered. Complaints and lawsuits were so futile that the process brought further expenses than compensation. The consequences of the insensitivity of the economic activity of the colonists, whether it was in the mining or agricultural sectors, were devastating and disrupted the Indians' "way of life, their routine of work, diet, and shelter, and, in taking them from their towns and homes, their wives and children, their repose and harmony."[33]

Critical of the Spanish colonial administration, he felt that the "multitude of laws, judges, viceroys, governors, presidentes, oidores, corregidores, alcades mayores, a million lieutenants, and yet other alguaciles" were incapable of correcting the wrongs done to Indian society. For their interests lay, for the most part, with the colonists. The undermining of the traditional authority of the Indian aristocracy ruined those political values of authority and obedience that he felt necessary for any community.[34] This was not entirely accurate. In the early stages of the colonization, Spaniards were more interested in tribute and gave the Indian nobility the responsibility of collecting the tribute. They proved to be no less insensitive than the colonists as they sought the means to buttress their own privileged status. Zorita contended that these Indian supervisors were not the "natural lords" but commoners and upstarts who did not possess the natural goodness and virtue and concern for the community that marked the pre-conquest aristocracy. In continuing to defend the concept of the rationality of the government of the indigenous society, he risked embellishing the Indian aristocracy when he already had abundant evidence to prove the irrational effects of the new colonial economic system. Be that as it may, the denigration of the Indian nobility was certainly one of the more lasting effects of colonization. As the native population declined, they were unable to collect the prescribed tribute and were often jailed and subsequently disgraced.

Painted in very dark colors, his analysis portrayed faithfully the fate of the native people at the moment of his departure from Mexico. But it failed to tell the story of the struggles of the reform movement in which he himself played a not inconsiderable part, or of the successes they achieved in getting the Crown to change its policy, however transitory in the long run.

Spanish encroachment on Indian community lands took place gradually.[35] Initially, the colonists demanded tribute and labor. Later, they saw the need for land in order to exploit the labor supply and for their large herds of cattle. The devastating effect this had on the Indian communities forced the viceroy and the missionaries to press for legislation to put a stop to this. Out of this early struggle arose the main features of an Indian policy that would be gradually defined. In nature protectionist, it aimed at preserving Indian communities from the encroachments of Spaniards, maintaining Indian social and economic institutions, and gradually to integrate them into the Spanish colonial system. The generally glowing description that Zorita presented of Indian communities must be seen in the context of this policy. His use of Spanish legal and theological notions to defend the rationality of the

Indian reflected the central strategy of the pro-Indian reformers which was to show the similarity of Spanish and Indian community traditions as they strove to first protect and then assimilate Indian communities to Spanish municipal institutions. Countless new towns were established with a "public square, then the town hall, prison, and community bank, the commons and municipal pastures".[36] The church was the most imposing building and streets were laid out at right angles to the square. This planning was not dissimilar to native villages which also were built around a central square. Indian in origin, too, was the idea of having community crops from which town officials were paid. These towns were administered by Indian officials - a town governor, two alcaldes, and several minor officials. The proper functioning of these towns depended to a large extent on the community banks. Missionaries took charge of these banks and worked hard to ensure that funds were constantly flowing into these banks in order to pay for expenses incurred by the town. The cultivation of maize, beans, and peppers, the development of the silk industry, sheep and goat raising, and certain joint ventures with Spaniards whereby Indian towns received two thirds of the harvest for supplying the land and labor and the Spaniards the other third for providing the oxen, plows, and other implements, were some of the ways Indian towns raised funds for their community banks. As for land tenure, it was again Indian precedent that formed the basis for Spanish policy. In the redistribution of land by viceroy Velasco I in 1550 at Metepec, each Indian was given 40 fathoms of land around his house. He and his descendants had the use of that land as long as they cultivated it. Tenure was untransferable and legal ownership was vested in the community, in accordance with the ancient *Calpulli* practice. However, the high hopes placed in this policy were not achieved. Indeed, the difficulty of instilling a spirit of profit among the Indians, Indian ignorance of livestock-raising, and epidemics were factors that contributed to the decline of Indian towns. Conceivably, the close supervisory control that the missionaries exercised over Indian life prevented these towns from developing.

But the underlying reason was the expansion of the colonists' sphere of economic interests. The intensification of livestock-raising and sugar cane cultivation started a process in which the colonists sought every means to appropriate land and extend their holdings. Untilled land was granted to the colonists and native nobility sold land from their vast estates under pressure of bribes and intimidation. Many Indian towns were in due course surrounded by Spanish fields, and eventually absorbed by the great estates or haciendas.

By 1546 the continuity of the encomienda was assured. Both the Crown and the reformers then directed their energy towards producing a more equitable tribute system. No question caused greater anguish than this as streams of complaints poured in about its inhumanity. Royal legislation implied that the tribute should be less than before the conquest and should not be accompanied by personal service, a law more honored in the breach than in its observance. The divergence between law and economic reality could be observed in the *visita* of Diego Ramirez made between 1551 and 1555. Despite royal efforts to put an end to the more oppressive aspects of the tribute system, he found that "(1) the audiencia made special grants to the encomenderos to collect more tribute than the amount stipulated on the tribute list; (2) The Indians were forced to pay more than they were assessed, either by their cacique, by the corregidor, or by the encomendero; (3) the Indians were overworked; (4) the Indians were forced to perform personal service; (5) the Indians were forced to carry heavy loads as beasts of burden; (6) land was taken from the Indians illegally; (7) the Indians were forced to carry their tribute from the town in which they lived to the encomenderos' places of residence; (8) old taxations were continued after a plague or something similar had depopulated the land; (9) the caciques were defrauding the Crown of its income by hiding many Indians when a new tax list was to be drawn up; after the taxation was made the Indians who had been hidden were forced by the cacique to pay tribute to him; (10) the corregidor and the cacique worked to deprive the Crown of income and to overtax the tribute paying Indians; (11) Indians hid themselves so that after the tax list was drawn up they could return and help their families pay the smaller taxation; and (12) the Indians made continual complaints, many unwarranted, asking for new taxations".[37]   The findings of Ramirez and later Zorita's treatise offered clear evidence that the Crown had failed to end the rampant abuses of the tribute system.

Zorita's proposals then were offered in the light of the failure of the prevailing policy. In castigating the encomenderos, he left no doubt that he shared Las Casas's view that the continuance of the encomienda was responsible for the demise of the native peoples. But the struggle to end it succumbed to the economic interests of the Crown and the colonists in the 1540's. The focus of pro-Indian activism shifted to reforming the tribute system. Zorita recommended that itinerant judges visit regularly the towns, farms, and textile factories to assess the value of their lands and products and to ascertain the population of each town.[38] They should also protect the ancient privileges and liberty of the Indian nobility by exempting them from tribute. Before determining what tribute each town should pay, a representative of the town, whether Indian or encomendero, should meet with judges to discuss the assessment and reach a consensus on the amount of tribute. In this way popular consent would be obtained before tribute was levied. An assessment should be the same for four or five years. If a town found it impossible to meet its tribute through an epidemic or crop failure, appeal should be made to the audiencia for relief. Since this process was likely to take time and money before resolution, Zorita suggested that the town official or religious report crop failures and epidemics as soon as they occurred. After the assessment had been made according to the economic activity and population of the town, the natural lords should be empowered to apportion to each member what he had to pay for they knew best what each person was able to pay. The tribute roll should then be sent to the corregidor and subsequently to the audiencia.

Members of the community should be assembled in the church in the presence of the corregidor and the priest who instructed and informed them of the amount of tribute the community as a whole and each one specifically must pay. Any surplus would remain with the community while a deficit would be made up by the community. For Zorita, popular understanding and agreement were necessary to prevent "the evil of suits and counts, and costs, assessments, and official visits they bring in their train". Tribute should be kept in a special community house to which the natural lord and two other town officials would have keys. A money box would remain in the house for the tribute that was paid in money and to keep the account books "in which is set down who are the tribute-payers for each year, what the tribute comes to, what was taken in or taken out of the house and box, what was expended, and by whose order, and the like".

To eliminate the abuses committed by the encomenderos, he suggested that their share of the tribute should come from the community treasury and that in no way should they be allowed to have business in Indian towns. They were accustomed to frequent Indian towns, demanding service and supplies without pay. Zorita felt that the only solution lay in preventing them from visiting Indian towns except on days appointed for the collection of tribute. Urging the Crown to return to the pre-conquest practice of soliciting tribute in the form of produce rather than money, he proposed that land be specifically set aside for this purpose. The encomendero would provide the seeds of crops the Indians were to grow while the Indians would be responsible for sowing and cultivating the fields, harvesting and storing the crops in the provincial capital.

Zorita insisted that this would not only ameliorate the burdens imposed on the Indians but it would make the economy more rational and beneficial to the whole society. Payment of tribute in money had forced the Indians to abandon their traditional agricultural activity in favor of commerce. The result was a shortage of food. If the Indians were allowed to plant maize, beans, and chili peppers, there would be an abundance of food for the whole society. Moreover, the material condition of the Indians would become better since these products were in demand. To cover the expenses of the community and to provide for the upkeep of the lord, Zorita recommended the cultivation of pieces of land in a similar fashion.

He questioned the excessive demands of the encomenderos for labor and charged that it was their insatiable thirst for luxury and extravagance that warranted it. After all, he contended, they possessed mines, estates, and other profitable businesses. If they were not satisfied, they should seek gainful employment. Zorita was of the opinion that the satisfaction of the labor demands of Spanish towns could be carried out more advantageously for the Indians than was the practice. Indian towns should be ordered to send a fixed number of laborers to Spanish towns every week for hire together with loads of fuel and vegetables. However, wages and prices should not be fixed and the Indians should be allowed to sell their labor and produce at the market price, as opposed to the current practice of fixed wages and prices whereby they received one-half of what they received in their own towns. In this way "the assignment of people for labor in the Spanish towns will be made with due regard for the needs of the Indian town in which they live and of the Spanish towns where they are to work".

In determining a more just tribute policy, Zorita proposed a system that was for the most part similar to that practiced in Indian society before the conquest. The pre-conquest system was not based on equality. Indeed, it might appear to have been arbitrary. The burden of tribute fell on the commoners, the *macehuales*, and not on the more privileged classes of nobles, magistrates, and distinguished warriors who along with the sick, the poor and the young were exempt from tribute. However, Zorita understood the complexity of the issue. What was clearly needed was a system that would make the transition from the native economy to the Spanish monetary economy less disruptive to the Indian communities than was the case during the early years of colonization. His recommendation of the main lines of preconquest tribute, unequal though it was, was based on the awareness that the underlying motivation of the Indian system was to provide order and harmony in the community.

Zorita has been accused of being unfair in his criticism of the Spaniards, and exaggerating the felicity of Indian society.[39] But his analysis of the social and economic conditions in Mexico agreed with others of his own time. The visitador, Diego Ramirez, found that "the economic needs of the Spaniards, their dependence upon Indian labor and its produce, seldom allowed the enlightened laws of the Crown to be put in operation". It was true that through the efforts of the reformers the Crown enacted legislation to limit the excesses of the colonists. But the gap between law and reality was great, as the report of Ramirez demonstrated. Moreover, what more convincing proof of Zorita's analysis could there be than the astounding decline of the Indian population? A study of the population trends between 1550 and 1570, the period between the two great epidemics of 1544-1546 and 1575-1579, showed that the population declined at a rate of 2 to 4 percent a year, thereby corroborating Zorita's analysis that the increasing labor demands and social dislocation were the primary reasons for the population decline.

If Zorita painted pre-conquest Indian society too brightly, one must remember the intense political debate that prevailed at the time over the rationality of Indian society. Perhaps he was unaware that at the beginning of the sixteenth century Indian society had evolved into a complex structure where "urban life, the increasing complexity of functions, the increase of the dominions and the accompanying task of administration, and the emergence of commerce all ineluctably and irremediably changed the ancient ways".[40] When he came to Mexico he had already seen the catastrophic effects of Spanish colonization in the islands. His experience in Mexico had filled him with horror that the same fate would befall the native Mexican people. Embellished though his treatment of the Indian nobility might be, his description of the dynamics of Indian society and its emphasis on social relations placed in stark relief the cruelty of early Spanish colonial society, and afforded posterity the valuable opportunity to see that Indian culture, "so suddenly destroyed, is one of those that humanity can be proud of having created".

In 1561 Zorita and Fray Jacinto de San Francisco proposed a plan to pacify the warlike Chichimec Indians who had been at war with the Spaniards since the opening of the silver mines at Zacatecas in 1546. Faithful to the philosophy of non-violence of Las Casas, they proposed to invite the Indians to settle in towns where all lay Spaniards would be prohibited from entering. Here they would change their nomadic ways and follow a peaceful, agricultural life. Following the rejection of this request, Zorita returned to Spain in 1566. He continued his interest in colonial matters and corresponded with his friends in the pro-Indian movement.

NOTES

Chapter 8

1. See Ricardo G. Villoslada, *La Universidad de Paris durante los estudios de Vitoria*, Analecta Gregoriana, XIV, (Rome 1938); Marcel Bataillon, *Erasme et l'Espagne*, (Paris, 1937).

2. Alonso de Zorita, *The Lords of New Spain*, trans.and an introduction by Benjamin Keen, (London, 1965). It is not known when Zorita wrote this treatise. Keen suggests that it was written before 1570.

3. *Ibid.*, 60-63. The life and works of Fray Bartolome de las Casas are well known. See my article in *ZMR* 61(1977) 128-136; Fray Bernardino de Sahagun studied at the university of Salamanca and professed as a Franciscan friar in 1529 when he set out for Mexico. He learned the Mexican languages and wrote a monumental work on the rites, customs, and mode of government of the natives. See Bernardino de Sahagun, *General History of the Things of New Spain, Florentine codex*, translated from Aztec into English by A.J.O. Anderson and C.E. Dibble, (Salt Lake City, 1950-55). Fray Toribio Benavente Motolinia (Fray Toribio took the name Motolinia, "poor man", in Mexico) came to Mexico in 1524 as one of the original twelve missionaries requested by Cortes. In addition to his missionary activity, he made an intensive study of the Indian languages, customs and history. See F.B. Steck, *Motolinia's History of the Indians of New Spain*, (Washington, Academy of the American Franciscan

History, 1951); Fray Francisco de las Navas came to Mexico as an aide to Bishop Juan de Zumarraga in 1528. He wrote a grammar of the Mexican language. See the translation by Remi Simeon, *Grammaire de la langue Nahuatl ou Mexicaine*, (Paris, 1875); Pablo Nazareo was one of the Indian graduates of the college of Santa Cruz de Tlaltelolco. He translated the epistles of Paul and the Gospels into Mexican. See F.B. Steck, *El Primer Colegio de America, Santa Cruz de Tlaltelolco*, (Mexico, 1944).

4. *Ibid.*, 89ff., 300 n. 22; R.S. Chamberlain, "The Concept of the Señor Natural as revealed by Castilian law and administrative documents," *Hispanic American Historical Review*, XIX (1939), no 2, 130-137; C. Gibson, *Spain in America*, (New York, 1966), p. 26. Gibson saw the Aztec aristocracy as aggressive expansionists, engaged in "human sacrifice and the methodical exaction of tribute."

5. *Ibid.*, 90.

6. *Ibid.*, 96.

7. *Ibid.*, 98-101; for a discussion of speeches as a genre of Aztec literature see A.M. Garibay K, *Historia de la literatura Nahuatl*, 2 vols. (Mexico, 1953-59), vol. 1, 411-448.

8. B. Hamilton, *Political Thought in Sixteenth Century Spain*, (Oxford, 1963) 11-29.

9. Aquinas, *Summa Theologica*, I, II, 90, 91.

10. Hamilton, *op. cit.*, p. 16.

11. Zorita, *op.cit.*, 103-105.

12. *Ibid.*, 106-111; for a discussion of the Calpulli see M. Moreno, *La Organizacion politica y social de los Aztecas*, (Mexico, 1931); A. Monzon, *El Calpulli en la organizacion social de los Tenocha*, (Mexico, 1941); H. Driver, *Indians of North America*, (New York, 1961).

13. *Ibid.*, 187.

14. *Ibid.*, 163.

15. *Ibid.*, 165.

16. *Ibid.*, 167.

17. *Ibid.*, 135-152.

18. *Ibid.*, 138; Alfonso Caso, *The Aztecs: People of the Sun*, trans. by L. Dunham (Oklahoma, 1958) 85-88.

19. Zorita, *op.cit.*, 141-151.

20. Genaro Garcia, *Documentos inéditos o muy raros para la historia de Mexico*, (Mexico, 1907) 237-258.

21. Zorita, *op.cit.*, 126.

22. Hamilton, *op.cit.*, 157.

23. Hamilton, *op.cit.*, 157.

24. *Ibid.*, 161.

25. J.H. Parry, *The Spanish Seaborne Empire*, (New York, 1970), 99-135.

26. F. Braudel, *The Mediterranean and the Mediterranean World in the Age of Phillip II*, trans. by S. Reynolds (New York, 1972), vol. 1, 462-542; Earl J. Hamilton, *American Treasure and the Price Revolution in Spain, 1501-1650*, (Boston, 1934), 301.

27. L.B. Simpson, *The Encomienda in New Spain*, (Berkeley, Cal., 1929), 82; S.A. Zavala, *La Encomienda Indiana*, 2nd. ed. (Mexico, 1973), p. 48.

28. Zorita, *op.cit.*, 206.

29. S.. Cook and W. Borah, *The Indian Population in Central Mexico, 1531-1610*, (Berkeley, Cal., 1960); C. Gibson, *Spain in America*, (New York, 1966), p. 63.

30. Zorita, *op.cit.*, 209.

31. *Ibid.*, 219-229; J. Miranda, *El tributo Indígena en la Nueva España durante el siglo XVI*, (Mexico, 1952).

32. Zorita, *op. cit.*, 212.

33. *Ibid.*, 174-179.

34. Simpson, *op.cit.*, 80-179.

35. *Ibid.*, 191ff.

36. R. Ricard, *The Spiritual Conquest of Mexico*, trans. by L.B. Simpson, (Berkeley, Cal., 1961), 153.

37. W.V. Scholes, *The Diego Ramirez Visita*, (Columbia, Missouri, 1946), 48.

38. Zorita, *op cit.*, 243-249.

39. J. Garcia Icazbalceta, *Nueva Colección de Documentos para la Historia de Mexico*, vol. 3, (Mexico, 1941), XVIII.

40. J. Soustelle, *Daily Life of the Aztecs on the Eve of the Spanish Conquest*, trans. by P.O. Brian (Stanford, Cal., 1961) 86.

Chapter 9

BARTOLOME DE LAS CASAS AND THE ISSUES OF THE GREAT DEBATE OF 1550-1551

In late 1550, an assembly of jurists and four theologians met with the council of the Indies in Valladolid at the request of the king to hear the opposing views of Bartolome de Las Casas and the noted Spanish Aristotelian scholar, Gines de Sepulveda, on the conquest of America.[1] This debate encapsulated the often conflicting Spanish responses to the conquest. Sepulveda himself never came to America, but relied for his information on historians like Oviedo who had taken a dim view of Indian rights. In light of the tense political situation in Peru and Mexico following the New Laws of 1542, Sepulveda became the darling of the colonists for his support of a militant imperialism in America. For the advocates of the rights of native Americans, Las Casas's defense was one of the splendid moments of their struggle. For Las Casas himself, it represented the maturation of his reflections on the consequences of the clash between European and American civilizations. He was seventy-six years old. Although he remained in contact with his friends in America and was still active in Spain in support of Indian causes, he had left America for good in 1547.

News about the uproar caused by his *Confesionario*, twelve rules for confessors, urging the denial of absolution to colonists who held encomiendas and Indian slaves until they made restitution to the Indians, had already reached Spain. No sooner had Las Casas arrived in Spain in 1547 than he learned that the emperor saw the *Confesionario* as implying criticism of the Crown's role in the colonization of America and demanded an explanation in writing. Las Casas then hurriedly composed his *Thirty Propositions* in which he argued that the purpose of Europe's mission in the new world was to preach the message of Christianity to its peoples. Using the familiar argument of pope Innocent IV, he stated that the pope had "the authority and power of Jesus Christ...over all human beings, Christians and non-Christians, insofar as he determined what is necessary to guide and direct them to the end of eternal life and remove obstacles to it."[2] The bulls of donation of Alexander VI were intended to coopt the Iberian monarchs in the project of "expanding and protecting the faith, the Christian religion, and converting the infidels." For Las Casas, the principal reward of the Crown would be in advancing the spiritual purpose of the Spanish presence in America, not in its material and commercial ambition.

Native rulers, he insisted, could not be deprived of their sovereignty. They preserved the right to lordship, dignity, and royal preeminence in accordance with "natural law and the law of nations." In his mind, those who opposed this view have encouraged unspeakable theft, violence, and tyranny. Idolatry did not constitute a just cause for seizing the property of native lords or their subjects. After all, the gospel had not been previously preached to them. They should therefore not be punished except those who "with malice prevent the preaching of the faith." Native rulers were expected to recognize the Spanish Crown as universal lords and sovereigns after they freely chose to become Christian. They could not be punished, if they chose not to convert. The colonists did not have a just cause to make war against "the innocent natives who were secure and peaceful in their own lands and homes." Armed conquests had no basis in law and "were, are, and will be unjust, iniquitous, tyrannical, and condemned by every law from the time of the discovery of the Indies till today." As for the labor systems, he felt that the devil himself could not have invented a more effective way to destroy the world of native Americans than the encomienda and the repartimiento which forced the Indians to work for Spaniards in the mines and as carriers over two hundred leagues. He reminded the king that he had the responsibility of "protecting native laws and customs which were just, changing those which were not, and helping them overcome the defects in their system of governing."

The New Laws of 1542 and the refusal of missionaries to grant absolution to the colonists unless they made restitution to wronged Indians made the political climate charged with emotion. The king's sensitivity to Las Casas's criticism of the Spanish conquest was mild compared to the storm that threatened from the treatise, *Democrates Secundus*, by Gines de Sepulveda.[3] An Aristotelian scholar who had written several works of history and literature, Sepulveda had written the *Democrates Secundus* probably in 1544 to defend the Crown's military conquests in America. His political views were already well-known. In 1529 he had exhorted the emperor Charles V to undertake a crusade against the Turks; he had supported the militant position of his patron Alberto Pio, prince of Carpi, against the pacifism of Erasmus.

After receiving initial support for the publication of *Democrates Secundus* from the council of Castile, the book was sent in 1547/48 to a commission of theologians at the universities of Salamanca and Alcala who condemned it. Sepulveda was certain that Las Casas was behind the decision. He sent a summary of the book to the papal court where it was published in the form of an *Apologia*. All copies of this work were ordered to be burned in Spain. Las Casas in turn wrote his own *Apologia* to counter Sepulveda's justification of Spanish military conquests. Las Casas's *Confesionario* on the one hand, and Sepulveda's *Democrates Secundus* on the other, rivetted the minds of those who were interested in America and caused the emperor to convene a meeting of theologians and jurists in Valladolid and have them decide the merits of the two views of the conquest of America. In 1550 and 1551, Las Casas and Sepulveda presented their arguments. After Sepulveda summarized the main points of his thesis, Las Casas read from his *Apologia* for several days. Although both claimed victory in the debate, no formal decision was taken by the commission.

Though a former student of Pomponazzi at the Spanish college in Bologna, Sepulveda was hardly an enlightened humanist. Anthony Pagden described his mind as "rigidly orthodox and highly chauvinistic."[4] He agreed that conversion of native Americans to Christianity was an important purpose of the encounter, but he felt that military conquest was appropriate because it facilitated the task of conversion. Dispossession of Indian sovereignty and property was justified because Indians were cultural barbarians and must submit to their European cultural superiors. To support his argument, he borrowed heavily from Aristotle's notion of natural slavery as well as Augustine's definition of slavery as punishment for sin. Native idolatry, human sacrifice, and cannibalism were in his mind the evidence to support his position. The use of Aristotle's notion of natural slavery to justify war against the Indians had a long history. Until Vitoria, Las Casas, and the Salamancan theologians constructed arguments against it, theologians like John Major and Palacios Rubios made significant use of it in elaborating their views of the Spanish conquest. Sepulveda's use of this argument demonstrated its persistence and significance for those who supported militant imperialism. The tone of Sepulveda's work was extremely deprecating to native Americans. Part of the reason was his dogmatic, ideological mind. One could see this in his earlier defense of Alberto Pio against the pacifist views of Erasmus; but, resentment against him arose because he chose to write his work in the form of a dialogue rather than in the scholastic manner. The polarities of civilized and barbarian were used for good literary effect, but were not in the process nuanced. For him, Indians had weak minds and practiced barbarous customs. They were capable of improvement through Christian and European rule and customs; they could as natural slaves even become friends of their civilized rulers. While their talents might improve beyond those of monkeys or bears, their mental limitations could not transcend those of bees or spiders. Indians were not human beings in his opinion; they had only the appearance of men. He contrasted the courage, magnanimity, and civilized virtues of Spaniards with the savagery of native Americans who rejected civilized life. For him, Hernan Cortes was noble and courageous; Moctezuma, cowardly. He articulated this moral polarity between civilized Europeans and barbarous Indians to serve his argument that Spanish masters were morally and politically justified in ruling over native Americans. This notion of natural slavery placed limits on the usefulness of the concept of civilization for human development. How different was Vitoria's view of the alleged savagery of native Americans. Vitoria stated that the description of some of the native cultures of America resembled the cultural level of peasants in Europe. It was culture, not natural slavery, that was responsible for the diversity and strangeness of Indian customs.

Las Casas's defense of native Americans and their cultures rested on the *Apologia* from which he read and his *Apologetica historia*, completed after 1551.[5] Las Casas had hoped that these works would have a wider audience than the commission at Valladolid. His purpose was to demonstrate by argument and the evidence of his experience that Indian peoples were members of the human community and that their pre-conquest societies were true civil societies, in spite of the differences of their customs. As Anthony Pagden has pointed out, Las Casas's work was original because he sought to prove that "beneath the glaring cultural differences between the races of men there existed the same set of social and moral imperatives."

Las Casas accepted Sepulveda's paradigm for determining human development. Civil society and Christianity were the keys to cultural transformation and the realization of human potential. He argued that the splendid cities of the Aztecs and Incas were eloquent witnesses of Indian civil society before the Spanish conquest. But he defined civil society more broadly. Where groups of families came together and built houses, there existed true civil society. This intellectual move was of course calculated to include all Indian societies, even those in the Caribbean and Florida, in his definition of civil society. Conversion to Christianity was important for native development, but their societies were already sufficiently developed that their consent was necessary. They could therefore be converted only by peaceful means.

This philosophy of conversion was enunciated in his first major work on the Indies, the *De Unico Vocationis Modo*. Completed between 1538 and 1539 while in Mexico to attend a conference on ecclesiastical reform, it included pope Paul III's papal bull, *Sublimis Deus*, which claimed that native Americans were rational and endowed with liberty and free will. Conversion by peace and kindness was advocated by Las Casas from his early years as a Dominican friar. That was essentially the spirit behind his failed colonizing attempt in Cumana in 1521, although Spanish soldiers were a part of that project. Critics like Oviedo never stopped chiding him with biting sarcasm about the Cumana experiment. The *De Unico Vocationis Modo* was inspired, however, by a significant success. Las Casas proposed that a small contingent of friars alone and unaccompanied by soldiers be allowed to bring the Indians of an unconquered region of Guatemala, Tuzulutlan, under Spanish rule peacefully and to preach the gospel to them. The Franciscan, Jacobo de Tastera, had already had success with a similar project in the Yucatan. On May 2, 1537, the project began. Some verses of poetry covering Christian doctrine were composed in Quiche and set to music and given to four Christian Indian merchants to memorize. They recited the verses and sang before the cacique of Tuzulutlan for eight days, answering questions as well. The cacique invited the friars to come to his town, built a church, and himself converted to Christianity. It was with confidence, then, that Las Casas would assert his method of evangelization, a method that had a certain resonance with the thirteenth-century Majorcan, Ramon Llull: "One and only one is the method that Divine Providence instituted in all the world and at all times to teach men the true religion, namely, that which persuades the understanding with reason and gently attracts the will, and this is common to all men without any difference."

Angel Losada reminded us that Las Casas was not a pacifist. He felt that war was sometimes a necessary evil, especially some wars against Muslims and heretics. Las Casas did not dismiss lightly Sepulveda's reasons for arguing that Spain's wars in America were just. In a sense, the center of the controversy was fixed on the Aristotelian distinction between civilized and barbarian peoples and the presumed rights of the former to rule over the latter. War against the natives was justified if they refused to accept Spanish imperial rule, according to this line of argument. Las Casas found this argument unacceptable. He argued that Sepulveda's definition of barbarian was too simple. There were many definitions of barbarian. If the term barbarian was used for non-Christians, then the Indians were barbarians. But in no way were they cruel or inhumane and incapable of self-government, which was the definition offered by Sepulveda. He insisted that native Americans did not belong to the class of barbarians that Aristotle recommended be hunted and brought forcefully to civilized life. Peaceful means was the only legitimate way. Indeed, Indian arts and crafts and their ability to learn the European liberal arts constituted proof that Indians were rational and capable of governing themselves.

Las Casas's argument against conquest and dispossession on the grounds of idolatry, human sacrifice, and cannibalism showed a skilful mind at home in history, law, and theology. Military intervention could take place, he argued, only if the occupying power had jurisdiction over that territory. But neither the pope nor Christian rulers possessed universal political jurisdiction. In his mind, freedom, not force, was the more defensible Christian approach to religious differences. Citing the examples of Christian practices towards Muslims and Jews in Europe, Las Casas showed that although Jewish and Muslim minorities were under the political jurisdiction of Christian rulers in Europe, they could not be punished for their religious rituals. The infidelity of Jews and Muslims was more serious than that of American Indians because Jews and Muslims had been exposed to Christian teachings. Yet, Las Casas emphasized that they possessed rights against forced labor and oppression. Was intervention not justified to save innocent victims from ritual sacrifice? Las Casas accepted the principle that human beings were responsible for other human beings and were obligated to come to the assistance of the innocent against suffering and death. But he defended all the same the native American case as different. For one thing, he contended that the wars of conquest in America had caused greater human destruction than ritual human sacrifice. The lesser evil was in the circumstance more appropriate than the destruction of kingdoms and cities. Correction or reform was the objective of punishment. It would have been more useful to pardon their past practice of human sacrifice. After all, he reminded his audience, the ancient Spaniards, Greeks, and Romans practiced ritual human sacrifice. In addition, Abraham's offer to sacrifice his son demonstrated the significance of the idea of sacrifice to divine worship. The appeal to abandon human sacrifice like all religious conversion should be made by rational teaching and persuasion, not by force.

In an interesting twist to the question of ritual human sacrifice, Las Casas argued that it demonstrated a deep religious devotion on the part of native Americans. Indians had some knowledge of God and loved God more than themselves: "They offered to their Gods their most precious and beloved of possessions, namely, the sacrifice of their children."[6] Those societies which "ordained by law and custom that human sacrifice be offered to their Gods at certain times...had a more noble concept and esteem of their Gods." Human sacrifice was not opposed to natural reason; it was an error rooted in natural reason itself. Indians could not be expected to abandon the religion of their ancestors until they were persuaded by peaceful means of a better alternative. Las Casas concluded: "If such sacrifices offend God, it is for God alone to punish this sin, and not for men." For Las Casas, then, the conditions essential for the mission to civilize and Christianize America were respect for the culture and beliefs of native Americans and that they should be allowed to choose freely to accept or reject Christianity.

The acrimony of this debate was caused in large part by the chain of events arising from the reform legislation of 1542. In the hearing before the council of the Indies in 1541, Las Casas gave an oral presentation of his *Very Brief Relation of the Destruction of the West Indies.*[7] Not one to mince his words or to compromise, he accused the Spanish colonists of exterminating the Indians in region after region of the Americas. He framed his argument by establishing a dualism between evil Spaniards and good Indians. From the perspective of Las Casas, the stakes were too high to have faith in quiet diplomacy. The catastrophe that befell the natives of the Caribbean and the terror practiced in Mexico and Peru left Las Casas no alternative but to paint the colonization of America in black and white. In his mind, the social consequences of the search for riches were ruining the mission to Christianize the native people. He placed hope in convincing the king to issue laws to protect them. He found the peoples of America "patient," "humble," and "peaceful." They possessed a lively intelligence and were willing "to receive our holy catholic faith and to be endowed with virtuous customs."[8] Into this flock of peaceful native people came the Spaniards like "hungry wolves, tigers, and cruel lions...for forty years they have torn them to bits, killed them, caused them anguish, affliction, and torment, and destroyed them." As evidence, Las Casas drew attention to the fact that only 200 natives of Española remained and that the population of Puerto Rico and Jamaica were similarly ravaged and destroyed: "We should realize the truth that in forty years some twelve million souls of men, women, and children have died unjustly and tyrannically at the hands of the Christians." The cause of this destruction, he felt, was the insatiable thirst and ambition for gold. Initially, the Indians thought that the Spaniards had come from heaven until they were subjected to vexations of every kind.

In his *Entre Los Remedios*, Las Casas proposed solutions to create a more humane order in America. The eight remedy was considered the most significant in that it exercised a major influence on the New Laws of 1542. Las Casas argued that America should be integrated into the Spanish kingdom and all its peoples be incorporated as free subjects and vassals of the Spanish Crown.[9] He warned that they should not be entrusted to individual Spaniards. America and its people should be under the jurisdiction of the Crown. "...not now, nor ever in perpetuity can they be taken or alienated from the Crown, nor given to anyone as vassals in encomienda or as feudal vassals." Insisting that the immediate abolition of the encomienda become a principle that all future monarchs should swear to uphold, Las Casas gave twenty reasons to support his point of view. He reminded the king that the purpose of the Spanish presence in the new world was to convert the Indians to Christianity: "As the purpose of the rule of Your Majesty over these peoples is no other than the preaching and establishment of the faith among them, and their conversion and knowledge of Christ...Your Majesty is obliged to remove all the obstacles in the way of this project." He then went on to show that the encomienda had hindered this purpose. He reminded the king that queen Isabella herself had ordered Columbus in 1499 to return the Indian slaves he had brought to Spain, exclaiming angrily: "What power does the Admiral have to give my vassals to anyone."

It seemed to him that the objectives of the missionaries were at odds with those of the colonists. Control over the native people was important to the world of the colonists because the labor of the native people was indispensable for the acquisition of wealth. But such a world, Las Casas argued, inspired only fear on the part of the Indians. Missionaries were witnesses of this and were resented by the colonists as "disturbing their temporal interests." The encomienda did not create a viable society because husbands were separated from their wives and fathers from their children to work far from their communities. If this system was conceived as a way of teaching the Indian civilization, he was convinced that it was a failure. The colonists were more like an enemy than teachers. Their efforts to uplift those under their care were nothing but "pretentious, false, and deceitful." Indians did not need teachers in civil affairs; they needed people to preach the tenets of Christianity and to provide responsible government for free communities and people. The burden of serving the Crown and the colonists in addition to their native lords was overwhelming and unbearable: "All the peoples and communities of the [New] World are free. They do not lose their freedom when they observe Your Majesty as their universal lord. Even if before they suffered defects to their republics, it was incumbent upon Your Majesty to remedy these defects so that they would enjoy a better quality of liberty...there is no power on earth which sanctions making the condition of the free worse and less free; only blame. The key of justice does not err; Liberty is the most precious and highest of all the temporal goods of this world." In the actual functioning of the encomienda, the condition of the Indians had changed from freedom to slavery. Indian towns were destroyed and their peoples made into abject slaves, reduced to "pure beasts," crushed "like salt in water," in a world where their consent and free will played no part.

He was of the opinion that the initial allocation of native people in Española lacked any authorization from the Crown. The encomienda, therefore, exceeded the terms of the agreement in establishing the colony on Española. When governor Ovando came to Espanola in 1502, he was instructed to treat the Indians as "free human beings with much love, affection, charity, and justice." In order to satisfy the wishes of those who came with him, he distributed Indians among them. He defended this practice by informing the Crown that the native people did not want to communicate with Spaniards and that this practice was necessary to encourage contact. Las Casas insisted that this report was a blatant lie. Relations between the native people and the Spaniards had actually improved before Ovando arrived. He confessed that there were even marital relations between Spaniards and Indians. To the historical argument that the institution of the encomienda was established against the orders of the Crown was added a more philosophical line to which Las Casas would repeatedly return. The encomienda was illegal because it did not receive the "consent of all those peoples who were not called, heard, or defended...as required by natural, divine, canon, and imperial law." He warned the king that unless the encomienda were abolished and the Indians taken from the control of the colonists, they would perish shortly and the vast lands of the new world would be empty of the native inhabitants. The private allocation of Indians to individual colonists worked against the interests of the Crown. He insisted that if the native people were treated as free vassals of the Crown, the new world would bring prosperity to Spain. The death, suffering, and demoralization of the Indians that resulted from the encomienda brought neither riches nor glory. If the Indians were placed under royal jurisdiction, they would feel great joy and consolation, knowing that they would no longer be "condemned to perish, and that life and happiness would come to them."

The abolition of the encomienda would give Spain the opportunity to atone for the destructiveness of the conquest of America. The whole world should know that the "money, gold, and wealth taken from the Indies were robbed, usurped, and seized violently and unjustly from the native owners." Las Casas concluded this treatise by repeating the warning that unless the tyrannical institution of the encomienda were abolished, all the Indies would in a few days be barren and depopulated like Española and other islands of the Caribbean. Then "God will send horrible punishments and perhaps will destroy all of Spain."

Contemporary historians agreed that the New Laws issued in 1542 reforming Spanish policies in America were inspired largely by Las Casas. Future Indian slavery was forbidden and existing slaves were to be freed unless their owners could show legitimate title. Indians could not be used as carriers. As for Indians held in encomienda, all public officials were to transfer immediately their Indians to the jurisdiction of the Crown. The encomiendas of private colonists who could not show legal title were also revoked. More significantly, the encomienda was to be gradually suppressed. No new ones were to be granted and, on the death of existing owners, their encomiendas were to be transferred to the Crown. There were other important measures. Explorers had to have a license for future discoveries. Religious had to be taken along and, above all, the native people were to be treated with respect. Las Casas complained about the policy of gradual abolition, but these laws were nevertheless impressive. The problem lay in putting them into effect. The resentment on the part of the colonists was deep. There were protests, riots, and open rebellion. Delegations of colonists and their sympathizers hurried to Spain to protest the New Laws. In the meantime, Las Casas was consecrated bishop of Chiapas in 1544 with the expectation of carrying out a more humane kind of encounter between Spaniards and native Americans with the assistance of the spirit of the New Laws. On his way to Central America to take up his post, he learned that the New Laws were not put into practice and that there was a movement, backed by some religious, to have the laws revoked. When he reached Chiapas and urged the colonists to free their Indian slaves, Las Casas was harassed and subjected to abuse. There were also threats to his life. It was the rebellion in Peru, however, that convinced the king that the New Laws threatened the survival of his empire in America. The viceroy of Peru, Nuñez Vela, was unable to enforce the laws; Gonzalo Pizarro refused to recognize him and considered himself king of Peru. Bowing to pressure, the emperor revoked the law dealing with the inheritance of the encomiendas on Oct. 20, 1549. In early 1546, Las Casas had decided to give up the office of bishop. The anger of the colonists that was directed at him made his work as bishop ineffective. He journeyed to Mexico to participate in a conference of bishops to discuss doctrinal matters. When this was over, he convened a meeting of Franciscans, Dominicans, and Augustinians to discuss the vexing problem of Indian slavery.

In his treatise on Indian slavery, Las Casas argued that all Indian slaves were held unjustly.[10] The temper of that age had permitted slavery provided that the slaves were captives in a just war. His argument was built on the premises that, first, the wars against the native Indians were not just and, second, that the Crown did not issue any authorization permitting slavery. Reiterating once more that the native Americans were different from Turks and Moors in that the Indians had no history of causing injury to Christians or taking their lands, he implied that the objective of reconquest, legitimate in the cases of Spain and Jerusalem, was invalid in America. Spanish presence in America was legitimate only in its mission to evangelize the native Americans. No divine or human law permitted war to advance this cause. As for the reason of the defense of innocent Indian victims against ritual human sacrifice, Las Casas contended that it was not worth much comment because "our Spaniards never went to war for this purpose, but to kill, despoil, and rob the innocent; to usurp their lands, their homes, their states, and their dominion." While Las Casas built his argument within the framework of the medieval European canon and civil law tradition, his use of concrete and extreme language to narrate his story and illustrate his analysis was designed to persuade the authorities of the reality of the human destructiveness in the Americas.

To an extent, the debate over the European encounter with America was conducted in too theoretical a manner. Early in the sixteenth century, the question of Spain's right to dominion over America was raised, especially after Montesinos and the Dominicans had voiced criticism of Spanish policies. The first responses of John Major, Matias de Paz, and Palacios Rubios were conceived broadly within the context and traditions of Europe.[11] The injunction called the *Requerimiento* which the king asked Palacios Rubios to draw up and which had to be read to the native people prior to intervention was meant to convince Europeans that the Spanish conquest was based on legal principles. For Las Casas, the reading of the injunction that "God chose S. Peter as leader of mankind...to establish his seat in all parts of the world and rule all people, whether Christians, Moors, Jews, Gentiles or any other sect" was nothing but hypocrisy. The proclamation that the pope had granted the Spanish Crown dominion over America and that, unless they complied, war would be waged against them was unjust and detestable. Las Casas exonerated Palacios Rubios whom he described as favoring the Indian cause. He saw instead the influence of the opinion of Hostiensis that non-Christians had no right to dominion. James Muldoon has argued persuasively that the *Requerimiento* was inspired more by the views of Innocent IV than Hostiensis.[12] The injunction was conceived to counteract possible charges by other European countries that the Spanish conquest was based on the views of John Wyclif that dominion depended on Christian grace which was condemned at the council of Constance in 1414. What the *Requerimiento* said in effect was that native American communities possessed real dominion, but that native dominion could be superseded by the right of evangelization. One might add that this was the theoretical framework that influenced the Salamancan theologians and jurists. The example of the *Requerimiento* highlights the difficulty of evaluating the sincerity of the laws that were passed to ameliorate Indian exploitation. The significance of the efforts of Las Casas and his supporters was to make the intellectual debate in Europe respond to the actual conditions of colonial life in America.

Wars against native Americans were unjust also because they were not authorized by the Crown. Indeed, Spanish colonists made little effort to put into practice laws and decrees that were passed to protect the welfare of the Indians. It was therefore illegal to make slaves of Indian captives. When the labor supply became scarce, some colonists would sail with two or three ships to the islands of Española, Puerto Rico, and Cuba, and also to the mainland. They would attack Indian villages at night in order to seize captives. They would pack three to four hundred people in one ship with the hope of selling them as slaves. Other colonies arbitrarily demanded Indian labor and products. Slaves were sometimes branded and chained. Las Casas remarked that he had seen this with his own eyes. Whole regions were depopulated by the kidnapping of Indians as slaves. What Las Casas described was, from the perspective of the Indians, a state that practiced terror. Indian slavery was but one form of terror. To the question whether slavery practiced by native Americans was milder than Spanish slavery, Las Casas maintained that there was no equivalence between Indian and European slavery. Slavery practiced by Indians was "a light burden"; it connoted a person who had a greater obligation to help and serve. An Indian who was a slave of other Indians was little different from a master's son because "he had his home, his herd, his wife, and children, and enjoyed liberty as other free subjects." Where Indian practices went beyond the boundaries of justice, Las Casas urged them to remember that it was the Christian practice to preserve good native laws and customs and extirpate evil ones. In this general thesis on slavery, he exhorted his audience to be mindful that liberty was the most precious and worthy possession after life itself. It must be pointed out that when Las Casas wrote this denunciation of slavery, he had not yet condemned African slavery. In fact, his slave, Juanillo, often accompanied him to ferry him across rivers. It was after the anti-slavery conference in Mexico in 1546 that he confessed that African slavery was as unjust and cruel as Indian slavery.

Las Casas drew several conclusions from his argument condemning all Indian slavery as unjust. He urged the king to free all Indians held as slaves by Spaniards; bishops were obliged to plead before the Crown and council of the Indies to free Indian slaves from tyranny and oppression and "if necessary, to risk their lives." Finally, he asked Franciscan, Dominican, and Augustinian religious to refuse to absolve any Spaniard who held Indian slaves unless he was examined by the Audiencia in accordance with the New Laws.

At the second conference of the friars in Mexico, Las Casas presented his *Confesionario*.[13]   As bishop of Chiapas, he had already put into practice several of the measures he recommended.   His refusal to absolve slaveowners was already well-known.   This formulary for confession was meant to apply to conquistador, encomendero, slaveholders, and merchants who were engaged in selling arms.   The central theme was the imperative of restitution before absolution could be given.   The antagonism of the colonists to Las Casas was not surprising.   On his deathbed or healthy, the penitent had to execute a legal document in the presence of a public notary empowering the confessor to free all Indian slaves, if he had any, and to distribute all his property to the Indians he had exploited or their survivors.   After all, Las Casas contended, he had brought nothing from Spain.   All that he had accumulated in America was through the labor of the Indians.   No property was to be granted to the conquistador's heirs.   Even if he had one hundred legitimate children, they were not to receive one cent.   To add to his humiliation, he had to acknowledge that he had participated in "such and such conquests or wars against Indians in these Indies, and that he was an accomplice in the robbery, violence, death, and captivity of Indians as well as the destruction of many of their towns and villages."   Even colonists who were not conquistadors but who had Indians allocated to them had to restore whatever they had taken as tribute and services to the surviving Indians, their heirs, or the villages where they lived.   It is worthwhile underscoring the two principles that he insisted on.   First, he urged freedom for all who were enslaved or exploited; second, restitution and compensation had to be given to the victims.   Manuscript copies of this work circulated in America and Spain.   Sepulveda had no hesitation in labeling the work "scandalous and diabolical."

Did these rules have any impact?   Guillermo Lohmann Villena has presented evidence that in Peru the Lascasian teaching on restitution did produce fruit.[14]   The publication of several of his works in 1552 circulated the ideas of Las Casas.   In addition, his friends and supporters, especially Fray Tomas de San Martin and Fray Domingo de Santo Tomas in Peru, had nurtured the spiritual climate of Peru by their sermons on the need for restitution.   Tomas de San Martin had written a stinging criticism of the encomienda to the king in 1551, and in 1553 wrote a manual on confession for conquistadors and encomenderos.   He wrote this work in Seville at the same time that Las Casas was there.[15]

It is possible to see the hand of Las Casas in this work. For San Martin, the conquistadors obtained their wealth unjustly and both biblical and canon law traditions had counselled restitution of ill-gotten goods as the price of moral reintegration. Encomenderos came in for a more realistic approach in that they were entitled to receive tribute with an easy conscience provided that they treated their Indians humanely and followed the required rules governing the use of Indian services. Fray Domingo de Santo Tomas, professor of theology at the university of San Marcos in 1553 and successor to Tomas de San Martin as bishop of Charcas, similarly identified with Las Casas in his actions and ideas.[16] When he visited Spain between 1555 and 1561, he kept up a correspondence with Las Casas. The archbishop of Lima, Jeronymo de Loaysa, also corresponded with Las Casas. The Lascasian vision therefore found fertile soil in Peru. Another reason why some conquistadors observed the rule of restitution was, Guillermo Lohmann Villena pointed out, that the Spanish colonists were not the monolithic, greedy, and cruel exploiters as Las Casas painted them. To be sure, they were thirsty for wealth. But some were moved by the suffering of the Indians. The picture of the conquistador Francisco Pizarro that we get from his will (1537) showed a man who set aside funds "to rescue Christian captives from the Turks, to pay a cleric to teach Indians, and to offer masses for the soul of Indians who died in the campaigns."[17]

In a document witnessed by Fray Domingo de Santo Tomas in 1563, Nicholas de Ribera declared that "I have taken account and searched my conscience and consulted with theologians and experts in moral questions. I confess that I owe the Indians of my encomienda a debt and I am responsible for paying eight thousand gold pesos...I ask that they be paid from my property." It seemed that Las Casas's censure of the wealth of the colonists and their treatment of the Indians troubled the consciences of the conquistadors and clerics. With the passing of the first conquistadors, the admonitions of Las Casas lost their force only to revive again in the 1560s. The right of the encomenderos to receive tribute became once more an important issue. Las Casas's doctrine of restitution was for a time an effective instrument in regulating the greed of the colonists.

When Las Casas sailed for Spain in 1547, his writings and political activity were already well known. His uncompromising moral stance, the harshness of his rhetoric, and the severity of his solutions did not endear him to conservatives like Sepulveda. That was why the debate at Valladolid did not illuminate the question or lead to the possibility of a compromise. The manichaean shape of the arguments of both Las Casas and Sepulveda made discourse difficult. Yet, in 1550 most of the contemporaries of Las Casas were recording the destruction of the Indies and the astounding deaths of the native people. The chronicles and histories concluded that the search for gold and wealth was the overriding motivation. It is difficult to dispute Las Casas's narrative. His analysis of the human catastrophe was not unreasonable. He made an excellent case for attributing the causes of destruction to the nature of the conquests and the establishment of forced labor systems. The number of deaths was too enormous and Indian suffering too moving to permit him to be tender with conquistadors and encomenderos. He had hoped that only by a brutal analysis could he expect a more humane policy. The defense of the dignity of native Americans was an important struggle; so too were his concern and projects for Indian cultural and social development. The abolition of forced labor systems was the prerequisite for both causes.

Although he never returned to America, Las Casas became the representative of Indian reform at the court of Spain. He corresponded frequently with his friends like Tomas de San Martin and Domingo de Santo Tomas in Peru, or Alonso de la Vera Cruz and Alonso de Zorita in Mexico. Whenever he learned that there were moves to reimpose the encomienda, he was quick to organize his political network to block these measures. This was not an easy time for Phillip II who found the treasury with scarce resources at his accession to the Spanish throne in 1556. He decided to grant encomiendas in perpetuity as a way of raising new funds. Las Casas immediately presented a petition showing that more funds could be raised if the king freed the Indians and restored native rulers. This was not accepted, of course. But it effectively blocked Philip's initial policy until the royal commission decided to allow perpetual encomiendas only for the first conquistadors, one lifetime for some colonists, and others to revert permanently to the Crown. Due to Las Casas's life-long struggle, royal legislation was able to control the arbitrariness of the encomenderos. In some cases, as under the administration of judge Zorita, Indian tribute was actually lowered.

Yet, the Indians did not benefit a great deal from these changes. Phillip II's desperate need for greater financial revenue led generally to increased taxation. The dramatic decline in Indian population should have lowered the tax burden for Indian communities. But, despite protective legislation, tax rolls were padded. Some Indian communities that had been exempt from tribute, lost this status. That was why Las Casas continued to criticize the encomienda with no less vigor that when he first raised the issue in 1515. Consider, for example, the memorandum he sent to the council of the Indies in 1562; "For days upon days, years upon years we have overlooked the two kinds of tyranny by which we have destroyed countless republics; one called conquest when we first entered...The other was and is tyrannical government...to which they gave the name repartimiento or encomienda."[18] The conclusion of this work summed up well Las Casas's perspective on the encounter between Europeans and native Americans: "First, all the wars which were called conquests were and are unjust. Second, we seized unjustly all the kingdoms and governments of the Indies. Third, encomiendas or repartimientos of Indians are cruel, in themselves evil, and therefore tyrannical. Fourth, all who grant them or receive them are in mortal sin. If they do not give them up, they will not be saved. Fifth, the king...cannot justify the wars and theft against the native people...any more than the Turks can justify their wars and plunder against Christian towns. Sixth, all the gold, silver, pearls, and other riches which have come to Spain...have been stolen. Seventh, unless they make restitution...they will not be saved. Eight, the native peoples of the Indies...have the right to make a just war against us and to drive us from the face of the earth. This right will last until the day of judgement." These were the issues he fought for throughout his long life. The doctrine of restitution became more urgent in his later years. In his very last work, a petition to pope Pius V, he asked the pope to excommunicate anyone who said that the war against the Indians was just only because of their idolatry. He urged the pontiff to demand that those bishops, friars, and clergy who have enriched themselves and lived magnificently "make restitution of all the gold, silver, and precious stones they have acquired."[19]

During his retirement, he completed his major work, *The History of the Indies*. Although the narrative ended in the early 1520s, it presented a story of the conquest of the Caribbean that was coherent, comprehensible, and sad. He minimized the effects of diseases on the decline of the native population, to be sure. But, the weight of the evidence for his argument that the Spaniards were responsible for the destruction of the Indians was massive. It was the experience of the cruelties of the Caribbean encounter that influenced his later political activity and writings. Criticism of the colonists remained unrelieved by

any distinctions.   A general condemnation of Spaniards seemed
unwarranted. Was he not favored at court? Was his influence among
the theologians and jurists at the universities of Spain not profound? In
America, he must have been aware that he was respected by most of the
religious. It was true that the outstanding Franciscan missionary, Fray
Toribio de Motolinia, had written a harsh letter about him to Charles V
in 1555, but that was in response to Las Casas's criticism of the practice
of mass baptisms of native Americans.   Franciscans like bishop
Zumarraga and Jacobo de Tastera were keen supporters of his
missionary methods. The tone of bitterness in his works would suggest
that his efforts were solitary and attended by failure.   But that
conclusion would miss the major significance of his work which was
that he created a reform movement which confronted the advocates of
militant imperialism in Spain and America. Wherever and whenever the
burdens of the labor system and Indian servitude became overwhelming,
Las Casas and his supporters challenged the system.   Anton de
Montesinos and Pedro de Cordoba in the Caribbean, Tomas de San
Martin and Domingo de Santo Tomas in Peru, Jacobo de Tastera in
Central America, Alonso de la Vera Cruz and Alonso de Zorita in
Mexico, Marcos de Niza in the borderlands, and Francisco de Vitoria
in Spain were among those who respected Las Casas and supported the
cause of Indian rights and peaceful conversion. Las Casas could not be
unaware how deep an influence he had. The plan of judge Zorita and
the Franciscan Jacinto de San Francisco to pacify and convert the
nomadic tribes to the north of Mexico was inspired by Las Casas's
successful experiment in Tuzulutlan, Guatemala.[20] Zorita corresponded
frequently with Las Casas. Indeed, it was Las Casas and the Franciscan
Alonso Maldonado de Buendia who presented Zorita's plan to the
council of the Indies in 1562. The council was still committed to
conquest as the means of pacification and offered faint support. They
approved it provided that financial support came out of Zorita's pocket.
The plan did not get off the ground then, but when the policy of "war
by fire and blood" proved a failure, Zorita's Lascasian plan was later
put into effect with some success and would inspire the creation of the
mission system during the later Spanish expansion on the American
continent.

    Another consequence of the reform movement was the struggle to
transfer the sixteenth century European system of justice to America, to
give it teeth, and to direct colonial society in a more humane way. The
use of legal and theological arguments in the debates over treatment of

the native peoples seemed at times tiresome and irrelevant. But the intellectual context of Spain and Europe determined the forms of the debate. The European legal system, largely the legacy of the theological culture of the middle ages, was nevertheless an impressive achievement. If the obsession with legality was one aspect of this culture, a relatively broad area of freedom of expression was the other. The issue was to make the system of justice effective. The actions of the conquistadors during the initial conquests of the Caribbean, Mexico, the Yucatan, and Peru made one wonder whether they were constrained by any form of justice. As Vitoria had remarked, there were so many stories of massacres that it would be more appropriate to speak of power than justice.

The observations of Las Casas, Ramon Pane, and Bernardino de Sahagun, among others, showed that native American communities had effective systems of justice of their own. It would certainly have been appropriate and useful had they been allowed to contribute to the system of justice created in America. The insistence of Las Casas, Vera Cruz, and Zorita on the natural rights and liberty of the native communities was meant to preserve many of the features of Indian justice. As Spanish America was drawn more tightly into an imperial system, this part of Las Casas's movement came to an end. In any case, the logic of medieval Christianity with its dogma of superiority over all other religions made it unlikely that it would allow a different system of justice to operate alongside its own. The missionary orders were prepared to allow some aspects of the indigenous cultures to thrive, but not native religions. Like Europeans of that time, native American justice and morality sprang from their religious beliefs. It was easy to see the physical cruelty and death that resulted from slavery, the encomienda, and diseases; few were aware, however, of the cultural death that the native people suffered when their religion was deliberately destroyed.

A clear illustration of the enduring significance of the questions of the Spanish right of conquest and the natural rights of the native people was the Spanish right of conquest of the Philippines in 1571 by Miguel de Legaspi.[21] The Augustinian friars, led by Andres de Urdaneta, condemned the conquest as unjust. They argued that the two conditions for a just war, authorization from the king and native aggression, did not exist. Phillip II had specifically enjoined Legaspi to secure the friendship of the native communities by peaceful means. The issue of Spanish dominion remained unsettled. The Augustinians and Jesuits came to support Spanish rule over the Philippines on the basis of the papal grants. For the Dominicans, however, as was their history in America, that principle alone was not satisfactory. Under the first bishop, Domingo Salazar (1581), and Miguel de Benavides, the third archbishop of Manila, the Dominicans did not accept the political sovereignty of Spain. They argued that the Spanish Crown was only an instrument of the spiritual power of the pope. The remaining way open for legitimate jurisdiction was the free consent of the natives. This was possible, Benavides stressed, if missionaries were sent to convert the natives by peaceful means. In 1597 Phillip II issued a decree offering restitution of tribute unjustly taken from the native people of the Philippines who were not Christian. The decree asked that the people voluntarily consent to submit to the Crown of Spain.

Consent of the governed, authorization from a duly constituted ruler, protection of the innocent, and the right of evangelization became principles governing the relations between Christian Spain and the non-Christian worlds in the sixteenth century. They represented an early formulation of principles of international relations. Sixteenth-century Spanish political thought resonated with these ideas. It must be remembered, however, that these principles in all likelihood stemmed from the thirteenth century works of Aquinas, Ramon Llull, Ramon Penyafort, and pope Innocent IV, on the one hand, and the expansion of Western Europe on the other. By the middle of the seventeenth century, the question of the Spanish right to conquest was no longer important. Juan de Solorzano y Pereira (1575-1654) published in 1629 and 1639 his volumes on Spain's right to America entitled *Disputatio de Indiarum iure*. It was a detailed account and analysis of those who questioned Spain's conquest of the Indies. Solorzano did not share their judgment.[22] For him, Spain's conquest was justified. Spain had come to have jurisdiction over America by virtue of the papal donation; its dominion was achieved through subsequent occupation. His argument was derived from Roman law and was similarly used to justify ancient Roman conquests. What Solorzano's argument suggested was that the Spanish conquest of America was already consolidated and was not any longer problematical. The theory of natural rights had given way to legal rights obtained by a sufficiently long period of occupation. Solorzano's interests lay more in preserving the legitimacy of the Spanish monarchy's rule over the empire and the civilized legislation it inspired to govern the Americas than in articulating the rights of native peoples.

The central significance of Las Casas was his awareness of the human destructiveness that was taking place and his struggle to put a stop to it. Although he might have exaggerated the responsibility of human beings in the deaths of the native Americans and ignored the role of epidemics, the catastrophic decline of the native population was undeniable and was the context that shaped his sensibility and his politics. He had come to know, love, and sympathize with the native people. He obviously felt that a radical attack on the colonial system could reverse the genocide that was taking place.

Las Casas's writings criticizing the Spanish colonists were used by Spain's enemies as propaganda in the sixteenth-century conflicts between Protestant England and Catholic Spain, and in the struggle of the Protestant Dutch to become independent of Spain.[23]   The first English edition of *The Very Brief Relation of the Destruction of the West Indies* was published in 1583 in London; in 1578, the first Dutch edition. Of greater political consequences were the Latin (1598) and German (1599) editions of the same work published and illustrated in Frankfurt by Jean Theodore and Jean Israel de Bry. These editions carried the message of Spain's cruelty throughout Europe. The Spanish conquest, not Las Casas's struggle for justice, was emphasized in these editions. Conquest, not the struggle for justice, came to define the Spanish legacy in America, at least for the English-speaking world. If the European discovery of America became a major source of interest and inspiration in the first part of the sixteenth century, the schism within Christian Europe that resulted from the Protestant and Catholic reformations created ideological tensions and political conflicts in Europe and America. The political context in Europe explained in part the popularity of Las Casas's works. His critique of Spanish policies and defense of the rights of native Americans might make it appear that his struggle was against Spanish imperial civilization. But that would be to misunderstand him and his work. Placing his hopes for changes in policy on the Spanish monarchy, he remained close to the center of power at court throughout his political life. Through the efforts of his friends and sympathizers at the major universities of Spain, he was able to bring his ideas and causes into the mainstream of Spanish intellectual and political life. The distinction between Las Casas and Spanish civilization in America is questionable. Las Casas's struggle for justice for native Americans in the sixteenth century was also the Spanish struggle for justice. It was equally true, however, that, despite the laws and rules that were won to protect native Americans, their condition did not appreciably improve nor their near extinction significantly come to an end. The self-interest of the powerful colonists in America and the growing sense of the importance of American resources to the Spanish Empire were the dynamics that proved stronger than the laws to control these interests.

NOTES

Chapter 9

1. Angel Losada, "The Controversy between Sepulveda and Las Casas in the Junta of Valladolid," in *Bartolomé de Las Casas in History*, ed. by Juan Friede and Benjamin Keen, (DeKalb, Illinois, 1971) 279-307.

2. Las Casas, *Doctrina*, prologue and selections by A. Yañez, (Mexico City, 1982) 33-52. [cited as *Doctrina*]

3. Juan Gines de Sepulveda, *Demócrates Segundo*, ed. by Angel Losada, (Madrid, 1951).

4. See Anthony Pagden, *The Fall of Natural Man*, (Cambridge, 1982), 109-118 for a keen analysis of Sepulveda's presentation.

5. For Las Casas's argument, *ibid.*, 118-145.

6. Las Casas, *Apologética Historia*, in *Doctrina*, 19-21.

7. *Doctrina*, p. 4; there is a new edition of the 1974 translation of the *Brevíssima Relación*-Las Casas, *The Devastation of the Indies: A Brief Account*, (Baltimore, 1992). For a full discussion of this theme, see Lewis Hanke, *The First Social Experiments in America*, (Cambridge, 1935); -, *Aristotle and the American Indians*, (Bloomington, Ind., 1959).

8. Las Casas, *Tratado sobre las encomiendas*, in *Doctrina*, 55-83; see Juan Friede, "Las Casas y el movimiento indigenista en España y America en la primera mitad del siglo XVI," *Revista de Historia de América*, 34(1952) 339-411.

9. For the most part, the essential structure of the New Laws remained intact. The emperor sent secret orders to the viceroy not to grant new encomiendas. The laws against slavery were not revoked. See Wagner, *op.cit.*, p. 160.

10. Las Casas, *Tratado sobre la Esclavitud*, in *Doctrina*, 87-134; See Silvio Zavala, "*Bartolomé de Las Casas ante La esclavitud de los Indios*," *Cuadernos Americanos*, XXV(1966) 142-156.

11. *Ibid.*, p. 89; see Pierre Chaunu, "Francisco de Vitoria, Las Casas et la querelle des justes titres," *Bibliothéque d'Humanisme et de Renaissance*, XXIX(1967) 485-495.

12. See James Muldoon, "John Wyclif and the Rights of the Infidels: The Requerimiento Re-examined," *The Americas*, XXXVI(1980) 301-316; Lewis Hanke, *The Spanish Struggle for Justice in the Conquest of America*, (Phil., 1949) 31-36.

13. Las Casas, *Avisos y Reglas para los Confesores*, in *Doctrina*, 137-154.

14. Guillermo Lohmann Villena, "La Restitución por Conquistadores y Encomenderos: Un Aspecto de la incidencia Lascasiana en el Peru," *Anuario de Estudios Americanos*, XXIII(1966) 21-89.

15. L.A. Eguiguren, "Fray Tomás de San Martin," *Mercurio Peruano*, 32(1951) 195-204.

16. R. Porras Barrenechea, "Fray Domingo de Santo Tomás," *Comercio*, May 12, 1959.

17. Lohmann Villena, p. 36.

18. Las Casas, *Memorial al Consejo de Indias*, in *Doctrina*, 157-162; see also Venancio Carro, "Los postulados teológico-juridicos de Bartolome de Las Casas," in *Anuario de Estudios Americanos*, XXIII(1966) 109-246.

19. Las Casas, *Petición a Su Santidad Pio V*, in *Doctrina*, p. 165.

20. Ralph E. Vigil, "Bartolomé de Las Casas, Judge Alonso de Zorita, and the Franciscans. A Collaborative effort for the Spiritual Conquest of the Borderlands," *The Americas*, XXXVIII(1981) 45-57.

21. J. Gayo Aragón, "The Controversy over justification of the Spanish Rule in the Philippines," in *Studies in Philippine Church History*, ed. by Gerald Anderson, (Cornell, 1969) 3-21; see also John Leddy Phelan, *The Hispanization of the Philippines*, (Madison, 1959).

22. James Muldoon, "Solorzano's De Indiarum Iure: Applying a Medieval Theory of World Order in the Seventeeth Century," *Journal of World History*, 2 no. 1(1991) 29-46; see Anthony Pagden, *Spanish Imperialism and Political Imagination*, (New Haven, 1990) p. 34.

23. See Benjamin Keen, "Introduction: Approaches to Las Casas, 1535-1970," in *Bartolomé de Las Casas in History*, 3-60. For the debate on Las Casas's role in creating the "Black Legend" of Spain, see Charles Gibson, *The Black Legend: Anti-Spanish Attitudes in the Old World and the New*, (New York, 1971); see the arguments of Lewis Hanke and Benjamin Keen in *Hispanic American Historical Review*, 44(1964) 293-340; 49(1969) 703-719; 51(1971) 112-127, 336-355.

EPILOGUE

What was the truth of the European encounter with America from 1492? Was it the discovery of Columbus and the opportunities for the expansion of knowledge about "the fourth part of the world"? One of the consequences of Columbus's voyages was surely the incorporation of the Americas in the march of Western European scientific progress and commercial expansion. Columbus came to represent the bearer of European scientific progress, commerce, and civilization, as if America and its native peoples could only derive meaning and a purpose when it became tied to Europe. From Columbus to European writers like Hegel and Goethe in the nineteenth century, it was Europeans and European issues which shaped the image of the Americas. In his history of the polemic in the 18th and the 19th centuries on the nature of the new world, Antonello Gerbi described the arrogance of European writers who, measuring achievements by their doctrine of progress, saw in America only the immaturity and degeneracy of its natives, animals, plants, and ecology.[1] They couched their descriptions and narratives in the language of science, thereby giving their pronouncements the ring of truth. A later generation of scholars would find the dispute between civilization and barbarism tiresome. Much more significant today has been the inquiry into the concrete relations between Europeans and native Americans. The search for the truth of the experience of the conquest of America reveals, however incomplete, that an enormous human catastrophe took place and deserves to be comprehended with all its complexity with the hope that future encounters between different peoples and cultures would be less inhumane.

The main features of the European perspective of the encounter with the peoples of America were shaped as early as 1493 in Columbus's letter to the Spanish monarchs. The first woodcut illustration of the letter, published that same year in Basel, showed the native people naked giving offerings, presumably of gold, to one of the Spaniards. The European artists who illustrated the editions of Columbus's letter seemed captivated by the nakedness of the native people, no less than Columbus. A more powerful influence on the imagination of Europe was Amerigo Vespucci's letter to Lorenzo de Pier Francesco de Medici on his third voyage to South America between 1501 and 1502, describing the customs of cannibals and other groups of native Americans. That there were thirteen Latin editions of that letter between 1503 and 1504, and ten German editions between 1505 and 1506 demonstrates the interest this narrative stirred among the European public. The content of the letter as well as the illustrations describing the nakedness and cannibalistic practices of the Indians helped create the image Europeans had of native Americans. To some Europeans, this description brought echoes of a past golden age; to others, it confirmed that picture of Asian peoples presented in John Mandeville's *Book of Marvels*, published in 1483. Little attempt was made to differentiate the Tainos of the Caribbean from the Tupinambas of Brazil, or the Aztecs of Mexico and Incas of Peru. As Ricardo Alegria had pointed out, European artists were not interested in the ethnology of native Americans. The text of the letters was the point of reference.[2] The first representations of native Americans were to have a significant political impact. First of all, they served to confirm the European sense of superiority over native American culture; secondly, as the conquest proceeded, they became the justification for the conquest, colonization and Christianization of native Americans. The debates at European universities over the native peoples make for painful reading. Advocates of European imperialism defended European power by citing its superior culture when most narratives of the conquest showed only naked power.

The question whether nakedness, alleged cannibalism, and ritual human sacrifice made the European conquest of America just needs to be answered. While condemning ritual human sacrifice, sixteenth-century theologians argued that this practice did not justify seizing native lands nor denying them their human rights. These theologians, especially at the universities of Salamanca and Mexico, were of course in line with the more liberal trend of the medieval Christian theological tradition. It was, however, the French humanist, Michel de Montaigne, who hit the nail on the head in his essay "on Cannibals", written in 1580.[3] He saw clearly the cultural flaw in the European perspective in their belief that their particular, historical values and rules were universally binding on all peoples and cultures. He admitted that the alleged cannibalism was horrible but felt that Europeans "surpassed [them] in every sort of barbarism." For him, arrogance and a sense of superiority have blinded Europeans: "While rightly judging their misdeeds, we are very blind to our own." Like Thomas More's *Utopia*, Montaigne's essay was written in the context of the debate between the relative merits of civilized and primitive life. More and Montaigne were critical of the existing condition of civilized life in Europe. Influenced by Vespucci's *Mundus Novus* letter, especially his statement that native Americans lived in a state of nature, they were sympathetic to native American ways of life. The dreams and hopes of some Europeans for a return to a more natural life were centered in America. By the 1520s and the 1530s Europeans learned of the great cities of Mexico. Yet, the image of America as the home of natural man persisted.

The encounter was, however, more fateful than the imposition of European cultural hegemony. The almost incredible decline in the native population begs for an explanation. Epidemic diseases were certainly a major cause of the demographic disaster. In their long isolation, native Americans did not develop immunity against certain diseases. To appreciate the impact of diseases in world civilization one simply had to consider the effect of the "black plague" in the fourteenth century when one-third of Europe's population died. Still, we have to take seriously the charges of sixteenth century human rights advocates that the cruelty of European colonists was also a significant cause. Initiated by Anton de Montesinos and spearheaded by Bartolome de Las Casas, the human rights movement pinned the blame for the destruction on the imperial institutions and the Spanish colonists. It must be emphasized that the human rights struggle was an important movement in the sixteenth century which sought to change the exploitative character of Spanish imperialism in America. The inhumanity of the conquest, slavery, and the encomienda was condemned by sixteenth-century moralists; the issue did not have to wait for the twentieth century. In the context of the vast human destructiveness, the human rights movement was, arguably, the most precious European legacy of the early encounter. The same European civilizations which so arrogantly and brutally conquered the Americas also produced people who denounced and condemned the conquest. In the process they articulated concepts that would be useful in defining the rights of all peoples. Considered from the perspective of the vanquished, however, it is doubtful whether the memory of the human rights movement diminishes the sense of the human tragedy of the conquest. In his study of Indian-European relations in colonial Peru, Steve J. Stern offered an

ironic view of this struggle for justice for the Indians.[4]   The struggle
and the consequent establishment of laws "subjected a good many
colonials to constraints and hardships...What it could not do, however,
was challenge colonialism itself. Spanish justice in some instances and
on some issues favored the native against their oppressors. But for that
very reason, it set into motion relationships which sustained colonial
power, weakened the peasantry's capacity for independent resistance and
rooted exploitation into the enduring fabric of Andean society."

Vitoria and his students, Montesinos, Las Casas, Zorita, and Vera
Cruz were critical of European imperialism, but they were still
European voices. They believed that Spanish imperialism could be
benevolent and humane. For them, power could be restrained by virtue.
In studying the texts of their defense of the Indians, especially those
who came to the Americas, there is no denying their passion and anger.
They understood concretely the suffering of the native peoples, whether
it was the activist Las Casas or the academic Vera Cruz, and sincerely
hungered for justice. Yet, the perspective of the conquest would have
been more complete, if there had been more voices of the vanquished,
voices unmediated by European teachers. Indian resistance of course
spoke loudly about Indian rejection of Spanish imperial rule. The
figure of Enriquillo and his treaty with Spain offered an alternative
possibility of the encounter.

The conflicts between the pro-Indian activists, who were for the most
part religious, and the colonists concealed the fact that the religious
missionaries were also agents of the Crown's plan to impose its imperial
rule on native Americans.   Political and religious purposes were
organized in the same system. Five clergymen accompanied Columbus
on his second voyage. It was Columbus who asked Ramon Pane, the
Jeronymite priest, to report on the beliefs and practices of the Tainos of
Española, after the native insurrection of March 27, 1495 was put
down.[5] Once the Aztecs were defeated, Cortes ordered the removal of
the images of their important gods from the main temple in
Tenochtitlan. For Cortes, political subjugation could not be separated
from religious subjugation.[6] He presented the native Mexicans with
pictures of the Blessed Virgin and implored them to set them in place
of their idols. While the conquest of Peru was still going on, Pizarro
received orders to destroy Incan idols and have the sons of Incan rulers
educated in special religious schools.[7] Nor were the missionary friars
timid about using these methods to advance their own purposes. Fray
Toribio de Motolinia reported that, in 1525 in Texcoco, "...three friars,

from ten at night until dawn, frightened and put to flight all those who were in the abodes and halls of the devils..." and "after destroying these public idols, the friars went after the ones that were enclosed."[8]

If the initial attempts to convert the native peoples to Christianity were so coercive, why then did the Indians embrace Christianity? The contemporary sources are in agreement that the Indians accepted Christianity. Motolinia was enthusiastic about the multitudes who participated in Christian ceremonies. While Sahagun and Duran seemed pessimistic about Indian conversion, it was because, as rigorists, they lamented the Christian and native religious mix. Using fragments of sixteenth-century indigenous sources, Miguel Leon-Portilla has built a strong case for the sincerity of affection that native Mexicans felt for the Franciscans in particular.[9] The Dominican Duran and Judge Zorita both observed that the poor Indians who beg from door to door "just as the fathers of St. Francis do today" were especially fond of them. What the Mexican poet, Octavio Paz, said about Mexican Indians might well be true generally about Indian conversion to Christianity: "The flight of the gods and the death of their leaders had left the natives in a solitude so complete that it is difficult for a modern man to imagine it. Catholicism re-established their ties with the world and the other world. It gave them back a sense of their place on earth."[10] Indian achievements in scholarship at the college of Tlatelolco, their interest in medicine and the organization of hospitals, and their mural paintings in the cathedral of Cuernavaca, for example, bear witness to the fact that in colonial Mexico native Mexicans found in Christianity a source of hope.

It was possible that once the conquests of the Caribbean, Mexico, Central America, and Peru were completed, some native communities saw the dismantling of the severe Aztec and Inca states as positive, creating freedom to pursue their own economic interests.[11] Steve J. Stern has shown that in Peru alliances were established between Europeans and native elites and that Spanish authority was won by consent. All of this changed by the 1540s in Mexico and 1560s in Peru with the discovery of major silver and gold mines. To meet the expanding colonial economy, a centralized colonial system was put in place. Native Indians from different communities were grouped together in new villages or reductions, and a system of labor and tribute imposed.

Despite the successes in Mexico, one should not lose sight of the fact that the imposition of Christianity was a cultural battle to conquer the hearts of the native peoples. Beliefs and practices that were excluded in the process of Christianization re-emerged later under different conditions or were blended into Christianity. Duran felt that the old religion was "so old, so rooted, so solidly based that it has been impossible to obliterate it in fifty seven years."[12] It seemed that, as the missionaries sought to Christianize native Americans, the native peoples Americanized Christianity. Sahagun, who did not support religious hybridization, was convinced that Catholicism had "shallow roots, and with much labor little fruit is produced."[13] In her study of the Mayan and Spanish encounter in the Yucatan, Inga Clendinnen has shown that although the Maya experienced subjugation after their brutal conquest by the Spanish, they did not abandon their sense of autonomy. Mayan lords continued to call their people for secret meetings to celebrate their traditional rituals and histories.[14] Her portrayal of the Franciscan bishop, Diego de Landa, and his cruelty on learning of the survival of Mayan religious practices offers a note of caution to the more benevolent face of the missionary movement. Stung by a sense of betrayal, Landa ordered mass arrests and tortured thousands of Maya Indians.

Conquests throughout history have been brutal, whether internal like the Aztec and Inca conquests of their rivals or external like the Spanish conquest of America. Was the conquest of America unique or more exemplary than, say, the ancient Roman conquests? The decline of the native population, the dispossession and oppression of the surviving native peoples were probably unparalleled. At the same time, the conquests were interpreted as having a noble purpose, namely, extending Christianity and civilization. This mix of cruelty and idealism created a contradiction that has been difficult to reconcile. How seriously should the mission to civilize be taken in the face of the horrors of the destruction that took place? Although Las Casas and his movement struggled with sincerity against great odds to bring a humane purpose to the encounter, the anger that one could detect at the end of Las Casas's life was of course brought on by an awareness that his dream was not realized. He sensed that the legal victories that they had won had hardly alleviated the burdens of the native peoples. The consequence of conquest was colonialism, not liberty. European cultural and political institutions and values were imposed as the only acceptable ones.

By the end of the sixteenth century, the character of the population had begun to change. To the European and Indian population were added a growing mestizo and African population. The conquest was also a conquest of Indian women. As the Indian population declined, more and more Africans were brought as slaves. Each group developed dynamic and creative cultures, and contributed to the racial and cultural mixture of the Americas.

During the course of the following century, other European nations would carve out their own empires in America and like the Spanish and Portuguese impose the supremacy of their own national cultures. The doctrine of cultural supremacy needs to be challenged. In the case of Spain, this arrogance is perplexing. Conquered during its long history by Carthaginians, Romans, Visigoths, Arabs, and Berbers, Spanish society was a mixture of different peoples and cultures. Its struggles for liberation were celebrated in its rich history, not least from the Roman and Muslim conquests. Yet, their hatred of being dominated did not prevent them from dominating other peoples. They failed to see, too, that their multicultural society brought strength and vitality. Instead, they hastened to cleanse their society of those who were not Christian. The adoption of a statute demanding tests to determine purity of blood (*Limpieza de sangre*) for membership in certain corporations was but one example of this. The explanation was not hard to find. The resurgence of the crusading spirit propelled both the reconquest of Spain and the conquest of America. In his reflections on why Europe came to dominate the modern world, the historian Hugh Trevor-Roper saw the European crusading spirit of the twelfth century as initiating the expansion of Europe.[15] For him, the crusades constituted one of the great turning points of history, whereby the "irredeemable barbarians" of Europe of the Dark Ages would be catapulted on the stage of history as the main actors. He saw the wars against Islam in the Near East and in Spain, the German march eastwards against the Slavs, the conquest of Ireland by the Anglo-Normans, and the conquest of Constantinople by Western Europe as "an inseparable part" of European expansion. Using David Hume's description of the crusades as "universal frenzy", he felt that this "universal frenzy" which launched Europe against Asia and the "re-creation, in Italy, of commercial cities trading directly with the east" as another turning-point. The suggestion that Europe's progress was linked to the vitality that was ushered by the crusades is an interesting insight, but also disquieting. Are wars of conquest the most useful means to bring progress? Should not human suffering be a countervailing weight in any scale to measure progress?

These reflections on the initial European conquests, colonization, and Christianization of the Americas incline towards accepting Las Casas's view of what happened in the encounter and, in particular, his vision of the possibilities of the encounter. He could not accept the death, enslavement, and the immiseration of the native peoples. The contradiction between the wealth and power of Europeans and the harshness of their exploitation of native Americans was too stark to tolerate for those whose consciences were moved by a sense of justice. The Salamancan theologians and the Lascasian movement were right to keep stressing the severity of the Spanish conquests. In their vision of American societies, the humiliated and impoverished must be given due dignity and the means for self-development. The encounter produced a great tragedy. In their minds, the construction of new societies should begin with the awareness of the sense of tragedy because the noble mission to civilize failed utterly. Awareness of tragedy carried with it a sense of responsibility for the disaster. Las Casas took this line of argument even further, demanding restitution for the exploited. Missionary educators did studies of native societies, showing that native Americans were human beings with virtues and defects like all other human beings, and deserving of self-esteem. In their defense of native property rights and their campaigns against coerced labor systems like the encomienda, they wanted to abolish institutions that were responsible for the continuing debasement of the Indians and to create conditions for their uplift and advancement.

The social picture had of course changed dramatically. African slaves and people of mixed races joined the declining native Americans as the exploited. As the colonial system developed, the condition of the oppressed hardly improved. The vision of Las Casas of the possibility of European and native American living fraternally in liberty and with equality was attractive. Those of European ancestry came to see themselves as American. By an ironic and tragic twist of history, American Indians have been marginalized in most American societies and, in the imagination of the dominant peoples of America, have come to represent the quintessential Other. But Las Casas's faith in the imperial power's sense of responsibility to change radically the shape of colonial society was unrealistic. There were times when, nudged by Vitoria and Las Casas, the Spanish Crown did see it as their responsibility to defend the native peoples. We see this as early as Columbus's second voyage when queen Isabella demanded that the Indians whom Columbus brought back to Spain as slaves be returned to

America as free men. But, when the economic interests of the empire started to conflict with human rights issues, not surprisingly the issue of human rights was placed in the background.

As we look at American societies then and now, there have been major achievements. Slavery is now universally abolished and laws have been enacted against discrimination on the grounds of race and culture. In many Latin American societies, those of mixed race have made considerable social advances; in the Caribbean, descendants of African slaves now govern complex democratic societies. Immigrants from Asia have added to the diversity of American cultures. Indeed, the rich diversity of cultures and races has become one of the distinctive features of many American societies. Everywhere European cultural hegemony is being challenged. Culture, race, and color remain important considerations that divide American societies. But class seems to be an equally important key to understanding the persistence of social injustice today. The misery of the poor is no less wrenching than when Montesinos raised his voice in the early sixteenth century. Montesinos, Las Casas, Vera Cruz, Zorita, and others saw the inhuman consequences of the encomienda, the system that was established to produce wealth, and struggled for its abolition. Is not one of the most significant legacies of the conquest of America the cry for social justice, a cry that continues to resonate today?

NOTES

Epilogue

1 Antonello Gerbi, *The Dispute of the New World. The History of a Polemic, 1750-1900*, rev. ed. and trans. by Jeremy Moyle (Pittsburgh, 1973).

2 Ricardo E. Alegría, *Las Primeras Representaciones graficas del Indio Americano, 1493-1523*, (Instituto de Cultura Puertorriqueña, 1978).

3 Michael Palencia-Roth, "Quarta Orbis Pars: Monologizing the New World," *Comparative Civilizations Review*, (Spring, 1992) 4-42.

4 Steve J. Stern, *Peru's Indian Peoples and the Challenge of Spanish Conquest*, (Wisconsin, 1982), p. 137.

5 Antonio M. Stevens-Arroyo, *Cave of the Jagua*, (Albuquerque, 1988) 72-82.

6 H. Cortes, *Letters from Mexico*, trans. and ed. by Anthony Pagden, (New Haven, 1986), p. 106. See also Bernal Diaz del Castillo, *The Discovery and Conquest of Mexico*, trans. and ed. by A.P. Mauldsley, (New York, 1956), pp. 63,77,105,

7 A. Tibesar, *Franciscan Beginnings in Colonial Peru*, (Washington, D.C., 1953) p. 39.

8 T. Motolinia, *Motolinia's History of the Indians of New Spain*, (Berkeley, Cal., 1950) p. 92.

9 Miguel León-Pontilla, *Los Franciscanos Vistos por el Hombre Nahuatl*, (Mexico city, 1985) 75-79.

10 Octavio Paz, *The Labyrinth of Solitude* (New York, 1985), p. 94.

11 Miguel León-Portilla, *Aztec Thought and Culture*, trans. by Jack E. Davis, (Norman, Oklahoma, 1963). León-Portilla argued that while ritual human sacrifice was practiced before the Aztecs, it became widespread only after 1429 when the Aztecs came under the influence of a "mystico-militaristic" ideology. He distinguished between the ideological culture of the rulers and other aspects of Aztec civilization. Inga Clendinnen's *Aztecs* (Cambridge, 1991) is a provocative, well written, but a disturbing book. She constructs her thesis almost completely from Sahagun's Florentine Codex and subordinates Aztec education, philosophy, mercantile activity, and daily life to the oppressive Aztec state.

12 D. Duran, *Book of the Gods and Rites and the Ancient Calendar*, (Norman, Oklahoma, 1971), p. 240.

13 Bernardino de Sahagun, *General History of the Things of New Spain: The Florentine Codex*, trans. and ed. by A.J. Anderson and Charles Dibble (Santa Fe, 1950-82), pp. 93-94.

14 Inga Clendinnen, *Ambivalent Conquests*, (Cambridge, 1987), p. 161.

15 Hugh Trevor-Roper, *The Rise of Christian Europe*, (London, 1965), 9-32.

BIBLIOGRAPHY

Abadie-Aicardi, A., " La Tradición Institucional Salamantina de La Universidad de Mexico (1551-1821) en La Tradición Universitaria", in *Jahrbuch für Geschichte von Staat, Wirtschaft und Gesellschaft LateinAmerika*, 12(1975) 1-66.

Abu-Lughod, Janet. *Before European Hegemony: The World System A.D. 1250-1350*, New York, 1989.

Alegría, Ricardo E., *Las Primeras Representaciones Gráficas del Indio Americano, 1493-1523*, Instituto de Cultura Puertorriqueña, 1978.

_*Los Orígines de La Esclavitud Negra: Descubrimiento, Conquista, y Colonización de Puerto Rico, 1493-1599*, Barcelona, 1969.

Almandoz Garmendia, J.A., *Fray Alonso de la Vera Cruz y La Encomienda Indiana*, Rome, 1967.

Andrés Marcos, T., *Los Imperialismos de Juan Ginés de Sepulveda*, Madrid, 1947.

Andrews, Kenneth F., *The Spanish Caribbean: Trade and Plunder, 1530-1630*, New Haven, CT, 1978.

Aznar Vallejo, E., *La Integración de las Islas Canarias en La Corona de Castilla*, Sevilla, 1984.

Bataillon, Marcel, *Erasme et l'Espagne*, Paris, 1937.

Baumel, J., *Les Leçons de Francisco de Vitoria sur les problemes de la colonisation et de la Guerre*, Montpellier, 1936.

Bell, A.F.G., *Juan Gines de Sepulveda*, Oxford, 1925.

Beltrán de Heredia, Vicente, *Domingo de Soto, Estudio Biográfico Documentado*, Madrid, 1961.

_*Historia de la Reforma de la Provincia de España (1450-1550)*, Rome, 1939.

_ "El Maestro Juan de la Peña", in *La Ciencia Tomista*, 51(1933) 40-60, 145-178.

_ "Melchor Cano en la Universidad de Salamanca," in *La Ciencia Tomista*, 143(1933) 178-268.

_ *La Autenticidad de la Bula*, Santo Domingo, 1955.

Bethell, Leslie (ed.), *Colonial Spanish America*, Cambridge, 1987.

Beuchot, M. et al., *Homenaje a Fray Alonso de la Vera Cruz en el Cuarto Centenario de su Muerte (1584-1984)*, Mexico city, 1986.

Brady, Robert L., "The Role of Las Casas in the Emergence of Negro Slavery in the New World," in *Revista de Historia de America*, 61-62(1966) 43-55.

Braudel, Fernand., *Civilization and Capitalism: The Fifteenth to the Eighteenth Centuries*, New York, 1984.

_ The Mediterranean World in the Age of Phillip II, trans. by S. Reynolds, New York, 1972.

Brown Scott, James, *Fancisco de Vitoria and his law of Nations*, New York, 1939.

Bullon, E., *Un Colaborador de los Reyes Católicos. El Doctor Palacios Rubios y sus Obras*, Madrid, 1927.

Burns, Robert I., *Muslims, Christians, and Jews in the Crusader Kingdom of Valencia*, Cambridge, 1984.

Burrus, E.J., *The Writings of Alonso de la Vera Cruz*, VI vols., St. Louis, 1968.

_ "Alonso de la Vera Cruz's Defense of the American Indians, 1553-1554," *The Heythrop Journal*, IV(1963) 225-253.

_ " Las Casas and Vera Cruz: Their Defense of the American Indians Compared," *Neue Zeitschrift für Missionswissenschaft*, XXII(1966) 201-212.

_ "Alonso de la Vera Cruz, Pioneer Defender of the American Indians," *The Catholic Historical Review*, 70, no.4(1984) 531-546.

Carreño, A.M., *La Real y Pontificia Universidad de Mexico*, Mexico city, 1961.

Carpenter, Alejo, *The Harp and the Shadow*. English translation, San Francisco, 1979.

Carro, Venancio, "Los Postulados Teológico-Jurídicos de Bartolome de Las Casas," in *Anuario de Estudios Americanos*, XXIII(1966) 109-246.

Caso, Alfonso, *The Aztecs: People of the Sun*, trans. by L. Dunham, Oklahoma, 1958.

Cervantes de Salazar, Francisco, *Mexico en 1954. Tres Diálogos Latinos*, ed. by J. Garcia Icazbalceta, Mexico city, 1875.

Chavez, E.A., *Fray Pedro de Gante. El Primero de los Grandes Educadores de la America*, (Mexico city, 1934).

Chenu, M., *Introduction a l'etude de St. Thomas d'Aquin*, Paris, 1950.

Clendinnen, Inga, *Ambivalent Conquests*, Cambridge, 1987.

_ *Aztecs*, Cambridge, 1991.

Colon, Cristobal, *The Letter of Columbus on the Discovery of the New*

World, trans. by S.E. Morison, Los Angeles, 1989.

_ *Raccolta Colombiana*, I,vol.1 and 2 (Rome, 1892-1894), English trans. *Journal and Other Documents*, ed. by S.E. Morison New York, 1963.

Colon, Fernando, *The Life of the Admiral Christopher Columbus by his son Ferdinand*, trans. by Benjamin Keen, Rutgers, NJ., 1959.

Cook, S.F. and Borah, W., *Essays in Population History: Mexico and the Caribbean*, Berkeley, Cal., 1971.

Cox, George O., *African Empires and Civilizations*, New York, 1974.

Crone, G.R., *The Discovery of America*, New York, 1969.

Crosby, Alfred W. Jr., *The Columbian Voyages, the Columbian Exchange, and their Historians*, Washington,D.C., 1987.

_ *The Columbian Exchange: Biological and Cultural Consequences of 1492*, Westport, CT., 1972.

Diaz del Castillo, Bernal, *The Discovery and Conquest of Mexico*, trans. by A.P. Mauldsley, New York, 1956.

De Roover, Raymond, *The Medici Bank: Its Organization, Management, Operations and Decline*, New York, 1948.

_ *The Rise and Decline of the Medici Bank, 1397-1494*, Cambridge, Mass., 1963.

Dobb, Maurice, *Studies in the Development of Capitalism*, London, 1946.

_ *Modern Capitalism: Its Origin and Growth*, London, 1928.

Driver, H., *Indians of North America*, New York, 1961.

DuPlessis, Robert S., "The Partial Transition to World-Systems Analysis in Early Modern European History," in *Radical History Review*, 39(1987) 11-27.

Duran, D., *Book of the Gods and Rites and the Ancient Calender*, Norman, Oklahoma, 1971.

Duyvendak, J.L., *China's Discovery of Africa*, London, 1949.

Edmundson, Munro S, (ed.), *Sixteenth-Century Mexico, The Work of Sahagun*, New Mexico, 1974.

Eguiguren, L.A., *Alma Mater: Orígenes de la Universidad de San Marcos, 1551-1579*, Lima, 1939.

_ "Fray Tomás de San Martín," in *Mercurio Peruano*, 32(1951) 195-204.

Ehrenberg, Richard, *Capital and Finance in the Age of the Renaissance*, New York, 1963.

Elliot, J.H., *Imperial Spain, 1469-1760*, New York, 1963.

Ennis, Arthur, "Fray Alonso de la Vera Cruz," in *Augustiniana*, V-VII, New York, 1955-'57.

Esperabé Arteaga, E., *Historia Pragmática e Interna de la Universidad de Salamanca*, Salamanca, 1914-'16.

Estarellas, J., "The College of Tlatelolco and the Problem of Higher Education for Indians in 16th Century Mexico," in *History of Education Quarterly*, 2(1962) 234-243.

Esteban Deive, Carlos, *La Esclavitud del Negro en Santo Domingo (1492-1844)*, 2 vols., Santo Domingo, 1975.

Fernandez-Armesto, F., *The Canary Islands After the Conquest*, Oxford, 1982.

_ *Columbus*, Oxford, 1991.

Fernandez Duro, C. (ed.), *De Los Pleitos de Colon*, 2 vols., Madrid, 1892-'94.

Fernandez de Navarrete, Martin (ed), *Colección de los Viages y Descubrimientos*, 3 vols., Madrid, 1825.

Figgis, J.N., *Studies of Political Thought from Gerson to Grotius, 1414-1625*, Cambridge, 1931.

Foster, Herbert J. (ed.), *From the African Slave Trade to Emancipation: Readings in Black History 1450-1860*, New Jersey, 1974.

_ "The Ethnicity of Ancient Egyptians," in *Journal of Black Studies*, 5(1978) 175-191.

Fraginales, Manuel Moreno, *Africa en América Latina*, Mexico city, 1977.

Friede, Juan, *Los Welser en la Conquista de Venezuela*, Caracas, 1961.

_ "Las Casas y El Movimiento Indigenista en España y América en La Primera Mitad del Siglo XVI, in *Revista de Historia de America*, 34(1952) 339-411.

Friede, Juan and Keen, B. (eds.), *Bartolome de Las Casas in History*, De Kalb, III., 1971.

Fuentes, Carlos, *The Buried Mirror. Reflections on Spain and the New World*, New York, 1992.

Galvan, Manuel, *Enriquillo*, Santo Domingo, 1882.

Garcia, Genaro, *Documentos inéditos o muy raros para la Historia de Mexico*, Mexico city, 1907.

Garcia Icazbalceta, J., *Bibliografía Mexicana del Siglo XVI*, Mexico city, 1954.

_ *Nueva Colección de Documentos para la Historia de Mexico*, vol. 3,

Mexico city, 1954.

Garibay K.,A.M., *Historia de la Literatura Nahuatl*, 2 vols., Mexico city, 1953-'59.

Gayo Aragon, J., "The Controversy over Justification of Spanish Rule in the Philippines," in *Studies in Philippine Church History*, ed. by Gerald Anderson, Cornell University Press, Cornell, 1969.

Gerbi, Antonello, *The Dispute of the New World. The History of a Polemic, 1750-1900*, revised edition and trans. by Jeremy Moyle, Pittsburgh, 1973.

Getino, L., *El Maestro Fray Francisco de Vitoria y el Renacimiento Filosófico-Teológico del Siglo XVI*, Madrid, 1914.

Gibson, Charles, *The Aztecs Under Spanish Rule*, Stanford, 1964.

_ *The Black Legend. Anti-Spanish Attitudes in the Old World and the New*, New York, 1971.

_ *Spain in America*, New York, 1966.

Grijalva, J., *Cronica de la Orden de San Augustin en las Provincias de la Nueva España*, Mexico city, 1624.

Gilson, E., *History of Christian Philosophy in the Middle Ages*, New York, 1955.

Guedes, M.J. and Lombardi, J. (eds), *Portugal/Brazil. The Age of Atlantic Discoveries*, New York, 1990.

Hamilton, Bernice, *Political Thought in Sixteenth-Century Spain*, Oxford, 1963.

Hamilton, Earl J., *American Treasure and the Price Revolution in Spain 1501-1650*, Cambridge, Mass., 1934.

Hanke, Lewis, *The First Social Experiments in America*, Cambridge, 1935.

_ *Aristotle and the American Indians*, Bloomington, Ind., 1959.

_ *The Spanish Struggle for Justice in the Conquest of America*, Philadelphia, 1949.

Hernáez, F.J., *Colección de Bulas, Breves, y Otros Documentos Relativos a La Iglesia y Filipinas*, 2 vols., Brussels, 1879.

Hillgarth, J.N., *Ramon Llull and Llulism in Fourteenth-Century France*, Oxford, 1971.

History Today, May 1992.

Hulme, Peter, *Colonial Encounters*, London, 1986.

Iglesia, Ramon, *Columbus, Cortes, and Other Essays*, translated and edited by L.B. Simpson, Berkeley, Cal., 1969.

Jane, Cecil (ed), *Select Documents Illustrating the Four Voyages of Columbus*, 2 vols., London, 1930-'32.

Jimenez, Rueda, J., *Las Constituciones de la Antigua Universidad de Mexico*, Mexico city, 1951.

Johnson, James T., *Ideology, Reason and the Limitations of War: Religion and Secular Concepts, 1200-1740*, Princeton University Press, Princeton, 1975.

Jones, Gwyne, *The Norse Atlantic Saga*, Oxford, 1964.

Jos, E., "El Libro del Primer Viaje. Algunas Ediciones Recientes," in *Revista de Indias*, X(1950) 719-751.

Justenhoven, Heinz-Gerhard, *Francisco de Vitoria zu Krieg und Frieden*, Köln, 1991.

Klein, Herb S., "The Establishment of African Slavery in Latin America in the 16th Century," in *African Slavery in Latin America and the Caribbean*, New York, 1986.

Klor de Alva, J.J. et al., *The Work of Bernardino de Sahagun*, New York, 1988.

Lanning, John Tate, *Academic Culture in the Spanish Colonies*, Oxford, 1940.
_ *Reales Cédulas de la Real Pontificia de Mexico de 1551 a 1816*, Mexico city, 1914.

Las Casas, Bartolome, *Historia Apologética*, Madrid, 1909.

_ *Doctrina*, edited by A. Yañez, Mexico city, 1982.

_ *Historia de Las Indias*, 3 vols., edited by A. Millares Carlo, Mexico City, 1951; English trans. and selections by A.M. Collard, New York, 1973.

_ *The Devastation of the Indies: A brief Account*, Baltimore, 1992.

León-Portilla, Miguel, *Fray Anton de Montesinos*, Mexico city, 1982.

_ *Aztec Thought and Culture*, trans. by Jack E. Davis, Norman, Oklahoma, 1963.

_ *Los Franciscanos Vistos por el Hombre Nahuatl*, Mexico city, 1985.

Leturia, Pedro de (ed.), *Relaciones entre la Santa Sede e HispanoAmérica*, in Analecta Gregoriana, CI, Rome, 1959.

Litvinoff, B., *1492. The Year and the Era*, London, 1991.

Lopez de Gomara, Francisco, *Historia General de Las Indias*, Madrid, 1852.

Malagón-Barceló, J., "The Role of the Letrado in the Colonization of America," in *The Americas*, 18(1961) 1-72.

Maalouf, Amin, *Leo Africanus*, New York, 1992.

Mann, Horace K., *Lives of the Popes in the Early Middle Ages*, vol. 14, London, 1902-'32.

Manzano y Manzano, J., *Cristobal Colon: Siete Años Decisivos de su Vida*, Madrid, 1964.

Martyre Anghera, Peter, *De Orbo Novo. The Eight Decades of Peter Martyre Anghera*, 2 vols., ed. by F.A. MacNutt, New York, 1912.

_ *Epistolario*, ed. by J. Lopez de Toro, Madrid, 1953.

Martins da Silva Marques, J., *Descobrimentos Portugueses*, 3 vols., Coimbra, 1940-'71.

Matias de Paz, *De Dominio*, ed. by S. Zavala, Mexico city, 1954.

Miller, Joseph, *The Way of Death. Merchant Capitalism and the Angolan Slave Trade, 1730-1830*, Wisconsin, 1988.

Milhou, Alain, *Colón y Su Mentalidad Mesiánica*, Valladolid, 1983.

Miranda, J., *El Tributo Indígena en la Nueva España Durante el Siglo VI*, Mexico city, 1952.

Monzon, A., *El Calpulli en la Organizacion Social de Los Tenocha*, Mexico city, 1941.

Morales Padron, Francisco, *Jamaica Española*, Seville, 1952.

_ "Las Relaciones entre Colon y Martin Alonso Pinzon," in *Revista de Indias*, 21(1961) 95-105.

Moreno, M., *La Organización Política y Social de Los Aztecas*, Mexico city, 1931.

Moffitt Watts, P., "Prophecy and Discovery: On the Spiritual Origins of Christopher Columbus's Enterprise of the Indies," in *American*

Historical Review, 90(1985) 73-102.

Morison, S.E., "The Earliest Colonial Policy toward America: That of Columbus," in *Bulletin of the Pan American Union,* LXXVI(1942) 543-555.

_ (ed.and trans.), *Journal and Other Documents on the Life and Voyages of Christopher Columbus,* New York, 1963.

_ *Admiral of the Ocean Sea,* 2 vols., New York, 1942.

Muldoon, James, *Popes, Lawyers, and Infidels: The Church and The non-Christian World, 1250-1550,* Philadelphia, 1979.

_ "The Contribution of the Medieval Canon Lawyers to the Formation of International Law," in *Traditio,* 28(1972) 463-497.

_ "John Wyclif and the Rights of the Infidels: The Requerimiento Re-Examined," in *The Americas,* XXXVI(1980) 301-316.

_ "Solorzano's De Indiarum lure: Applying a Medieval Theory of the World Order in the Seventeenth Century," in *Journal of World History,* 2 no.1(1991) 29-46.

Needham, Joseph, *Science and Civilization in China,* vol. 1, London, 1954.

Ocaranza, F., *Historia de la Medicina en Mexico,* Mexico city, 1934.

O'Gorman, Edmundo., *The Invention of America,* Bloomington, Ind., 1961.

Oviedo Y Valdes, G. Fernandez de, *Historia General y Natural de Las Indias, islas y Tierra Firme del Mar Océano,* 5 vols., edited by J. Natalicio Gonzalez and Jose Amador de Los Rios, Paraguay, 1959.

Ozment, S., *The Reformation in Medieval Perspective,* Chicago, 1971.

Pagden, Anthony, *Spanish Imperialism and the Political Imagination,*

New Haven, CT., 1990.

_ *The Fall of Natural Man*, Cambridge, 1982.

_ (ed.), *The Languages of Political Theory in Early Modern Europe*, Cambridge, 1987.

Palacios Rubios, *De Las Islas del Mar Océano*, ed. by S. Zavala, Mexico city, 1954.

Paz, Octavio, *The Labyrinth of Solitude*, New York, 1985.

Palencia-Roth, Michael, "Quarta Orbis Pars: Monologizing the New World," in *Comparative Civilizations Review*, (Spring, 1992) 4-42.

Pannikar, K.M., *Asia and Western Dominance*, London, 1959.

Parry, J.H., *The Spanish Seaborne Empire*, New York, 1970.

Pennington, Kenneth J., Jr., "Bartolome de Las Casas and the Tradition of Medieval Law," in *Church History*, 39(1970) 149-161.

Pereña Vicente, Luciano, *Misión de España en América*, Madrid, 1956.

Phelan, John Leddy, *The Millennial Kingdom of the Franciscans*, 2nd. ed., Berkeley, Cal., 1970.

_ *The Hispanization of the Phillipines*, Madison, Wisconsin., 1959.

Phillips, Carla Rahn, *The Worlds of Christopher Columbus*, Cambridge, 1992.

_ "The Blurred Image: Christopher Columbus in the United States Historiography," in *Humanities News*, Jan. 1992.

Pike, Ruth, *Enterprise and Adventure. The Genoese in Seville and the Opening of the New World*, New York, 1966.

Pirenne, Henri, *Medieval Cities: Their Origins and the Revival of Trade*,

Princeton, 1925.

Porras Barrenechea, R., "Fray Domingo de Santo Tomas," in *Comercio*, May 12, 1959.

Reid, Anthony, *Southeast Asia in the Age of Commerce, 1450-1680*, New Haven, CT., 1983.

Ricard, Robert, *The Spiritual Conquest of Mexico*. English translation, Berkeley, Ca., 1966; originally published as *Conquête Spirituelle de Mexique*, Paris, 1933.

Rivera Pagan, Luis N., *Evangelización y Violencia: La Conquista de America*, San Juan, P.R., 1990.

Robles, Oswald, "El Movimiento Neo-Escolástico en Mexico," in *Filosofía y Letras*, 23(1946).

Roys, R.L. (ed.), *The Book of Chilam Balaam of Chumayel*, Norman, Oklahoma., 1967.

Rumeu de Armas, Anthony, *La Política Indigenista de Isabella*, Valladolid, 1969.

Sahagun, Bernardino de, *General History of the Things of New Spain. Florentine Codex*, trans. by A.J.O. Anderson and C.E. Dibble, Utah, 1950-'55.

Sale, Kirkpatrick, *The Conquest of Paradise*, New York, 1990.

Sardar, et.al., *The Blinded Eye: 500 Years of Christopher Columbus*, Goa, India, 1993.

Sauer, Carl O., *The Early Spanish Main*, Berkeley, Cal., 1966.

Scholes, W.V., *The Diego Ramirez Visita*, Columbia, Missouri, 1946.

Sepúlveda, Juan Gines de, *Democrates Segundo*, ed. by Angel Losada,

Madrid, 1951.

Serrano, Sanz M., *Orígenes de la Dominación Eapañola en America*, Madrid, 1918.

Shiels, William E., *King and Church: The Rise and Fall of the Patronato Real*, Chicago, 1961.

Simpson, L.B., *The Encomienda in New Spain*, Berkeley, Ca., 1929.

Smith, Alan K., *Creating a World Economy. Merchant Capital, Colonialism, and World Trade 1400-1825*, Colorado, 1991.

Snow, Phillip, *The Star Raft: China's Encounter with Africa*, New York, 1988.

Soustelle, J., *Daily Life of the Aztecs on the Eve of the Spanish Conquest*, trans. by P.O. Brian, Stanford, 1961.

Spitz, Lewis W. *The Renaissance and Reformation Movements*, 2 vols., St. Louis, Missouri, 1971.

Stavrianos, L.S., *The Global Rift*, New York, 1981.

Steck, F. Borgia, *Motolinia's History of the Indians of New Spain*, Washington, D.C., 1951.

_ *El Primer Colegio de America. Santa Cruz de Tlatelolco*, Mexico city, 1944.

Stern, Steve J., *Peru's Indian Peoples and the Challenge of Spanish Conquest*, Wisconsin, 1982.

Stevens-Arroyo, Anthony M., *Cave of the Jagua*, Albuquerque, N.M., 1988.

Sued Badillo, J., *Los Caribes: Realidad o Fábula*, Rio Piedras, P.R., 1978.

Thapar, R., *A History of India*, I, London, 1966.

Tibesar, Antonine, *Franciscan Beginnings in Colonial Peru*, Washington, D.C., 1953.

Tisnes, Roberto M., *Alejandro Geraldini*, Santo Domingo, 1987.

Todorov, T., *The Conquest of America*, English trans., New York, 1984.

Traboulay, David M., "Scholastic in the Wilderness: Alonso de la Vera Cruz," *Zeitschrift für Missionswissenschaft und Religion Wissenschaft*, 4(1974) 273-283.

Trevor-Roper, Hugh, *The Rise of Christian Europe*, London, 1965.

Tyler, S. Lyman (ed.), *Two Worlds: The Indian Encounter with the European*, Utah, 1988.

Van Sertima, Ivan, *They Came Before Columbus*, New York, 1976.

Vera Cruz, Alonso de, *Dialectica Resolutio*, Mexico city, 1954.

_ *Physica Speculatio*, Mexico city, 1957.

_ *De Decimis*, ed. and trans. by E. Burrus, St. Louis, 1968.

_ *De Dominio*, ed. by E.J. Burrus, St. Louis, 1968.

Vigil, Ralph E., "Bartolome de Las Casas, Judge Alonso de Zorita, and the Franciscans. A Collaborative Effort for the Spiritual Conquest of the Borderlands," in *The Americas*, XXXVIII(1981) 45-57.

Vespucci, Amerigo, *The Mundus Novus Letter to Lorenzo Medici*, trans. and introd. by G.T. Northup, Princeton, 1916.

Vignaud, H., *Toscanelli and Columbus*, London, 1902.

Villena, Guillermo Lohman, "La Restitución por Conquistadores y Encomenderos: Un Aspecto de la Incidencia Lascasiana en el Peru," in

Anuario de Estudios Americanos, XXXII(1966) 21-89.

Villoslada, R., *La Universidad de Paris durante Los Estudios de Francisco de Vitoria*, Rome, 1938.

Vitoria, Francisco de, *Doctrina Sobre Los Indios*, edicion facsimile, ed. by Ramon Hernández Martín, Salamanca, 1989.

_ *Relectio de Indis et De Iure Belli*, ed. by Ernest Nys, Washington, D.C., 1917

Wagner, Henry Raup, *The Life and Writings of Bartolome de Las Casas*, Albuquerque, 1967.

Walker, D.J.R., *Columbus and the Golden World of the Island Arawaks*, London, 1991.

Wallerstein, I., *The Modern World System*, 2 vols., 1974, 1980.

Warren, Fintan B., *Vasco de Quiroga and his Pueblo Hospitals of Santa Fe*, Washington, D.C., 1963.

West, Delno, "Medieval Ideas of Apocalyptic Mission and the Early Franciscans in Mexico," in *The Americas*, XLV(1989), 293-313.

Wilford, John Noble, *The Mysterious History of Columbus: An Exploration of the Man, the Myth, the Legacy*, New York, 1991.

Wilson, Ian, *The Columbus Myth*, New York, 1989.

Wolf, Eric, *Europe and the Peoples Without History*, Berkeley, Ca., 1982.

Zavala, S., "The American Utopia of the Sixteenth Century," *The Huntington Library Quarterly*, 10(1947) 337-347.

_ *La Encomienda Indiana*, Madrid, 1935.

_ "Bartolome de Las Casas ante La Esclavitud de los Indios," in

Cuadernos Americanos, XXV(1966) 142-156.

Zorita, Alonso, *The Lords of New Spain*, trans. with an introduction by Benjamin Keen, London, 1965.

INDEX

222

INDEX

Dr. David Traboulay is currently professor of History at the College of Staten Island and Liberal Studies at the Graduate Center of the City University of New York. A native of Trinidad and Tobago, where he received his primary and secondary education at Presentation College, he received his B.A. (Hons.) and M.A. from Dublin University, Ireland, and his Ph.D. from the Medieval Institute of the University of Notre Dame. He was a Fulbright Scholar to the University of Delhi, India in 1993.